Learning
Illustrator CS4

Ramesh Bangia
B.Sc., Dip. Comp. Sc.
Formerly: Managing Editor, Software Today
Formerly: Incharge Computer Centre, Hindustan Copper Ltd., New Delhi

KHANNA BOOK PUBLISHING CO. PVT. LTD.

Learning Illustrator CS 4 — Ramesh Bangia

Published by

Khanna Book Publishing Co. (P) Ltd.

Regd. Office:

1694-95 Nai Sarak, 1st Floor
Delhi - 110 006 (India)
Tel. 011-23283211, 23256658
Telefax: 011-23256658
Website: www.khannaedu.com
E-mail: contact@khannaedu.com

ISBN 978-93-80016-47-4

First Edition 2010

Printed in India by Seth Printers, Noida (U.P.)

Preface

Learning of a software is both easy and difficult. It depends upto what level you are planning to learn. If you are learning only for the working use, then it is very easy. But, when you try to go deep into it, then you realise how difficult it is to master it.

Illustrator CS4 is such a vast subject that it will take a lot of time to understand it fully. This book has been written in mind to make you aware of the options available in the software and how they can be used. It is like telling the child about the steps and stairs. You are the one who is to climb the stair. This book will just guide you how to use the stairs.

I am indeed debited to my publishers Khanna Book Publishing Co. Pvt. Ltd., specially Sheetal Khanna for their suggestions and encouragement given in producing this book.

I would like to thank my family specially my wife Sadhna, kids Mayank and Samarth, for without their criticism this book would not have seen the day.

Suggestions for improvement of the book are indeed welcome.

Ramesh Bangia

Contents

1. **Getting to know Illustrator CS 4** 1

Introduction 1
What is New in Illustrator CS4 1
Enriched workspace tools 1
- Multiple artboards in your documents 1
- Tabbed document windows and Document Arrangement panel 1
- Application bar and workspace switcher 1
- Practical smart guides 1
- Quick, easy, and obvious key object alignment 2

New drawing and color tools 2
- Blob Brush tool for merging paths 2
- Expanded Gradients panel and tool 2
- Transparency in gradients 2
- Separations Preview panel 2

Improved access to core functionality 2
- Clipping masks with clear simplified appearance and access 2
- In-panel Appearance editing 2
- Enriched Graphic Styles panel 3

Enhanced integration at export 3
- Support for Flex extensions 3
- Multiple artboard export support 3

Minimum System Requirements 3
- Installing the Software 3
- Uninstalling the Software 4

License activation 4
- Registration Information 4

Adobe Product Improvement Program 4
- Font Installation 5
  - Installed Fonts 5
  - Additional Fonts 5

The Beginning 6
Illustrator Screen 6
- Menu bar 8
- Toolbox 8
- Illustration Window 8
- Artboard 8
- Scroll Bars 8
- Size Option Box 9
- Status Bar 9

Menu Commands 9
File menu 9
Edit menu 12

Name 15
Raster/Vector balance 15
Line Art And Text Resolution 15
Gradient And Mesh Resolution 15
Convert All Text To Outlines 16
Convert All Strokes To Outlines 16
Clip Complex Regions 16
Tracing Presets 16
Preset 16
Mode 16
Threshold 16
Palette 16
Max Colors 17
Output To Swatches 17
Blur 17
Resample 17
Fills 17
Strokes 17
Max Stroke Weight 17
Min Stroke Length 18
Path Fitting 18
Minimum Area 18
Corner Angle 18
Raster 18
Vector 18
Select 18
Print Presets 18
Adobe PDF Presets 18
Illustrator Default (Illustrator only) 19
Oversized Pages (Acrobat only) 19
PDF/A-1b: 2005 (CMYK and RGB) (Acrobat only) 19
PDF/X 1a (2001 and 2003) 19
PDF/X 4 (2007) 20
Press Quality 21
Rich Content PDF 21
Smallest File Size 21
Standard (Acrobat only) 21
SWF Presets 21
Preset 21
Flash Player Version 22
Type Of Export 22
Curve Quality 22
Frame Rate 22
Loop 22

Preserve Appearance 22
Preserve Editability Where Possible 23
Compressed 23
Protect File 23
Text As Outlines 23
Color Settings 23
Assign Profile 24
Keyboard Shortcuts 24
Preferences 24
General Preferences 24
Selection and Anchor Display 27
Object Selection By Path Only 27
Snap To Point 27
Adding and Deleting Anchor Points 27
Type 28
Units and Display Performance 29
Guides and Grid 30
Smart Guides & Slices 31
Hyphenation Options 33
Plug-ins and Scratch Disk 34
User Interface 35
File Handling & Clipboard 35
Appearance of Black 37
Object menu 38
Type menu 40
Select menu 43
Effect menu 43
View menu 48
Window menu 52
Help menu 55
Using Palettes 57
Customizing a Palette's Appearance 58
Color Settings 58
2. Tools of Illustrator CS 4 61
Understanding Tools 61
Tear off 61
Selection Tool 61
Direct Selection Tool 62
Group selection 62
Magic Wand Tool 62
Direct Select Lasso Tool 63
Pen Tool 63
Add point 63
Delete point 63

Convert point 63
Type Tool 63
Area type 63
Path type 63
Vertical type 63
Vertical area type 64
Vertical path type 64
Line Segment Tool 64
Arc Tool 64
Spiral Tool 64
Rectangular Grid Tool 64
Polar Grid Tool 64
Rectangle Tool 64
Rounded rectangle 64
Ellipse Tool 64
Polygon 65
Star 65
Flare 65
Paintbrush Tool 65
Pencil Tool 65
Smooth 65
Erase 65
Blob Brush Tool 66
Blob Brush tool guidelines 66
Blob Brush tool options 66
Eraser Tool 67
Eraser tool options 67
Rotate Tool 68
Reflect 68
Twist 68
Scale Tool 68
Shear 68
Reshape 69
WarpTool 69
The twirl tool 69
The pucker tool 69
The bloat tool 69
The scallop tool 69
The crystallize tool 69
The wrinkle tool 69
Free Transform Tool 69
Symbol Spray Tool 70
Symbol Shifter tool 70
Symbol Scruncher tool 70

- Symbol Sizer tool ... 70
- Symbol Spinning tool ... 70
- Symbol Stainer tool ... 70
- Symbol Styler tool ... 70
- Symbol Screener tool ... 70
- Column Graph Tool ... 70
- Stacked column ... 71
- Bar ... 71
- Line ... 71
- Area ... 71
- Scatter ... 71
- Radar ... 71
- Mesh Tool ... 71
- Gradient Tool ... 71
- Eyedropper Tool ... 72
- Paint bucket ... 72
- Measure ... 72
- Blend Tool ... 72
- Autotrace ... 72
- Live Paint Bucket Tool/Live Paint Selection Tool ... 73

Artboard Tool ... 73
- Artboard options ... 74
- Slice Tool ... 74
- Hand Tool ... 74
- Page ... 74
- Zoom Tool ... 74

Using Drawing Tools ... 74
Points and Segments ... 75
Strokes and Fills ... 75
Drawing a Rectangle ... 75
- Using Numbers ... 76
- Rounding off a Rectangle's Corners ... 76
- Creating a Live Rounded Rectangle ... 76

Drawing an Ellipse ... 77
Simple Shapes at an Angle ... 78
Polygons, Stars and Spirals ... 78
Drawing a Regular Polygon ... 78
Drawing a Star ... 79
Creating Double Star ... 80
Creating a Spiral ... 80
- Controlling Spirals ... 81

Using Selection and Curves ... 82
Arrows and Lassos ... 82
The Plain Black Arrow Tool ... 82

Direct Selection Tool 82
Selecting using Lassos 83
The Black Lasso 83
The White Lasso 83
Adding More Lasso Selections 83
Selecting Everything 83
Other Selection techniques 83
Same Fill and Stroke 83
Same Fill Color 84
Same Stroke Color 84
Same Stroke Weight 84
Same Blending Mode 84
Same Opacity 84
Same Masks 84
Same Stray Points 84
Same Brush Strokes 84
Deselecting 84
Dragging 84
Dragging Points 85
Pen Tool 85
Pen Tool Basics 85
Path building 85
Adjusting a point 85
Closing the path 85
Leaving the path open 85
Extending an open path 86
Joining two open paths 86
Defining Points and Segments 86
Corner point 86
Straight segment 86
Smooth point 86
Curved segment 86
Straight segment followed by curved 86
Curved segment followed by straight 86
Cusp point 86
Modifying the Closing Point 87
Working with the Pen 87
Drawing Curves 88
Creating Corners 89
Converting Smooth Points to Cusps 90
Handling Corner Points 91
Adding Points to a Path 91
Removing Points from a Path 91
Converting Points between Corner and Smooth 92

Redo Undo Operations 94

3. **Handling Text in Illustrator CS 4** **95**

Introduction 95
Creating Text Objects 95
Text in Blocks 96
Resizing and Reshaping Text Blocks 97
Selecting and Editing Text 99
Selecting with the Type Tool 99
Adding Text 100
Formatting Text 100
Character-Level Formatting 101
    Selecting a Typeface 101
    Reducing/Enlarging Type 101
    Distance between Lines 102
Space between Characters 102
Changing Height and Width of Characters 103
Superscript and Subscript 103
Paragraph-Level Formatting 104
    Alignment 104
Indentation of Paragraphs 106
    Paragraph Spacing 106
Letters and Words Spacing 106
Activating Automatic Hyphenation 107
Working with Tabs 109
    Tabs Palette 110
The Text Eyedropper and Paint Bucket 110
    Sucking up Attributes with the Eyedropper 111
    Pouring out Attributes with Paint Bucket 111
    Configuring Eyedropper and Paint Bucket 112
Creating Various Text Effects 112
Merging Text with Curve 112
Shifting Type in Relation to Its Path 113
Using Vertical Type 114
    Taking out Alignment Handle 115
Wrapping Text to a Shape 115
Wrapping Type Around Graphics 116
Importing and Exporting Text 116
Spell Checking 117
Search and Replace 119
Replacing Fonts 120

4. **More Commands of Illustrator CS 4** **121**

Working with Lines and Brushes 121
    Stroking Type and Text Paths 121
Applying Stroke from the Stroke Palette 121

Line Weight 122
Line Caps 122
Line Joins 123
Dash Patterns 123
Using Brushes 124
Creating and Applying Brushes 125
Defining Calligraphic Brushes 126
Creating Scatter Brushes 127
Defining Art Brushes 128
Creating Pattern Brushes 128
Drawing Line and Arc Segments 131
Drawing Rectangular Grids 132
Drawing polar grids 133
Transformations 134
The Scale Tool 134
Scaling with the Shift Key 134
Duplicating Objects as You Scale Them 135
Scaling with the Bounding Box 136
Resizing by the Numbers 137
Scaling from the Transform Palette 137
Using the Scale Dialog Box 138
Scaling Partial Objects 139
Working with Colours 139
Onscreen Color controls 140
Using the Color Palette 140
Applying Colors 141
Using the Slider Bars 141
Using Swatches Palette 142
Setting the Swatches Palette Focus 143
Creating a Color Swatch 144
Adjusting Colors 145
Applying a Single Fill 146
Creating and Changing Gradient Swatches 146
Working with Compound Paths and Masks 147
Understanding Path Blends 148
Creating a blend 148
Creating Linear Blends 149
Blend Options 149
Using the Blend option 149
Blending Multiple Objects 150
Editing blends 150
Changing Blend Colors on the Fly 150
Moving a Blended Object 150
Editing a Blended Object 150

Adjusting the Blend Options 151
Expanding a Blend 151
Replacing the Spine 151
Reversing the Spine 151
Reversing Front to Back 151
Changing into filled shapes 151
Masking blends 151
Creating Color Blends 152
Multiple colors with linear blends 152
Creating Shape Blends 152
Computer Vents 153
Creating Realism with Shape Blends 153
Compound Paths 155
Creating compound paths 155
Masks 155
Crating Masks 156
Stroking and Filling Masking Objects 156
Releasing masks 156
Masks and Printing 156
Using Compound Paths and Masks in an Illustration 157
Creating a film strip 157
Flare 158
Create a default flare 158
Draw a flare 158
Create a flare using the Flare Tool Options dialog box 160
About Symbols 160
Create a symbol 160
Select the artwork you want to use as a symbol. 160
Create a Sketch using the Scribble Effect 161
Path Overlap 161
Variation (for Path Overlap) 162
Stroke Width 162
Curviness 162
Variation (for Curviness) 162
Spacing 162
Variation (for Spacing) 162
About Web Graphics 162
Create 3D Objects 163
Create a 3D object by Extruding 163
5. Keyboard Shortcuts of Illustrator CS 4 165
6. Questions 185

1 Getting to know Illustrator CS 4

Introduction

Adobe Corporation, which has sofware like Photoshop and PageMaker has Illustrator too. Its new version is CS4 which lives upto the challenge of the market, which is flooded with various graphics software. Its biggest competitor is CorelDRAW.

Well, I will refrain from comparing the two, but would certainly like to emphasize on the merits of Illustrator CS4 in this book. For CorelDRAW, I suggest you read my books on CorelDRAW 12 and X.3.

What is New in Illustrator CS4

Enriched workspace tools

Multiple artboards in your documents

Create multi-page files containing up to 100 artboards of varying sizes. You can create artboards that overlap, appear side-by-side, or are stacking on top of one another. You can also save, export and print artboards independently or together. Multiple artboards have replaced the Crop Area tool. (See Using multiple artboards.)

Tabbed document windows and Document Arrangement panel

Display multiple documents in a tabbed view or open them side by side so you can easily compare or drag items from one document to another. Simply click a document's tab to open it, or click Close (x) on a tab to close it. Use the intuitive Arrange Documents window to quickly arrange your open documents in a variety of configurations.

Application bar and workspace switcher

From the application bar at the top of each Creative Suite application, provides menus and options in one easy to access place. Use the workspace switcher to quickly jump to different workspace configurations to meet your specific needs. Also along this bar, you can access Adobe Bridge and the document arrangement panel.

Practical smart guides

Smart guides are now even more practical with unobtrusive appearance and behaviors. Instant pop-ups appear with alignment and measurement information, such as deltas between objects and angles of rotation (that you can specify) and when moving or transforming objects. Of course, objects still snap to any alignment you choose to make it easy to arrange and transform objects exactly how you want.

Quick, easy, and obvious key object alignment

The Align panel and Control panel now provide quick access to the key alignment option. A key object is the one object that you want other objects to align to. You specify a key object by selecting all the objects you want to align, including the key object, and then clicking again on the key object. When selected, the key objects appears with a thick blue outline, and the Align To Key Object icon appears in the Control panel and Align panel. Simply choose an alignment option, such as Horizontal Align Left or Vertical Align Center, and all the other selected objects align to the key object.

New drawing and color tools

Blob Brush tool for merging paths

Use the Blob Brush to draw paths that merge with existing artwork. The Blob Brush draws paths that are fill only - no stroke - and can merge with existing artwork that has the same fill, and no stroke. The Blob Brush can merge with existing artwork that has complicated appearances (as long as there is no stroke on the artwork and the Blob Brush is set up to paint with the exact same fill and appearance settings. For example, if you've created a yellow filled rectangle with a drop shadow applied, you can set up the Blob Brush with those attributes and then draw a path across the rectangle, and the two paths will be merged. You can easily select and edit the resulting shape. Use the Blob Brush together with the Eraser tool for truly intuitive vector painting.

Expanded Gradients panel and tool

Using the enhanced Gradient tool, you can interact with gradients on the object itself by adding or changing color stops, applying transparency to color stops, and changing the direction or angle of a linear or elliptical gradient (also new in CS4). The Gradient panel now provides a menu of all your saved gradients, directly access color panels, and apply transparency to individual color spots, among other things.

Transparency in gradients

Create gradients with two to many colors and define the opacity of any or all individual colors. By specifying different opacity values for the different color stops in your gradient, you can create gradients that fade in or out and reveal or hide underlying images.

Separations Preview panel

Preview your color separations on your monitor before printing to avoid color output surprises such as unexpected spot colors and unwanted overprinting. The Separations Preview panel lets you easily turn colors on and off so you can see how blending, transparency, and overprinting will appear in color-separated output.

Improved access to core functionality

Clipping masks with clear simplified appearance and access

Adobe Illustrator now displays only the masked area while you are moving or transforming a masked object. Double-click the masked object to open it in Isolation mode, where you can view and edit the mask independently of all other objects.

In-panel Appearance editing

Select an item in the Appearance panel to view and use the enhanced full-featured controls. Click hyper-links to open option dialog boxes for effects, strokes, and fills. Click a visibility icon for any attribute to easily turn it on or off.

Enriched Graphic Styles panel

The newly updated Graphic Styles panel provides you with a quick and easy way to view and apply styles to objects in your document. Use the Text For Preview option to view a style as it appears on text, or right-click a thumbnail to quickly preview how that style will look on a selected object on the artboard. Effect-only styles now display the outlines of the object on which the style was created, so you can recognize your effect-only styles at a glance. Merge a style with an object's existing style or merge two or more different styles on an object by simply using the Alt or Option key when applying the style.

Enhanced integration at export

Support for Flex extensions

Efficiently deliver more editable, workable content to developers for web, interactive, and RIA projects. For instance, use the Flex Skinning Design extensions for Illustrator to create and export vector skins in the Adobe Flex format.

Multiple artboard export support

Creating documents with multiple artboards now makes it easy to create multi-page documents for exporting. You can export artboards to any of the following formats: PDF, PSD, SWF, JPEG, PNG, TGA, and TIFF. Or import a multiple artboard Illustrator file into Adobe InDesign or Adobe Flash.You can now easily create multiple-page PDFs. When exporting to Flash SWF format, multiple artboards export as multiple files.

Minimum System Requirements

- 2GHz or faster processor
- Microsoft® Windows® XP with Service Pack 2 (Service Pack 3 recommended) or Windows Vista® Home Premium, Business, Ultimate, or Enterprise with Service Pack 1 (certified for 32-bit Windows XP and Windows Vista).
- 512MB of RAM (1GB recommended)
- 2GB of available hard-disk space for installation; additional free space required during installation (cannot install on flash-based storage devices)
- 1,024x768 display (1,280x800 recommended) with 16-bit or greater video card
- DVD-ROM drive
- Broadband Internet connection required for online services.

Installing the Software

1. Before you install, close all applications currently running on your system—including other Adobe applications, Microsoft Office applications, and browser windows. It is also recommended to temporarily turn off virus protection during the installation process.
2. You must have administrative privileges or be able to validate as an administrator.
3. Do one of the following:
- Insert the DVD in your drive, and follow the on-screen instructions. If the installer does not

launch automatically, navigate to the Adobe CS4 folder found at the root level on your disk and double-click Setup.exe to start the installation process.

- If you downloaded the software from the web, open the folder, navigate to the Adobe CS4 folder, double-click Setup.exe, and then follow the on-screen instructions.

4. If you are installing as an upgrade, the installer will check your system to find the valid upgrade product. If it cannot find it, it will ask you to input the serial number of the product being upgraded. You can also install the software in trial, then input your new and previous serial numbers in the serialization screen shown during launch.

Uninstalling the Software

1. Before you install, close all applications currently running on your system—including other Adobe applications, Microsoft Office applications, and browser windows. It is also recommended to temporarily turn off virus protection during the installation process.
2. You must have administrative privileges or be able to validate as an administrator.
3. Do one of the following:
   - Insert the DVD in your drive, and follow the on-screen instructions. If the installer does not launch automatically, navigate to the Adobe CS4 folder found at the root level on your disk and double-click Setup.exe to start the installation process.
   - If you downloaded the software from the web, open the folder, navigate to the Adobe CS4 folder, double-click Setup.exe, and then follow the on-screen instructions.
4. If you are installing as an upgrade, the installer will check your system to find the valid upgrade product. If it cannot find it, it will ask you to input the serial number of the product being upgraded. You can also install the software in trial, then input your new and previous serial numbers in the serialization screen shown during launch.

License activation

During the installation process, your Adobe software contacts Adobe to complete the license activation process. No personal data is transmitted. For more information on product activation, visit the Adobe website at www.adobe.com/go/activation.

A single-user retail license activation supports two computers. For example, you can install the product on a desktop computer at work and on a laptop computer at home. If you want to install the software on a third computer, first deactivate it on one of the other two computers. Choose Help > Deactivate.

Registration Information

When you install your software, be sure to register to get up-to-date product information, training, newsletters and invitations to Adobe events and seminars. You will also receive a complimentary benefit for registering.

Adobe Product Improvement Program

After you use your Adobe software a certain number of times, a dialog box may appear asking whether you want to participate in the Adobe Product Improvement Program.

If you choose to participate, data about your use of Adobe software is sent to Adobe. No personal information is recorded or sent. The Adobe Product Improvement Program only collects information about which features and tools you use and how often you use them.

You can opt in to or out of the program at any time:

To participate, choose Help > Adobe Product Improvement Program and click Yes, Participate.

To stop participating, choose Help > Adobe Product Improvement Program and click No, Thank You.

Font Installation

There are additional fonts on the installation disk.

Installed Fonts

Several OpenType fonts are included with Illustrator CS4. A subset of these fonts are installed by Illustrator for your convenience. Specific font faces from the following font families are installed:

- Adobe® Caslon™ Pro
- Adobe® Garamond® Pro
- Arno™ Pro
- Bell Gothic Std
- Bickham Script® Pro
- Birch® Std
- Blackoak® Std
- Brush Script Std
- Chaparral® Pro
- Charlemagne® Std
- Cooper Std
- Eccentric Std
- Garamond Premier Pro
- Giddyup® Std
- Hobo Std
- Kozuka Gothic® Pro
- Kozuka Mincho® Pro
- Letter Gothic Std
- Lithos® Pro
- Mesquite® Std
- Minion® Pro
- Myriad® Pro
- Nueva® Std
- OCR-A Std
- Orator Std
- Poplar® Std
- Prestige Elite Std
- Rosewood® Std
- Stencil Std
- Tekton® Pro
- Trajan® Pro
- Adobe Myungio Std
- Adobe Ming Std
- Adobe Song Std

These fonts are installed in the following locations:

[startup drive]\Windows\Fonts\

Additional Fonts

The following fonts and accompanying documentation are not installed, but included in the Documentation folder on the Illustrator CS4 product DVD (in the case of retail customers), or in the packaged download file (if you downloaded Illustrator CS4 from Adobe Store). For trial customers, this additional content will not be available until after purchase.

- Adobe® Caslon® Pro
- Bernhard Modern Std
- Caflisch Script® Pro
- Kozuka Gothic® Std
- Kozuka Mincho® Std
- News Gothic Std
- Wood Type Ornaments Std
- Ryo Display Std
- Ryo Gothic Std
- Ryo Text Std

Adobe Fansong Std Adobe Heiti Std

You will also find the fonts listed in the installed set above, but with a number of additional font faces not included in the installation. Anyone who cares about getting all of the available fonts should definitely take the time to install the additional set.

The Beginning

You can start Illustrator as you would do with any other software. From Start, go to the Programs and the select Illustrator from Adobe group.

After showing the opening logo of the company, as shown above, it would give rise to a blank slate for you to work on, as shown on next page.

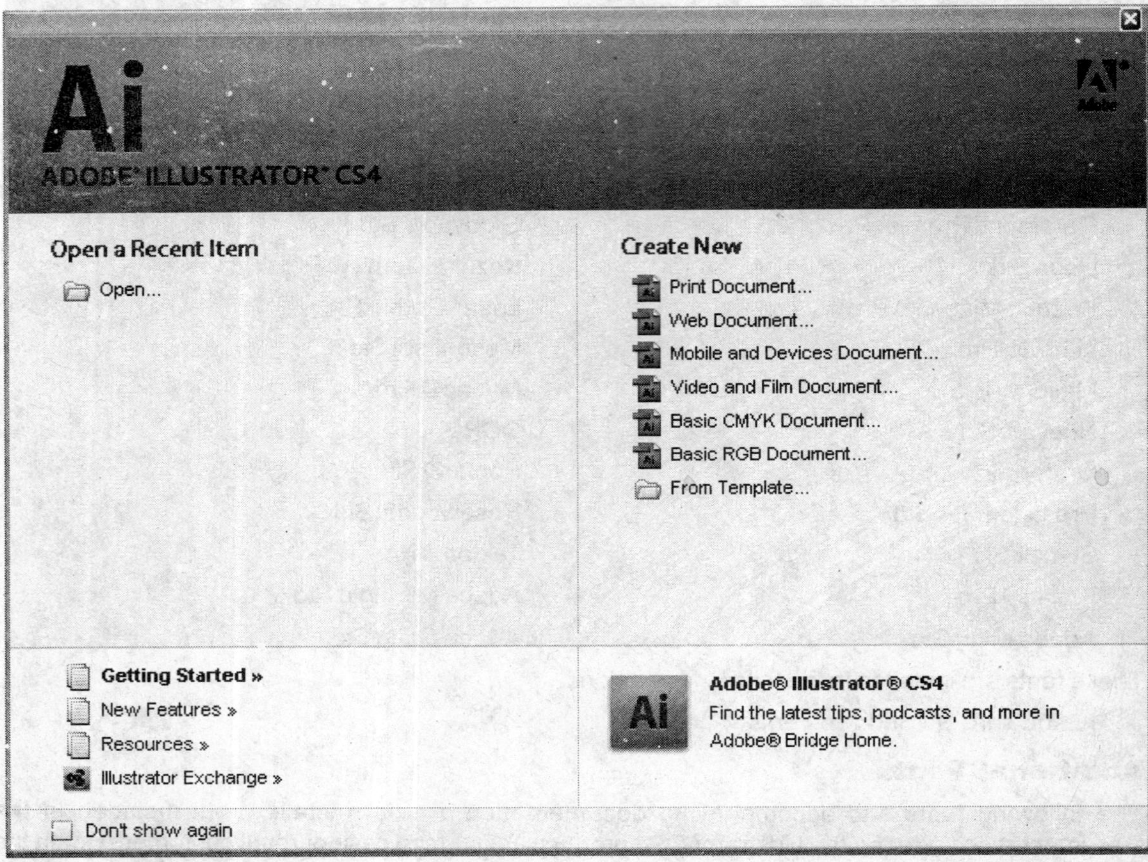

As you can notice, there are various tools in the toolbox to help you work in Illustrator and the menus which have various commands underneath them. As usual you can select these commands from the menu and run them.

Illustrator Screen

Let me first tell you what the Illustrator screen, actually has. You can see the various contents of the screen on the next page. Various items of the screen are described below:

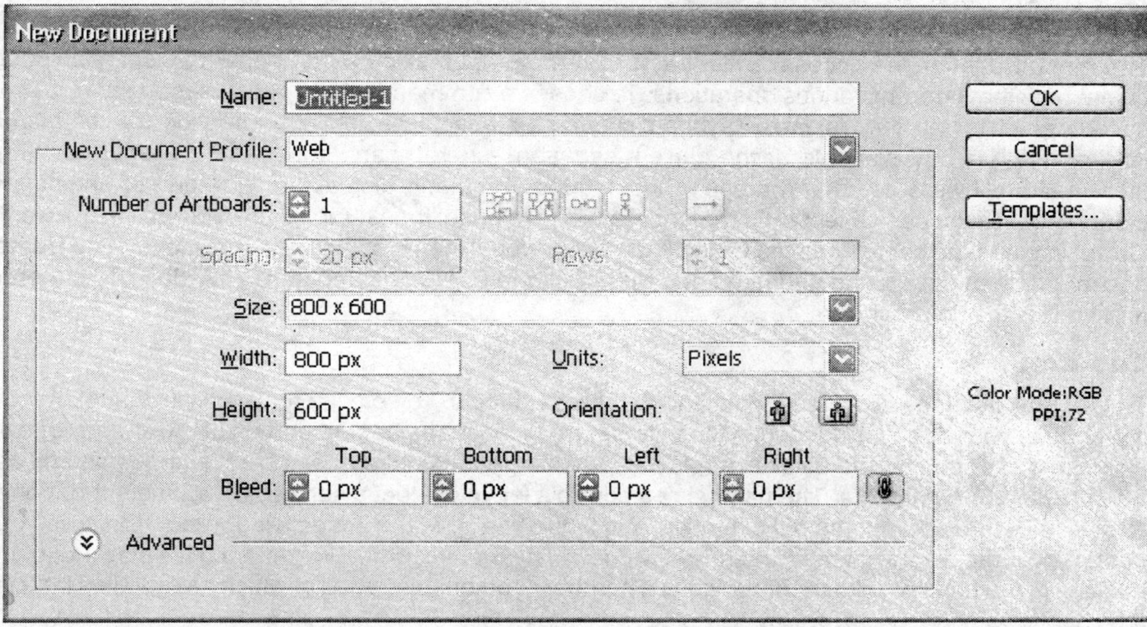
New Document
Name: Untitled-1
OK
Cancel
New Document Profile: Web
Templates...
Number of Artboards: 1
Spacing: 20 px
Rows: 1
Size: 800 x 600
Width: 800 px
Units: Pixels
Height: 600 px
Orientation:
Color Mode:RGB
PPI:72
Top
Bottom
Left
Right
Bleed: 0 px 0 px 0 px 0 px
Advanced

File Edit Object Type Select Effect View Window Help
ESSENTIALS
No Selection
Stroke: 1 pt
2 pt. Oval
Style:
Opacity: 100 %
Document Setup
Preferences
Untitled-1 @ 140% (RGB/Preview)
140%
Never Saved

Menu bar

The menu bar provides access to Illustrator's CS4 menus. Click a menu name to display a list of commands that perform various operations. To choose a command, drag your cursor on top of it so it becomes highlighted, then release. Keyboard shortcuts appear to the right of commands. If a command is dimmed, it is not available at the current situation and you can't choose it. If a right-pointing arrowhead follows a command name, choosing the command displays a submenu of additional commands. To choose Object>>Command Paths>>Release, for example, you would click the word Object in the Menu bar to open the Object menu. You would then move down to the Compound Paths command, then over to the submenu and then click the Release command. This closes the menu and applies the command.

Toolbox

The toolbox includes 26 default tools and 38 alternate tools. To select a tool, click its icon. Later in the chapter you will be introduced to these tools one by one. The bottom portion of the toolbox offers three sets of controls. The color controls let you change the colors of an object's stroke and fill as well as interchange colors. The paint styles controls let you select a solid color, a gradient or none (that is, see-through) for your fill or stroke. And in the final row, the image window controls give you control over the display of the foreground window. The toolbox is known generically as a palette. In addition to the tool box, Illustrator provides a number of other palettes all of which are detailed later in the chapter.

Illustration Window

The illustration window is the large window in the middle of the desktop. A window appears for every open illustration. The title bar lists the name of the document, the relative viewing size, the document color mode and the type of preview currently chosen. If the illustration has not been given a name, the name appears as "Untitled art," followed by a number.

You can move the illustration window by dragging the title bar. Close the illustration by clicking in the close box in the upper left corner (or in the upper right corner of the window to enlarge or reduce the size of the window manually. Click the zoom box again to reduce the window to its previous size. In Windows users, this corresponds to the maximize/restore box that sits just to the left of the close box. To the left of that, Windows provides the minimize box, which reduces Illustrator to a button on the Windows taskbar without quitting the program.

Artboard

The page with the drop shadow in the middle of the window is the art board. This represents the size of the drawing you want to create. Surrounding the artboard is the pasteboard. You can move objects out into the pasteboard if you like and these objects will be saved with your illustration, but they will not print. Experienced artists typically use the pasteboard as a storage area for objects they can't quite bear to delete. The dotted line around the image able area shows the portion of the artboard your printer can actually print. Most printers can't print to the extreme edges of a page. Together, the artboard and pasteboard are generically known as the drawing area.

Scroll Bars

The scroll bars appear along the right and bottom edges of the illustration window, as they do in most Windows applications. They allow you to move your drawing with respect to the window to better see various portions of your illustration. Click one of the arrows at the end of a scroll bar to nudge the drawing a small distance' click in the gray area of a scroll bar to move the drawing a greater distance. Drag the tab in either scroll bar to move the drawing manually.

Size Option Box

The size option box in the lower left corner of the illustration window lets you change the view size of your artwork. Simply click the size option box, enter any permitted value and hit Enter. You can reduce the view to as little as 3.13 percent of the actual size, allowing you to easily see the largest possible artboard size that Illustrator permits. Going to the other extreme, you can expand a square inch to a respectable 6-1/3 square feet by choosing 6400 percent.

Status Bar

The status bar just to the right of the size bar lists all kinds of moderately useful information about the program. Click the status bar to display a pop-up menu of status bar options, you can have the status bar list the active tool, the date and time, the amount of RAM going unused inside Illustrator, the number of available undos and redos or the type of color profile assigned to the document.

Now we come to learning the menu commands.

Menu Commands

One look at these menu commands and you know what is where.

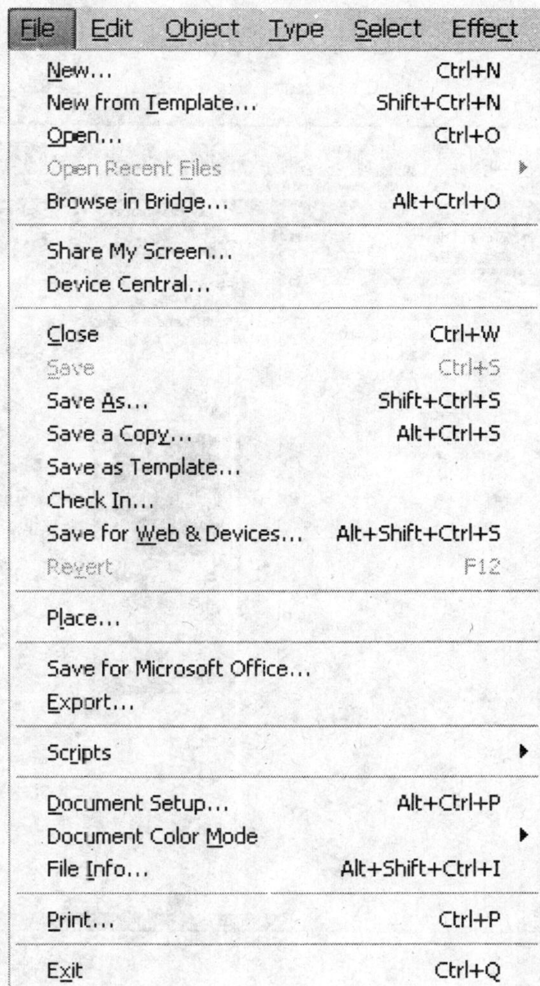

File menu

New: The New command lets you create a blank, untitled Illustration image. You can also use this command to create a new image with the exact same pixel dimensions as an image or selection that has been copied to the Clipboard.

New from Template: It gives you the option of openings an exiting template and then changing it according to your own liking.

Open: It allows you to open an existing file from either the hard disk or other media attached to the computer, floppy drive, CD drive, etc. This also gives rise to a dialog box, from where you can select the file, which you want to open.

Open Recent Files: It allows you to open a recently opened file.

Browse in Bridge: It allows you to browse through various files in the hard disk.

Share My Screen: It allows you to share the screen with other users over the Internet.

Device Central: Lets you preview how your document will appear on a particular mobile phone or device.

Close: It allows you to close the current illustrator file.

Save: It saves the current illustrator file.

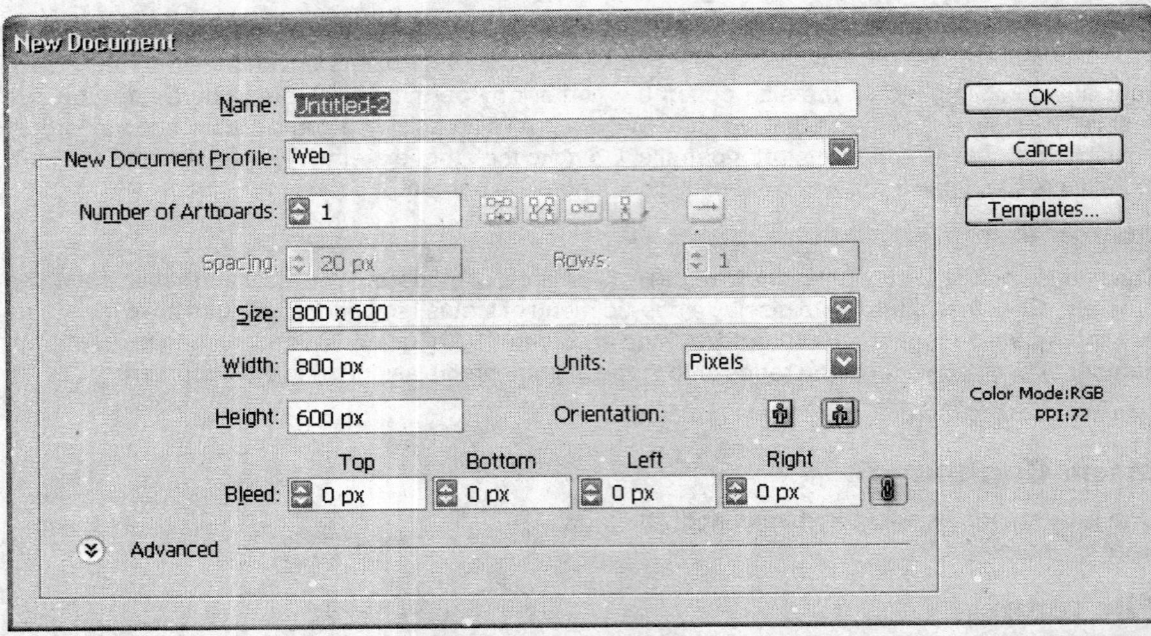
New Document
Name: Untitled-2
New Document Profile: Web
Number of Artboards: 1
Spacing: 20 px
Rows: 1
Size: 800 x 600
Width: 800 px
Units: Pixels
Height: 600 px
Orientation:
Top
Bottom
Left
Right
Bleed: 0 px 0 px 0 px 0 px
Advanced
OK
Cancel
Templates...
Color Mode:RGB
PPI:72

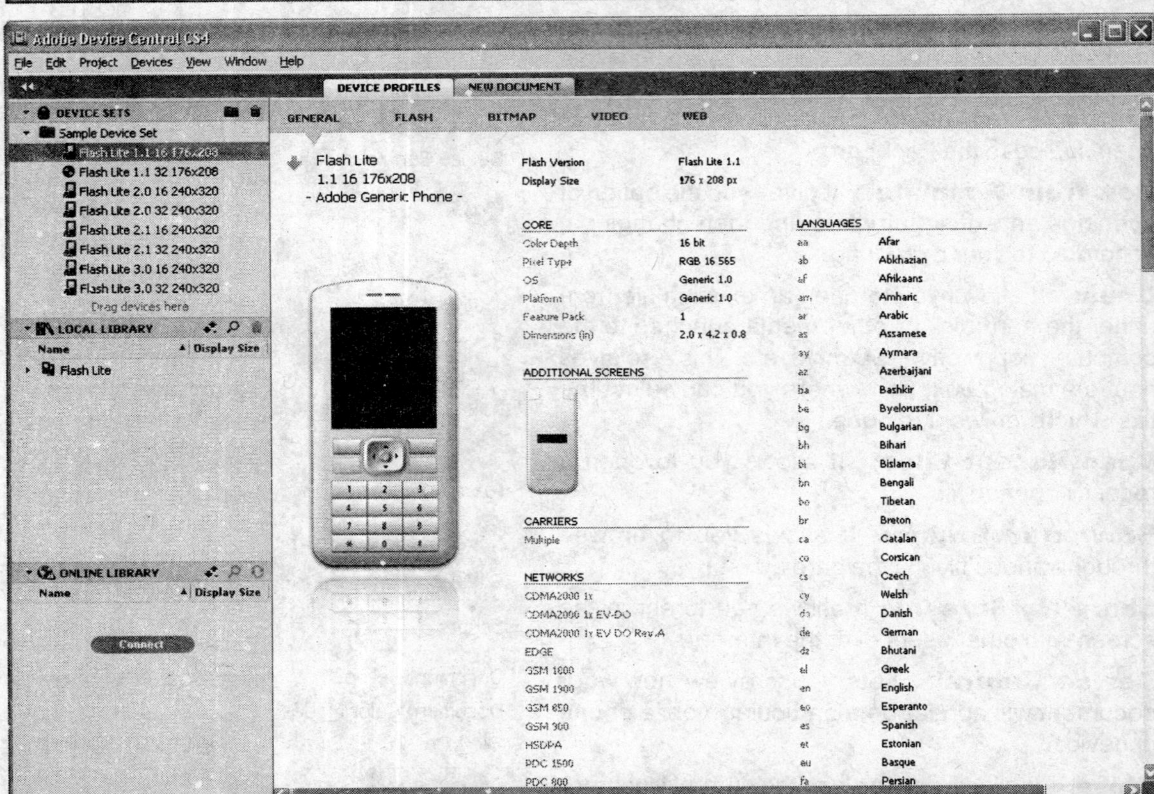
Adobe Device Central CS4
File Edit Project Devices View Window Help
DEVICE PROFILES
NEW DOCUMENT
DEVICE SETS
Sample Device Set
Flash Lite 1.1 16 176x208
Flash Lite 1.1 32 176x208
Flash Lite 2.0 16 240x320
Flash Lite 2.0 32 240x320
Flash Lite 2.1 16 240x320
Flash Lite 2.1 32 240x320
Flash Lite 3.0 16 240x320
Flash Lite 3.0 32 240x320
Drag devices here
LOCAL LIBRARY
Name
Display Size
Flash Lite
ONLINE LIBRARY
Name
Display Size
Connect
GENERAL
FLASH
BITMAP
VIDEO
WEB
Flash Lite
1.1 16 176x208
- Adobe Generic Phone -
Flash Version
Flash Lite 1.1
Display Size
176 x 208 px
CORE
Color Depth
16 bit
Pixel Type
RGB 16 565
OS
Generic 1.0
Platform
Generic 1.0
Feature Pack
1
Dimensions (in)
2.0 x 4.2 x 0.8
ADDITIONAL SCREENS
CARRIERS
Multiple
NETWORKS
CDMA2000 1x
CDMA2000 1x EV-DO
CDMA2000 1x EV DO Rev.A
EDGE
GSM 1800
GSM 1900
GSM 850
GSM 900
HSDPA
PDC 1500
PDC 800
LANGUAGES
aa Afar
ab Abkhazian
af Afrikaans
am Amharic
ar Arabic
as Assamese
ay Aymara
az Azerbaijani
ba Bashkir
be Byelorussian
bg Bulgarian
bh Bihari
bi Bislama
bn Bengali
bo Tibetan
br Breton
ca Catalan
co Corsican
cs Czech
cy Welsh
da Danish
de German
dz Bhutani
el Greek
en English
eo Esperanto
es Spanish
et Estonian
eu Basque
fa Persian

Save As: It allows you to save the current file under a new name or overwrite the current file or even with a different format.

Save a Copy: It allows you to make a copy of the existing illustrator file.

Save as Template: This command allows you to save the current file in the form of a template, which can be used later on.

Check In..: Allows you to check the spelling of the text in the document.

Save for Web & Devices: It allows you to save the current file as a Web page.

Revert: You can revert back to the earlier saved version.

Place: This command is used to place the text into the file.

Save for Microsoft Office: This command allows you to save for different programs of Microsoft Office constituents.

Export: Using this command you can export the selected text of the publication into a document file in the format selected by you.

Scripts: Illustrator provides prerecorded actions and scripts to assist you in performing common tasks. Prerecorded actions are installed as a default set in the Actions palette when you install the Illustrator application; default scripts appear in the File > Scripts submenu.

Document Setup: You can define here various options for your new illustrator file.

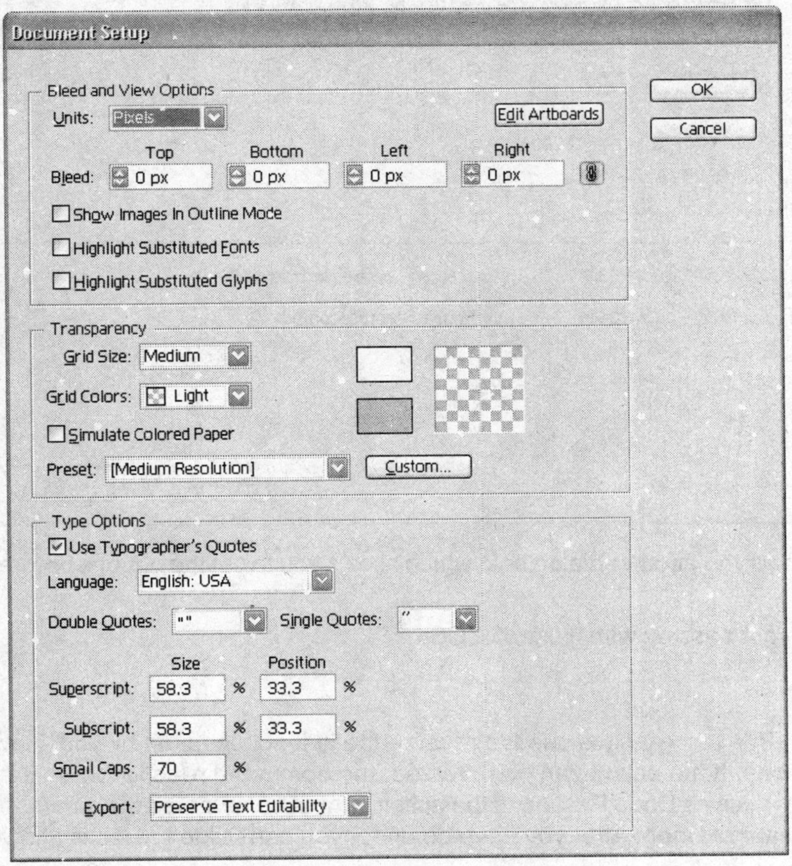

Document Color Mode: It allows you to toggle between CYMK and RBG colour mode.

File info...: Use it to provide information about the contents of a document and to preserve information about a document that will be opened in other Adobe applications.

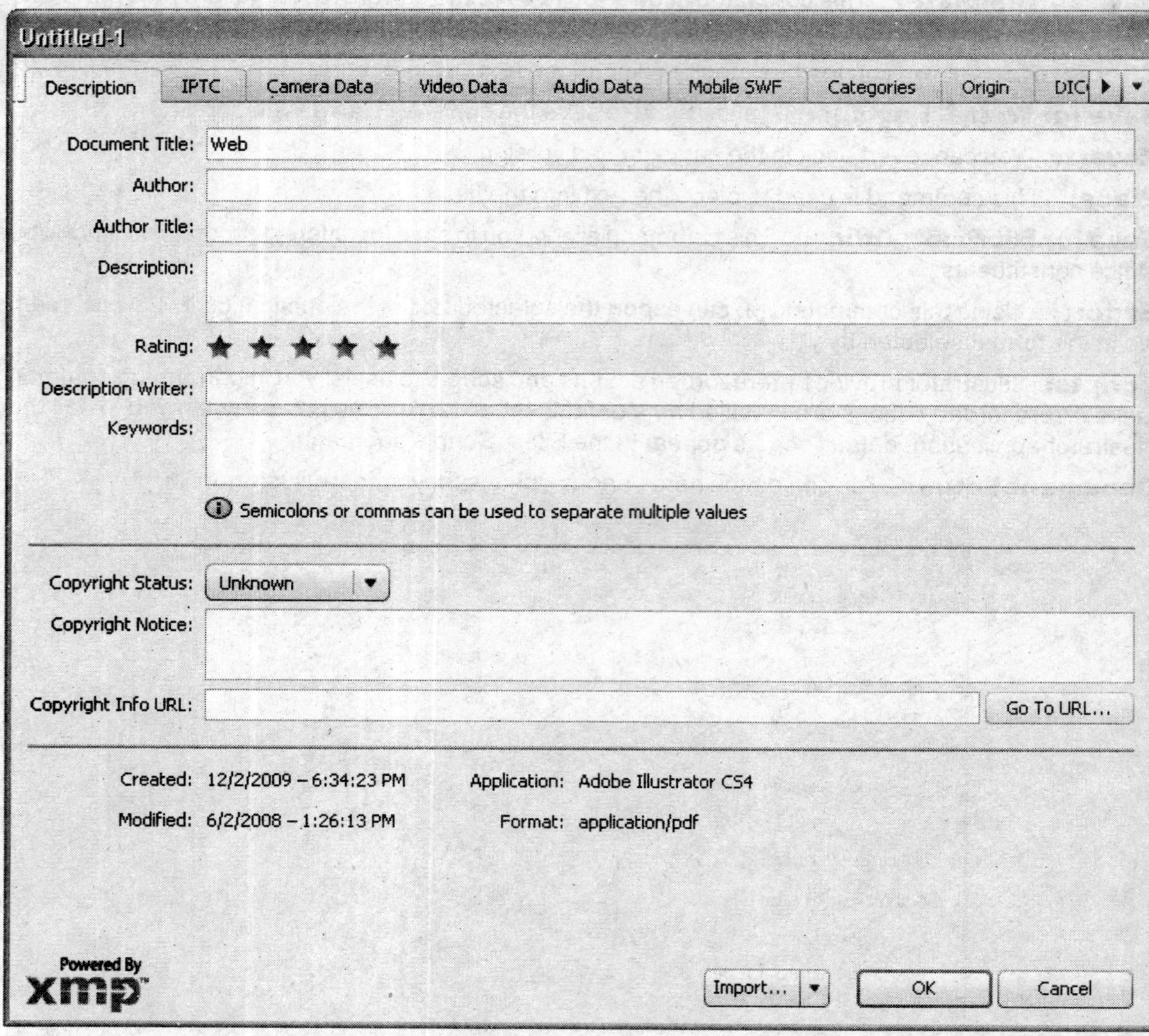

Print: This gives you another dialog box, which allows you to set the options before sending the file for printing.

Exit: Closes your session with Illustrator CS4.

Edit menu

Undo/Redo: This command is used to reverse the last action taken by you. However, you can't undo all the actions. If the action can be reversed, the command read Undo on the Edit menu and names the action such as Undo Pasting. If the action cannot be reversed the command is off and thus can be read as cannot Undo. After you have do undo, you can Redo too if it is allowed.

Cut: This command is used to cut the selected text or graphics from your file and keep it available for pasting it later to any other place in the same file or any other file or even any other software which supports the clipboard text.

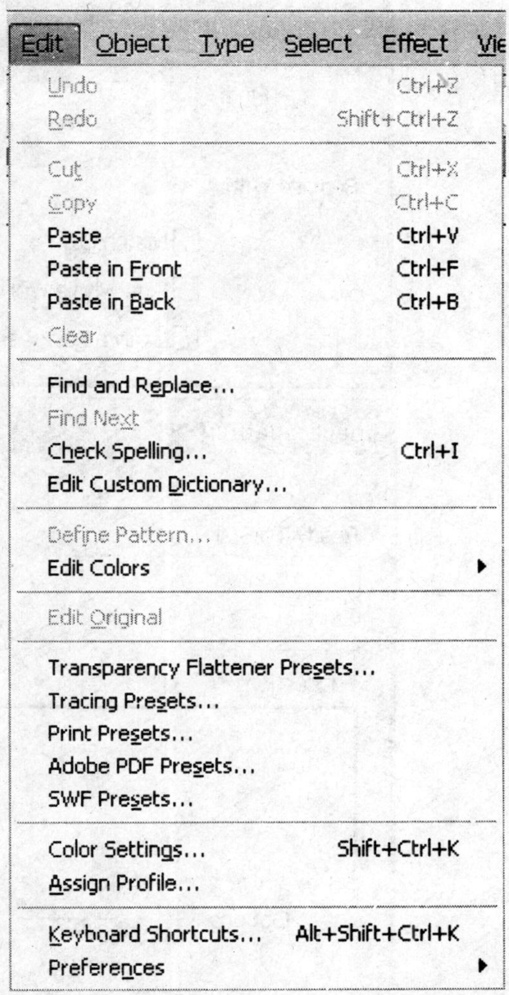

Copy: This command is also used to copy the selected text or graphics from your file and keep it available for pasting it later. Only difference it has from Cut command is that it leaves the original text as it is whereas in the case of Cut the original text is lost. When you have more than one publication open, you can copy objects between publications without using the Clipboard. Select an object in one publication, drag it to position in the other publication window and release the mouse button to create a copy.

Paste: This command is used to place the selected text or graphics from clipboard, where the text using the above Cut or Copy command has been kept.

Paste In Front: This command pastes a cut or copied selection outside another selection in the same image or different image. The source selection is pasted onto a new layer, and the destination selection border is converted into a layer mask.

Paste In Back: This command pastes a cut or copied selection inside another selection in the same image or different image. The source selection is pasted onto a new layer, and the destination selection border is converted into a layer mask.

Clear: This command is used to delete the current selection from your file without storing it in the Clipboard. This has the same effect as pressing Delete or Backspace.

Find and Replace: This command is used to find a portion of the text or an object and later replace it with another one.

Find Next: This command is used to find the next text the object after finding the first.

Check Spelling: Checks the spelling of the selected text using the dictionary available with the software.

Edit Custom Dictionary: This command allows you to edit the dictionary available with the software, adding or deleting the words mostly required by you.

Define Pattern: The pattern you define here is repeated as tiles within the selection. Each new pattern replaces the current pattern. If you want to reuse patterns, save a file of swatches for defining patterns. You can also use the pattern stamp tool to paint with a pattern.

Edit Colors: When you have artwork selected and you access the dialog box by clicking the icon in the Control panel, Swatches panel, or Color Guide panel, or when you choose Edit > Edit Colors > Recolor Artwork, the dialog box opens as the Recolor Artwork dialog box and you have access to the Assign tab and the Edit tab. When you do not have artwork selected and you access the dialog box

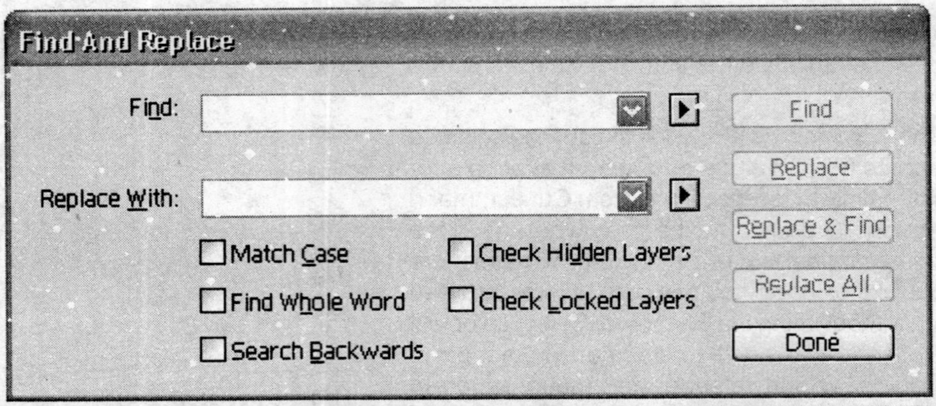
Find And Replace
Find:
Replace With:
Match Case
Check Hidden Layers
Find Whole Word
Check Locked Layers
Search Backwards
Find
Replace
Replace & Find
Replace All
Done

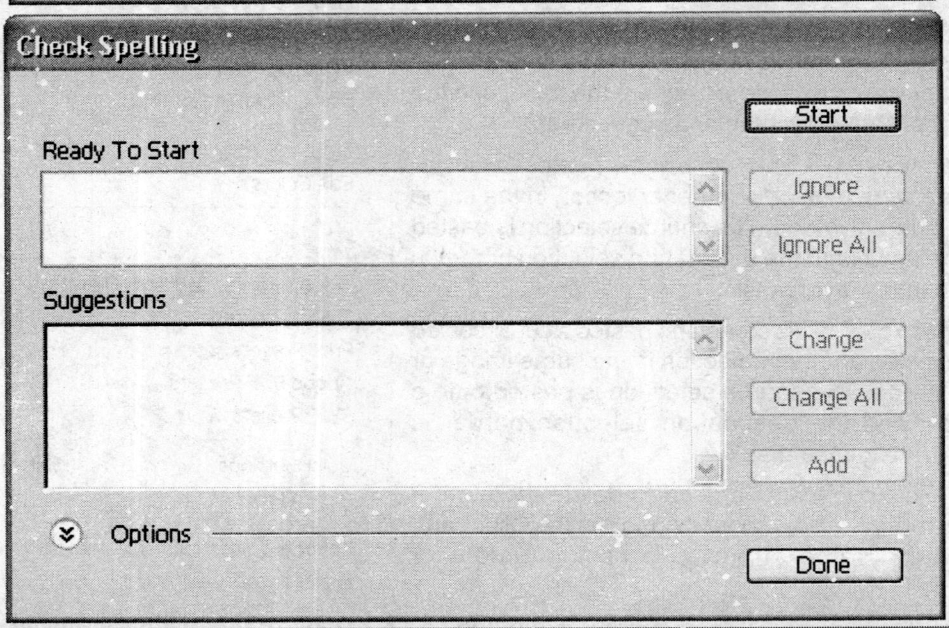
Check Spelling
Start
Ready To Start
Ignore
Ignore All
Suggestions
Change
Change All
Add
Options
Done

Edit Custom Dictionary
Entry:
Add
Delete
Change
Done

by clicking the icon in the Control panel, Swatches panel, or Color Guide panel, the dialog box opens as the Edit Colors dialog box and you have access to the Edit tab only. Regardless of which name appears at the top of the dialog box, the right side of it always displays the color groups for the current document, along with two default color groups: Print Color and Grayscale. You can select and use these color groups at anytime..

Edit Original: Specailly useful for the linked graphics when you have to edit the original graphics too.

Transparency Flattener Presets: You can set the following options in Transparency Flattener Preset Options dialog box.

Name

Specifies the name of the preset. Depending on the dialog box, you can type a name in the Name text box or accept the default. You can enter the name of an existing preset to edit that preset. However, you can't edit the default presets.

Raster/Vector balance

Specifies the amount of rasterization. The higher the setting, the less rasterization is performed on artwork. Select the highest setting to keep as much artwork as possible vector data; select the lowest setting to rasterize all the artwork.

Line Art And Text Resolution

Specifies the resolution for vector objects rasterized as a result of flattening.

Gradient And Mesh Resolution

Specifies the resolution for gradients and mesh objects rasterized as a result of flattening.

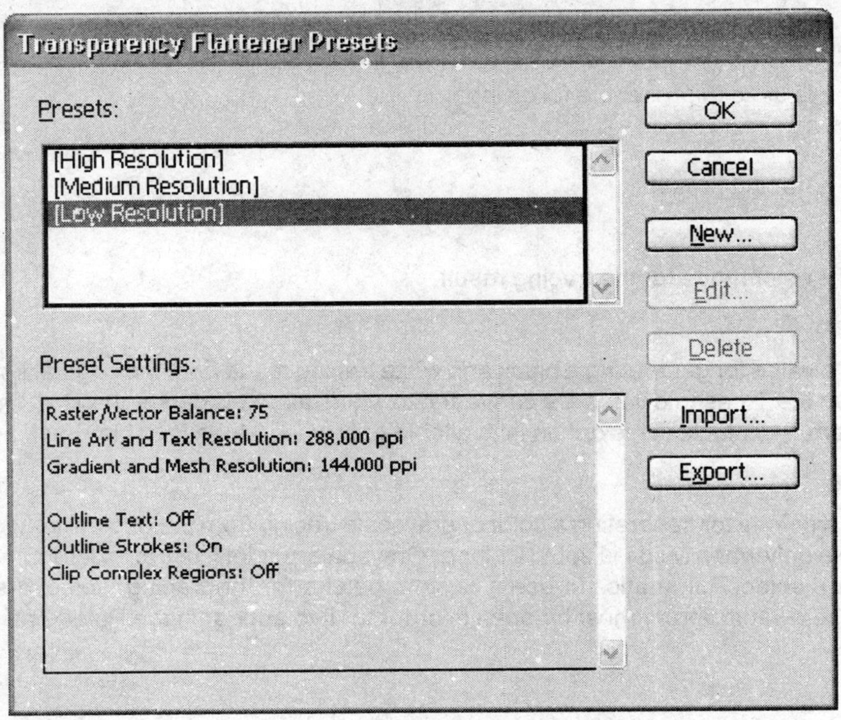

In most cases, a value of 300 is sufficient for Line Art And Text Resolution, and a value of 150 is sufficient for Gradients And Mesh Resolution. However, if small fonts or fine objects will be rasterized or if the output is a high-quality print, higher values (600 ppi or more) are necessary. Using very high values is not recommended because it can degrade performance without noticeably improving the quality of the artwork. Note that for both options, the Flatness setting in the Graphics portion in the Print dialog box affects the precision of intersections when flattening.

Convert All Text To Outlines

Converts all type objects (point type, area type, and path type) to outlines and discards all type glyph information. This option ensures that the width of text stays consistent during flattening. Note that enabling this option will cause small fonts to appear slightly thicker.

Convert All Strokes To Outlines

Converts all strokes to simple filled paths. This option ensures that the width of strokes stays consistent during flattening. Note that enabling this option will cause thin strokes to appear slightly thicker.

Clip Complex Regions

Ensures that the boundaries between vector artwork and rasterized artwork fall along object paths. Selecting this option reduces stitching artifacts that result when part of an object is rasterized while another part of the object remains in vector form. However, selecting this option may result in paths that are too complex for the printer to handle. Some print drivers process raster and vector art differently, and this can also result in color stitching. You may be able to minimize stitching problems by disabling some print-driver specific color-management settings. Because these settings vary with each printer, see the documentation that came with your printer.

Tracing Presets

This command is used to preset the following:

Preset

Specifies a tracing preset.

Mode

Specifies a color mode for the tracing result.

Threshold

Specifies a value for generating a black and white tracing result from the original image. All pixels lighter than the Threshold value are converted to white, all pixels darker than the Threshold value are converted to black. (This option is available only when Mode is set to Black and White.)

Palette

Specifies a palette for generating a color or grayscale tracing from the original image. (This option is available only when Mode is set to Color or Grayscale.) To let Illustrator determine the colors in the tracing, select Automatic. To use a custom palette for the tracing, select a swatch library name. (The swatch library must be open in order for it to appear in the Palette menu.)

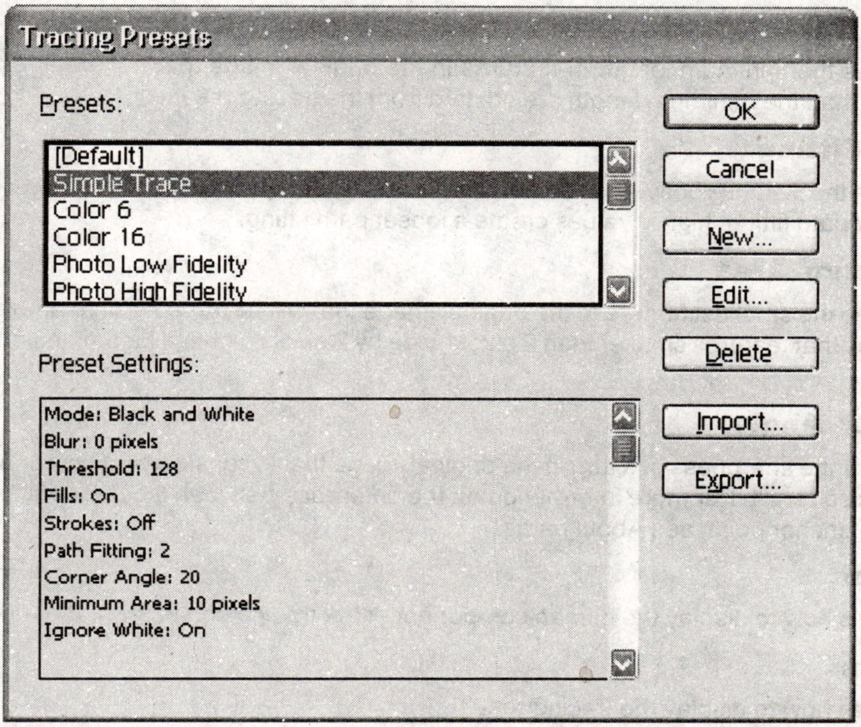

Max Colors

Specifies a maximum number of colors to use in a color or grayscale tracing result. (This option is available only when Mode is set to Color or Grayscale and when Palette is set to Automatic.)

Output To Swatches

Creates a new swatch in the Swatches palette for each color in the tracing result.

Blur

Blurs the original image before generating the tracing result. Select this option to reduce small artifacts and smooth jagged edges in the tracing result.

Resample

Resamples the original image to the specified resolution before generating the tracing result. This option is useful for speeding up the tracing process for large images but can yield degraded results.

Fills

Creates filled regions in the tracing result.

Strokes

Creates stroked paths in the tracing result.

Max Stroke Weight

Specifies the maximum width of features in the original image that can be stroked. Features larger than the maximum width become outlined areas in the tracing result.

Min Stroke Length

Specifies the minimum length of features in the original image that can be stroked. Features smaller than the minimum length are omitted from the tracing result.

Path Fitting

Controls the distance between the traced shape and the original pixel shape. Lower values create a tighter path fitting; higher values create a looser path fitting.

Minimum Area

Specifies the smallest feature in the original image that will be traced. For example, a value of 4 specifies that features smaller than 2 pixels wide by 2 pixels high will be omitted from the tracing result.

Corner Angle

Specifies the sharpness of a turn in the original image that is considered a corner anchor point in the tracing result. For more information on the difference between a corner anchor point and a smooth anchor point, see About paths.

Raster

Specifies how to display the bitmap component of the tracing object.

Vector

Specifies how to display the tracing result.

Select

Preview in the Tracing Options dialog box to preview the result of the current settings.To set the default tracing options, deselect all objects before you open the Tracing Options dialog box. When you're finished setting options, click Set Default.

Print Presets

If you regularly output to different printers or job types, you can automate print jobs by saving all output settings as print presets. Using print presets is a fast, reliable way to print jobs that require consistently accurate settings for many options in the Print dialog box. You can save and load print presets, making it easy to back them up or to make them available to your service providers, clients, or others in your workgroup. Once you select a print preset, you can view the settings for it in the Print Presets dialog box.

Adobe PDF Presets

A PDF preset is a group of settings that affect the process of creating a PDF. These settings are designed to balance file size with quality, depending on how the PDF will be used. Most predefined presets are shared across Adobe Creative Suite components, including InDesign, Illustrator, Photoshop, and Acrobat. You can also create and share custom presets for your unique output requirements.

A few of the presets listed below are not available until you move them—as needed—from the Extras folder (where they are installed by default) to the Settings folder. Typically, the Extras and Settings folders are found in (Windows) Documents and Settings\All Users\Application Data\Adobe\Adobe PDF or (Mac OS) Library/Application Support/Adobe PDF. Some presets are not available in some Creative Suite components.

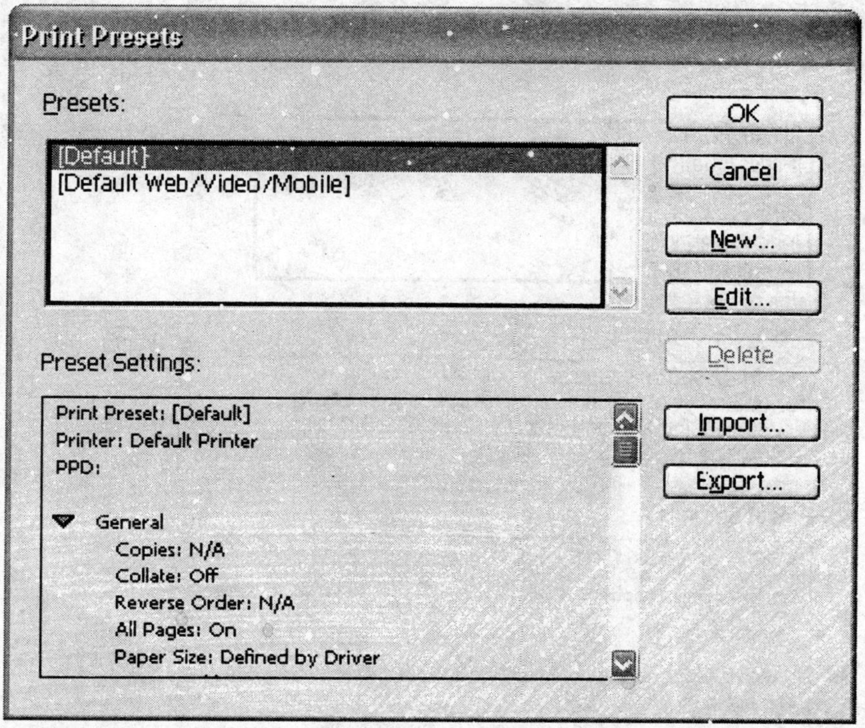

Review your PDF settings periodically. The settings do not automatically revert to the default settings. Applications and utilities that create PDFs use the last set of PDF settings defined or selected. High Quality Print

Creates PDFs for quality printing on desktop printers and proofing devices. This preset uses PDF 1.4 (Windows) or PDF 1.6 (Mac OS), downsamples color and grayscale images to 300 ppi and monochrome images to 1200 ppi, embeds subsets of all fonts, leaves color unchanged, and does not flatten transparency (for file types capable of transparency). These PDFs can be opened in Acrobat 5.0 and Acrobat Reader 5.0 and later. In InDesign, this preset also creates tagged PDFs.

Illustrator Default (Illustrator only)

Creates a PDF in which all Illustrator data is preserved. PDFs created with this preset can be reopened in Illustrator without any loss of data.

Oversized Pages (Acrobat only)

Creates PDFs suitable for viewing and printing of engineering drawings larger than 200 x 200 inches. These PDFs can be opened in Acrobat and Reader 7.0 and later.

PDF/A-1b: 2005 (CMYK and RGB) (Acrobat only)

Used for long-term preservation (archival) of electronic documents. PDF/A 1b uses PDF 1.4 and converts all colors to either CMYK or RGB, depending on which standard you choose. These PDFs can be opened in Acrobat and Reader versions 5.0 and later.

PDF/X 1a (2001 and 2003)

PDF/X 1a requires all fonts to be embedded, the appropriate PDF bounding boxes to be specified,

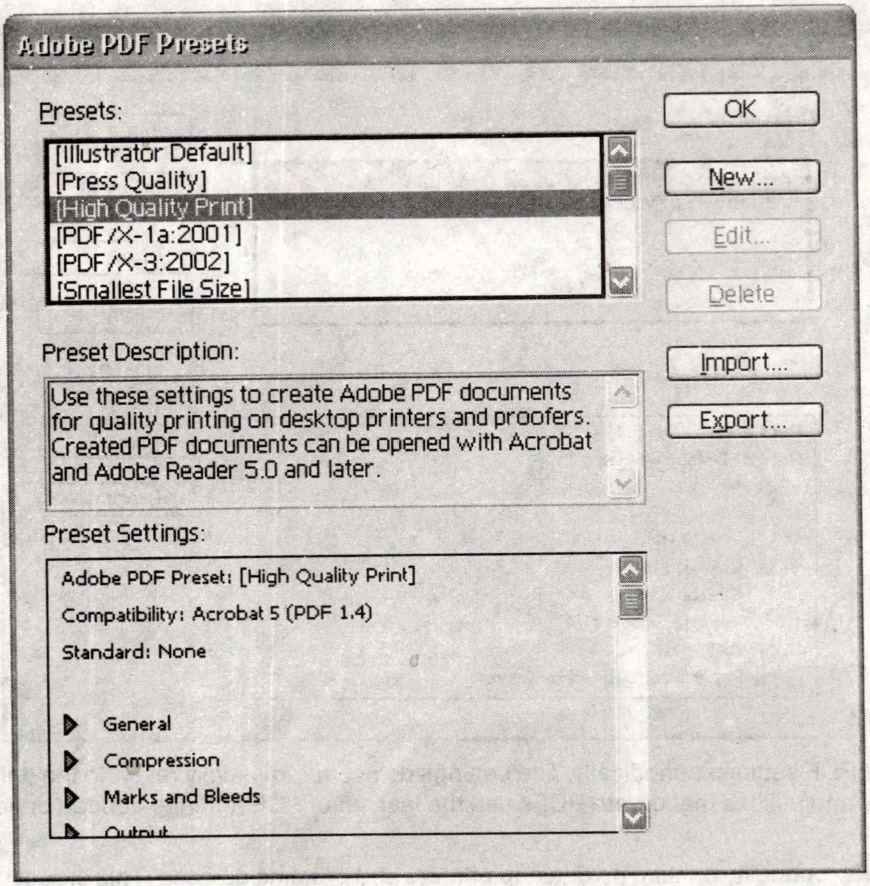

and color to appear as CMYK, spot colors, or both. Compliant files must contain information describing the printing condition for which they are prepared. PDF files created with PDF/X 1a compliance can be opened in Acrobat 4.0 and Acrobat Reader 4.0 and later. PDF/X 1a uses PDF 1.3, downsamples color and grayscale images to 300 ppi and monochrome images to 1200 ppi, embeds subsets of all fonts, creates untagged PDFs, and flattens transparency using the High Resolution setting.

The PDF/X1 a:2003 and PDF/X 3 (2003) presets are placed on your computer during installation but are not available until you move them from the Extras folder to the Settings folder.

PDF/X 4 (2007)

In Acrobat 8, this preset is called PDF/X 4 DRAFT to reflect the draft state of the ISO specification at Acrobat ship time. This preset is based on PDF 1.4, which includes support for live transparency. PDF/X 4 has the same color management and International Color Consortium (ICC) color specifications as PDF/X 3. You can create PDF/X 4-compliant files directly with Creative Suite 3 components (Illustrator, InDesign, and Photoshop). In Acrobat 8, use the Preflight feature to convert PDFs to PDF/X 4 DRAFT.

PDF files created with PDF/X 4 compliance can be opened in Acrobat 7.0 and Reader 7.0 and later.

Press Quality

Creates PDF files for high-quality print production (for example, for digital printing or for separations to an imagesetter or platesetter), but does not create files that are PDF/X-compliant. In this case, the quality of the content is the highest consideration. The objective is to maintain all the information in a PDF file that a commercial printer or print service provider needs in order to print the document correctly. This set of options uses PDF 1.4, converts colors to CMYK, downsamples color and grayscale images to 300 ppi and monochrome images to 1200 ppi, embeds subsets of all fonts, and preserves transparency (for file types capable of transparency).

These PDF files can be opened in Acrobat 5.0 and Acrobat Reader 5.0 and later.

Note: Before creating an Adobe PDF file to send to a commercial printer or print service provider, find out what the output resolution and other settings should be, or ask for a .joboptions file with the recommended settings. You might need to customize the Adobe PDF settings for a particular provider and then provide a .joboptions file of your own.

Rich Content PDF

Creates accessible PDF files that include tags, hyperlinks, bookmarks, interactive elements, and layers. This set of options uses PDF 1.5 and embeds subsets of all fonts. It also optimizes files for byte serving. These PDF files can be opened in Acrobat 6.0 and Adobe Reader 6.0 and later. (The Rich Content PDF preset is in the Extras folder.)

This preset was called eBook in earlier versions of some applications.

Smallest File Size

Creates PDF files for displaying on the web or an intranet, or for distribution through an e mail system. This set of options uses compression, downsampling, and a relatively low image resolution. It converts all colors to sRGB, and (for Distiller-based conversions) does not embed fonts. It also optimizes files for byte serving.

These PDF files can be opened in Acrobat 5.0 and Acrobat Reader 5.0 and later.

Standard (Acrobat only)

Creates PDF files to be printed to desktop printers or digital copiers, published on a CD, or sent to a client as a publishing proof. This set of options uses compression and downsampling to keep the file size down, but also embeds subsets of all (allowed) fonts used in the file, converts all colors to sRGB, and prints to a medium resolution. Note that Windows font subsets are not embedded by default. PDF files created with this settings file can be opened in Acrobat 5.0 and Acrobat Reader 5.0 and later.

SWF Presets

The Adobe Flash (SWF) file format is a vector-based graphics file format for the creation of scalable, compact graphics for the web. Because the file format is vector-based, the artwork maintains its image quality at any resolution. The SWF format is ideal for the creation of animation frames, but you can also save raster images in SWF format or mix raster and vector graphics.

Preset

Specifies the preconfigured set of options you want to use for export. You can create new presets by setting options as desired, and then choosing Save Settings from the panel menu. (To open the panel menu, click the triangle to the right of the Preset menu.)

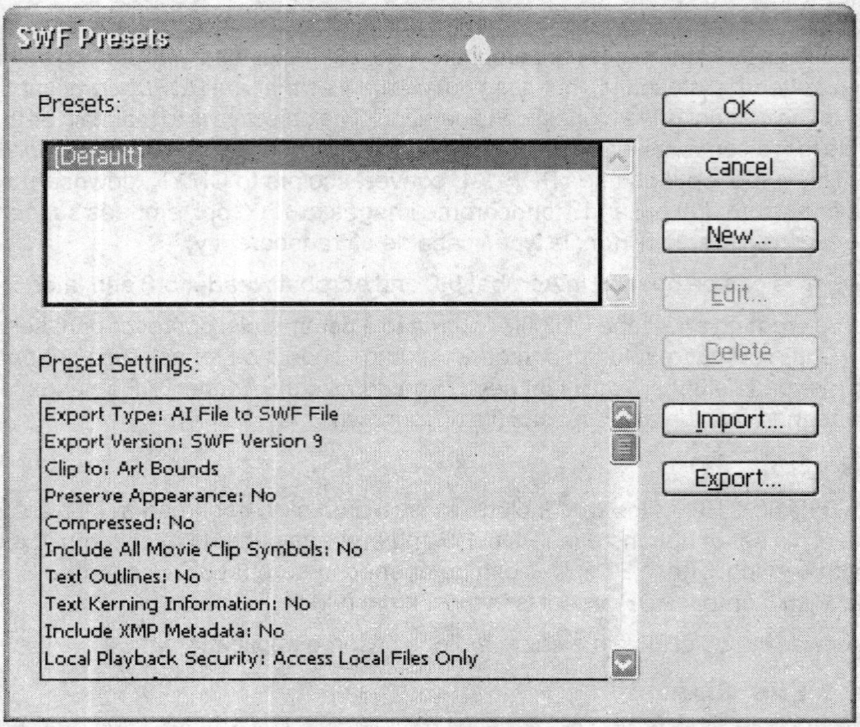

Flash Player Version

Specifies the earliest version of Flash Player that will support the exported file.

Type Of Export

Determines how layers are exported. Select AI File To SWF File to export the artwork to a single frame. Select Layers To SWF Frames to export the artwork on each layer to a separate SWF frame, creating an animated SWF.

Select AI File To SWF File to preserve layer clipping masks.

Curve Quality

Specifies the accuracy of the bezier curves. A low number decreases the exported file size with a slight loss of curve quality. A higher number increases the accuracy of the bezier curve reproduction, but results in a larger file size.

Frame Rate

Specifies the rate at which the animation will play in a Flash viewer. This option is available only for Layers To SWF Frames.

Loop

Causes the animation to loop continuously, rather than play once and then stop, when played in a Flash viewer. This option is available only for Layers To SWF Frames.

Preserve Appearance

Expands strokes into stroke-shaped fills and flattens any blending modes and transparency that SWF doesn't support.

Preserve Editability Where Possible

Converts strokes to SWF strokes, and approximates or ignores transparency that SWF doesn't support.

SWF supports object-level opacity only.

Use the Export command instead of the Save For Web & Devices command to maintain artwork's stacking order by exporting each layer to a separate SWF file. You can then import the exported SWF files into Adobe Flash simultaneously.

Compressed

Compresses the exported file.

Protect File

Protects the file so that it cannot be imported by applications other than Flash.

Text As Outlines

Converts all text to outlines to maintain appearance. If you plan to edit the text in Flash, don't select this option.

Color Settings

For most color-managed workflows, it is best to use a preset color setting which has been tested by Adobe Systems. Changing specific options is recommended only if you are knowledgeable about color management and very confident about the changes you make.

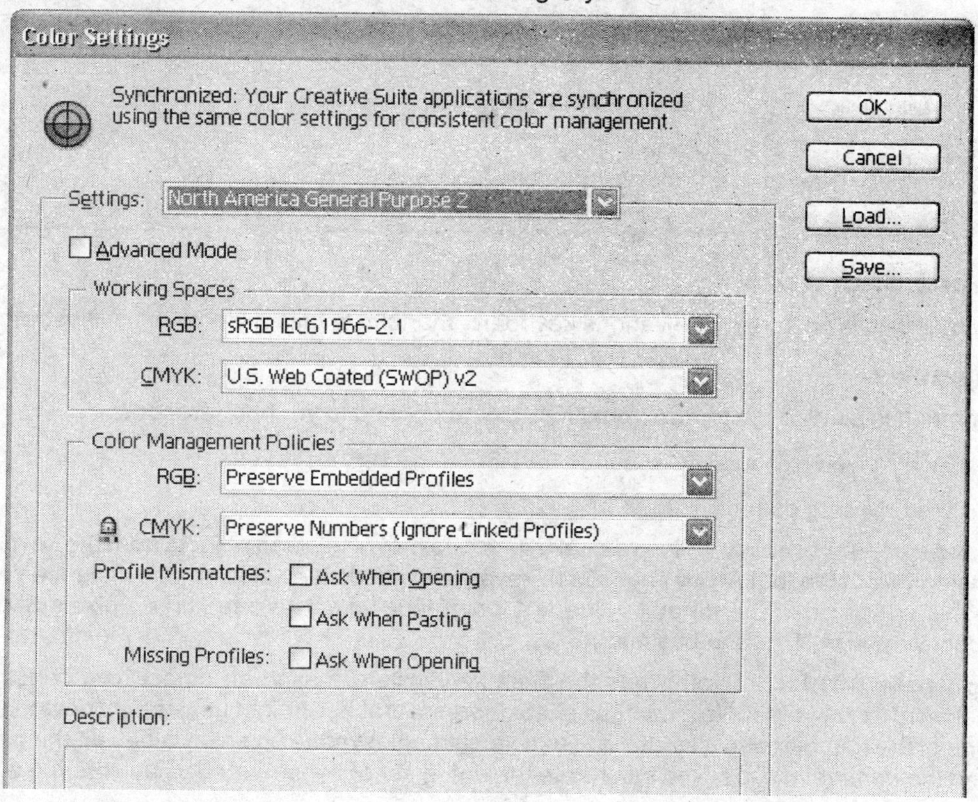

After you customize options, you can save them as a preset. Saving color settings ensures that you can reuse them and share them with other users or applications.

To save color settings as a preset, click Save in the Color Settings dialog box. To ensure that the application displays the setting name in the Color Settings dialog box, save the file in the default location. If you save the file to a different location, you must load the file before you can select the setting.

To load a color settings preset that's not saved in the standard location, click Load in the Color Settings dialog box, select the file you want to load, and click Open.

Assign Profile

This command has the following options.

Don't Color Manage This Document to remove the existing profile from the document. Select this option only if you are sure that you do not want to color-manage the document.

Working Color Model: working space> to assign the working space profile to a document that either uses no profile or a profile different from the working space.

Profile to reassign a different profile to a color-managed document. Choose the desired profile from the menu. Illustrator assigns the new profile to the document without converting colors to the profile space.

Keyboard Shortcuts

This command calls on screen the various keyboard shortcuts available for using in Illustrator.

Preferences

This command is used to customize your Illustrator according to your preferences.

General Preferences

It has the following options.

Keyboard increment: Illustrator allows you to move selected objects from the keyboard by pressing one of the four arrow keys. Each keystroke moves the selection the distance you enter into this option box. The default value is 1 point, equivalent to one screen pixels at the 100 percent view size. That's subtle nudge.

Constrain Angle: If you press the Shift key while dragging an object, you constrain the direction of its movement to a multiple of 45 degrees; that is, straight up, straight down, left, right or one of the four diagonal directions. These eight angles make up an invisible, er, thingamabob called the *constraint axes*. You can rotate the entire set of constraint axes by entering a value –

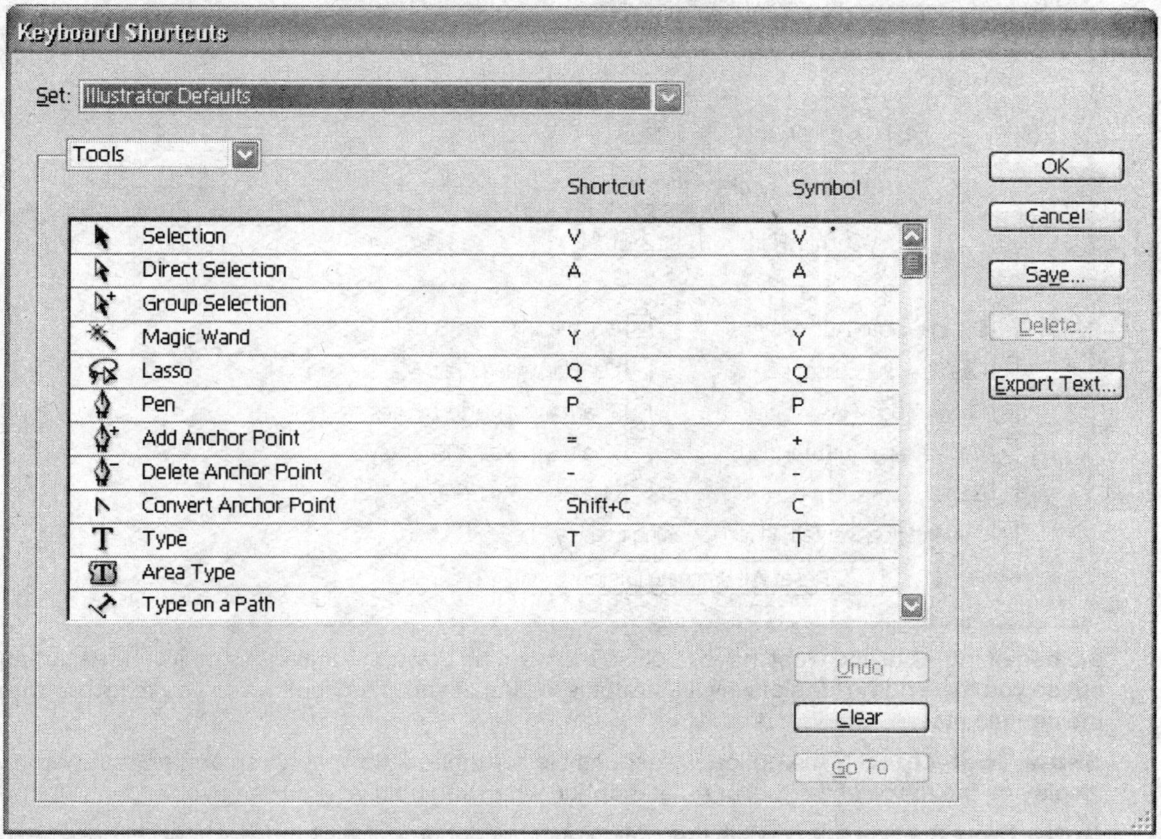

measured in degrees – in the Constrain Angles option box. This value affects the creation of rectangles, ellipses and text blocks, as well as the performance of transformation tools.

Corner Radius: This option sets the default roundness for the rounded rectangle tool. A value of 0 creates perpendicular corners; larger values make for progressively more rounded rectangles. However, this is just the default setting. You can change the amount as you are working using the Rounded Rectangle dialog box. You never need to come back here to change the setting.

Use Area Select: This option controls how you go about selecting filled objects in the preview mode. When it's checked, you can click anywhere inside an object to select the object, so long as the object is filled. When the option is off, you can select an object only by clicking on its points and segments. You can leave this option off so they can select objects behind other objects easily without the fills getting in the way.

Use Precise Cursors: When this option is checked, Illustrator displays crosshair cursors in place of the standard cursors for all drawing and editing tools. These special cursors let you better see what you're doing, but they're not so fun to look at.

Disable Warnings: Checking this box commands Illustrator to resist its temptation to tell you incessantly that you don't know what you are doing. For instance, clicking even slightly off an objects' point with the convert point tool will by default result in Illustrator's scolding you. Disabling this warning won't correct the problem – you will still have to repeat the operation from

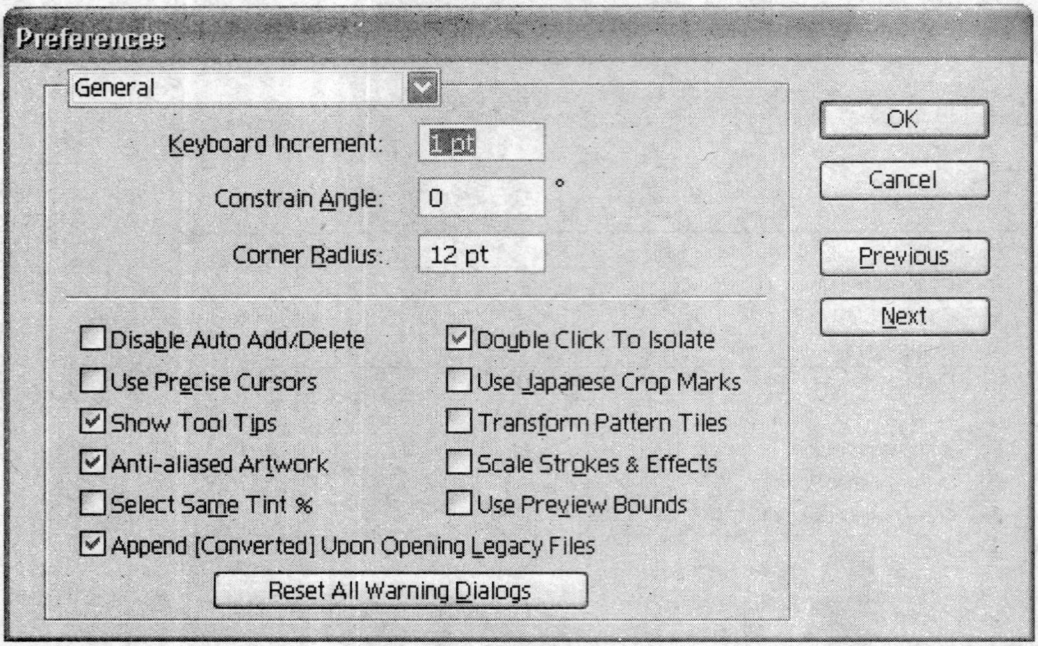

the beginning – but you wont' have to close the warning box first. Leave this on if you're starting out so you have some idea of why Illustrator is yelling at you. Turn it off when you're fed up with the complaints.

Show Tool Tips: This option is responsible for those little yellow rectangles that pop up displaying the name of the tool or palette option when you hold your cursor over it.

Anti-aliased Artwork: With this option on, your document will have a smoother on-screen appearance. This gives you a better idea of what your vector artwork will look like when printed on a PostScript printer, because your final hardcopy will not have all the jagged imperfections that show up on screen.

Paste Remembers Layers: Select this check box if you want to paste objects back onto the layers from which they were originally copied. When this option is turned off, Illustrator pastes all objects onto the current layer, regardless of where they came from. This is just the default setting, though. There's a command in the layers palette that lets you override this setting.

Select Same Tint Percentage: This command lets you select two objects having different tint colours.

Disable Auto Add/Delete: By default, the pen tool will automatically change to the add point tool or delete point tool as the situation demands. For example, if you position the pen tool over a point of a selected path, the pen tool will temporally transform into the delete point tool, ready to out the damn spot. If you prefer the pen tool to limit its personalities to only one identity, check this box.

Japanese Crop Marks: Instead of the typical crop makes you get when you choose Object>> Cropmarks>>Make, you'll get the Japanese-styled ones when this option is active. With this option selected, trim marks will also conform to Japanese styling. Japanese crop marks are a bit more involved and provide an additional center mark along each side, but they function just the same as the regular did crop marks.

Transform Pattern Tiles: When an object is filled or stroked with a tile pattern, you can specify whether the pattern moves, grows, shrinks or rotates as you move, scale or rotate the object. Fortunately you can turn this option on or off in the transformation tools dialog boxes. This setting only effect transformations created manually.

Scale Strokes and Effects: This is the new name for the old Scale Stroke Weight. When you scale an object proportionally – so that both height and width grow or shrink the same amount – Illustrator can likewise change the thickness of the stroke or effects such as feathering that are assigned to the object. If you are working on a project where all strokes must be half a point, you want to turn this option off. Like the transform pattern tiles, you can turn this setting on and off in the transformation tools dialog boxes.

Use Preview Bounds: This is the new name for the old Add Stroke Weight command. By default, both the Transform and Info palettes display a selected path's physical attributes without considering the path's stroke weight. For example, the Info palette would normally list a 40 point by 20 point rectangle with a 10 point stroke as having a width of 40 points and a height of 20 points. With the Use Preview Bounds upon on, the Info palette would list this same rectangle with a height of 50 points and a width of 30 points. The 10 point stroke would add 5 points to each side. The reason for the name change is that the preview bounds can also apply to effects such as drop shadows, glows and other effects that extend far beyond the boundaries of the original object.

Reset All Warnings Dialogs: As you work in Illustrator, you will encounter various dialog boxes that Adobe thinks are giving you important information that will make you a happier and smarter Illustrator person. After a few dozen times reading the same dialog box, you may find yourself cursing at the screen. Sometimes, however, there is a little box that says "Don't show again." If you click that you will never see that specific dialog box again. Unless you click this major button in the preferences – then you get to re-read all those informational messages you had forgotten.

Selection and Anchor Display

Selecting paths and points in complex images can be challenging. Using the Selection and Anchor Display preferences, you can specify the tolerance for pixel selection and choose other options that can make selection easier for a particular document.

Choose Edit > Preferences > Selection & Anchor Display.

Specify any of the following Selection options: Tolerance

Specifies the pixel range for selecting anchor points. Higher values increase the width of the area around an anchor point that you can click to select it.

Object Selection By Path Only

Specifies whether you can select a filled object by clicking anywhere in the object or whether you have to click a path.

Snap To Point

Snaps objects to anchor points and guides. Specify the distance between the object and anchor point or guide when the snap occurs.

Adding and Deleting Anchor Points

Adding anchor points can give you more control over a path, or it can extend an open path.

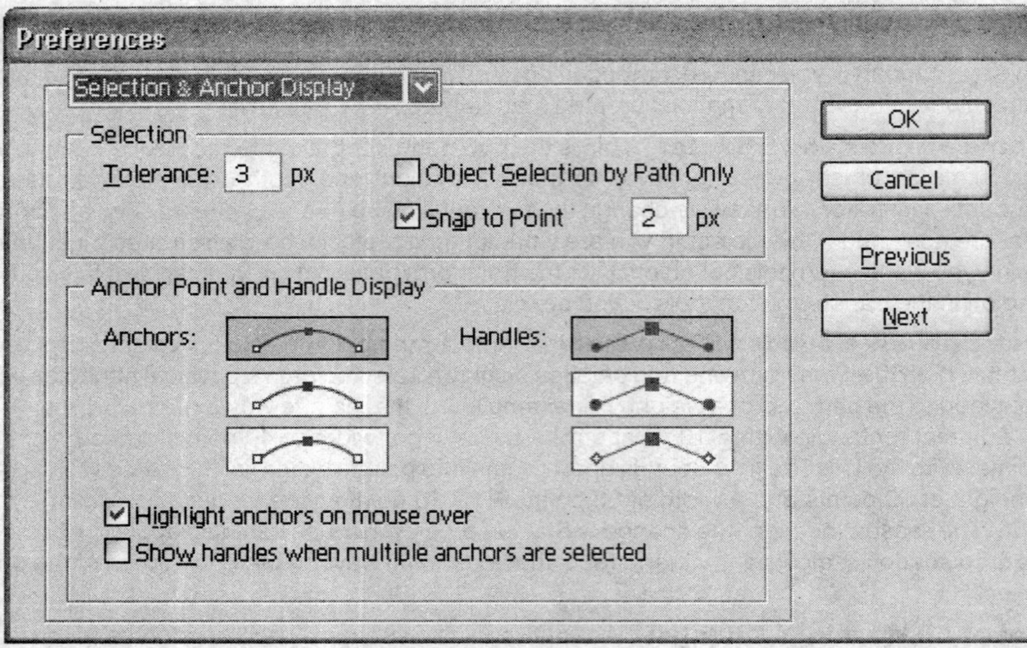

However, it's a good idea not to add more points than necessary. A path with fewer points is easier to edit, display, and print. You can reduce the complexity of a path by deleting unnecessary points. Adding and deleting anchor points works similarly in Adobe applications.

The Tools panel contains three tools for adding or deleting points: the Pen tool , the Add Anchor Point tool , and the Delete Anchor Point tool . In addition, the Control panel has a Remove Selected Anchor Points button

By default, the Pen tool changes to the Add Anchor Point tool as you position it over a selected path, or to the Delete Anchor Point tool as you position it over an anchor point.

Don't use the Delete, Backspace, and Clear keys or the Edit > Cut and Edit > Clear commands to delete anchor points: these keys and commands delete the point and the line segments that connect to that point.

Type

The next preference command, File>>Preferences>>Type, displays the lovely and functional dialog box as shown below. In this box you will find options related to text manipulation.

Size/Leading: Just as you can nudge objects from the keyboard, you can likewise adjust the size and leading of selected text with keystrokes. To define the increment of each keystroke, enter a value.

Baseline Shift: Baseline shift raises and lowers characters relative to the baseline, ideal for creating superscript and subscript type. To determine the increment for raising and lowering selected type, type a new value into this option box.

Tracking: To keep large text looking good, you may want to adjust the amount of space between neighbouring characters, called kerning or tracking. You can modify the kerning from the keyboard by the increment you enter in this option box. This value is always measured in 0.001 em space. An em space is as wide as the current type size is tall, or the width of character w.

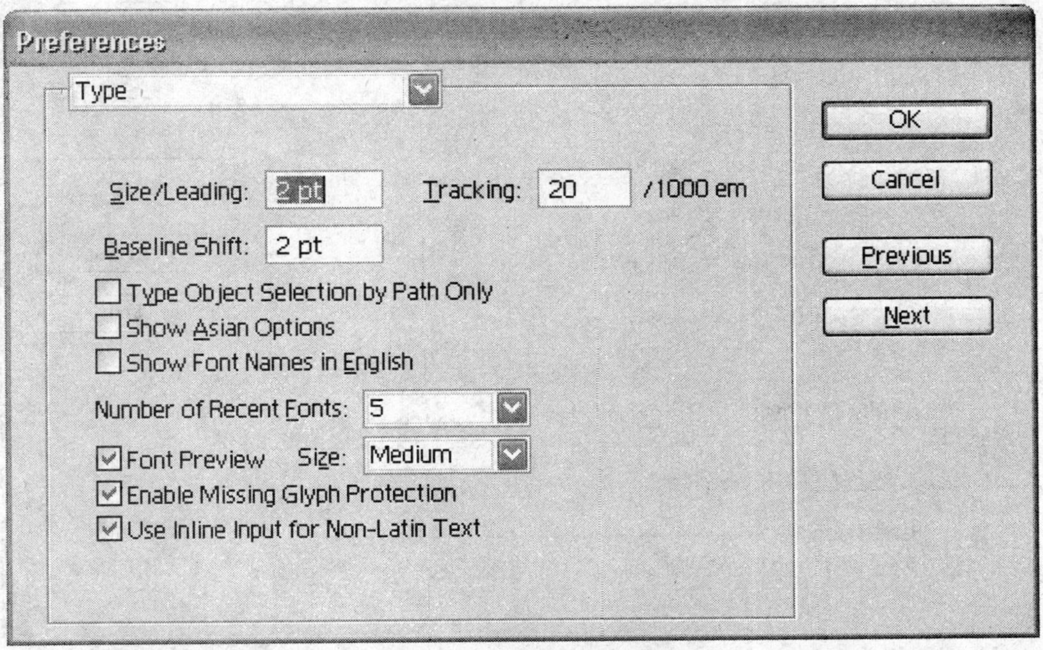

Greeking: If text smaller than this value Illustrator shows the text blocks as gray bars, an operation called greeking. Both type size and view size figure into the equation, so that 6-point type greeks at 100-percent view size and 12-point type greeks at 50 percent. Greeking speeds up the screen display because gray bars are easier to draw than individual characters.

Type Area Select: Just as the Area Select option of General Preferences gives you control over how you go about selecting filled paths, the Type Area Select option lets you choose just how careful you have to be when you're trying to select text and text blocks. When this option is deactivated, you have to click the path in which the type resides. With this option checked, you have a bit more freedom, since you need to click only within the bounding box that envelopes the type.

Show Font Names in English: If you have fonts loaded on your system that use alphabets other than the Latin alphabet, checks this option to force Illustrator to show the font in its English equivalent. This assumes that the font contains this information in its code; Illustrator cannot translate the fonts' names on its own.

Auto Trace Tolerance: This complex little option controls the sensitivity of both the pencil and the autotrace tools. Any value between 0 and 10 is permitted and it is measured in screen pixels. Low values make the tools very sensitive, so that a pencil path closely matches your cursor movements or an autotrace path closely matches the form the imported template.

Tracing Gap: Tracing templates frequently contain loose pixels and rough edges. Using the Auto Trace Gap option, you can instruct Illustrator to trace over these gaps. A value of 0 turns the option off, so that the autotrace tool traces rough edges as they appear in the template. A value of 1 allows paths to skip over single-pixels gaps; a value of 2 (the highest value allowed) allows paths to hurdle two-pixel gaps.

Units and Display Performance

The next option in Preferences is Units and Display Performance. The File>> Preferences>>Units

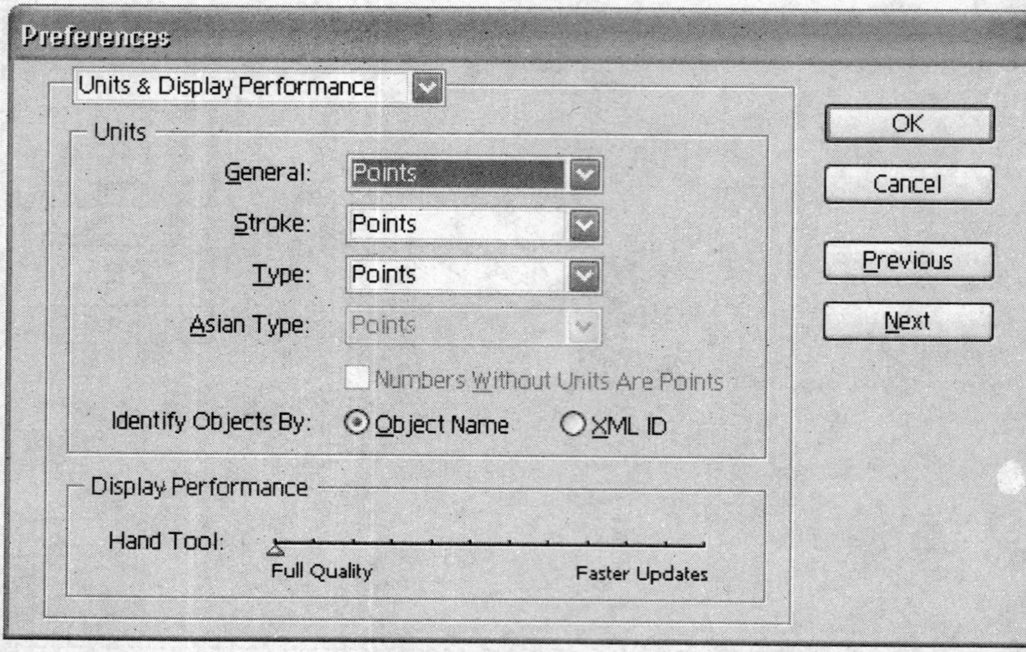

and Display Performance command focuses on the units that Illustrator uses in different dialog boxes, as well as the number of undos that are at your disposal. Dialog box of this is shown next.

General: Select Points/Picas, Inches, Centimeters or Millimeters from this pop-up menu to specify the system of measurement to use throughout all dialog boxes (including this one) as well as in the horizontal and vertical rulers. Unlike the similar option in the Document Setup dialog box – which affects just the one drawing you're working on – this option applies to all future illustrations in addition to the one you're working on.

Stroke: If you think in inches, then obviously you would set the general measurement to inches. But do you really want to specify stroke weights in inches? Not unless you enjoy thinking in hundredths of an inch. The setting gives you the luxury of defining strokes as points.

Type: You could select an option from this pop-up menu to specify the measurement system used specifically for type. But no one in his ight mind would do this, since points are the standard for measuring type in nearly every corner of the globe leave this option set to Points/ Picas, the default.

Asian Type: With this box you can use the asian types only if you have used the option of using the asian fonts while loading.

Numbers Without Units Are Points: With this box checked, Illustrator will assume that any number you enter into an option box without specifying a unit, such as 72 instead of 72 pt., should be in points and not picas. Otherwise, Illustrator will convert unitless numbers to picas – 72 becomes 6p0 (6 picas and no points).

Identify Object By: You have the option of using the object name or its XML identification.

Display Performance: You can set here the option of displaying the hand tool faster.

Guides and Grid

Next in line is Guides and Grid. This dialog box, as shown on the next page, allows you to choose the color and style of both guides and grids. You can also set the size and spacing of a grid. To see the actual guides and grid, you must choose the corresponding Show command in the View menu.

Various other options are:

Color: From this pop-up menu, choose from eight predefined colors for your guides and grids. If you prefer to define your own color, then either choose Other form the Pop-up menu or double-click the color box just to the right of the menu. The Color dialog box will display, where you construct your own color by clicking on the spectrum in the upper right portion of the box. Also, you can save the colour created by you by clicking the Add to Custom Color button.

Style: From these pop-up menus, you decide whether your guides and grid will appear as dashed or solid lines. If you select the Dots option, you will see only the major gridlines and not all the additional subdivisions.

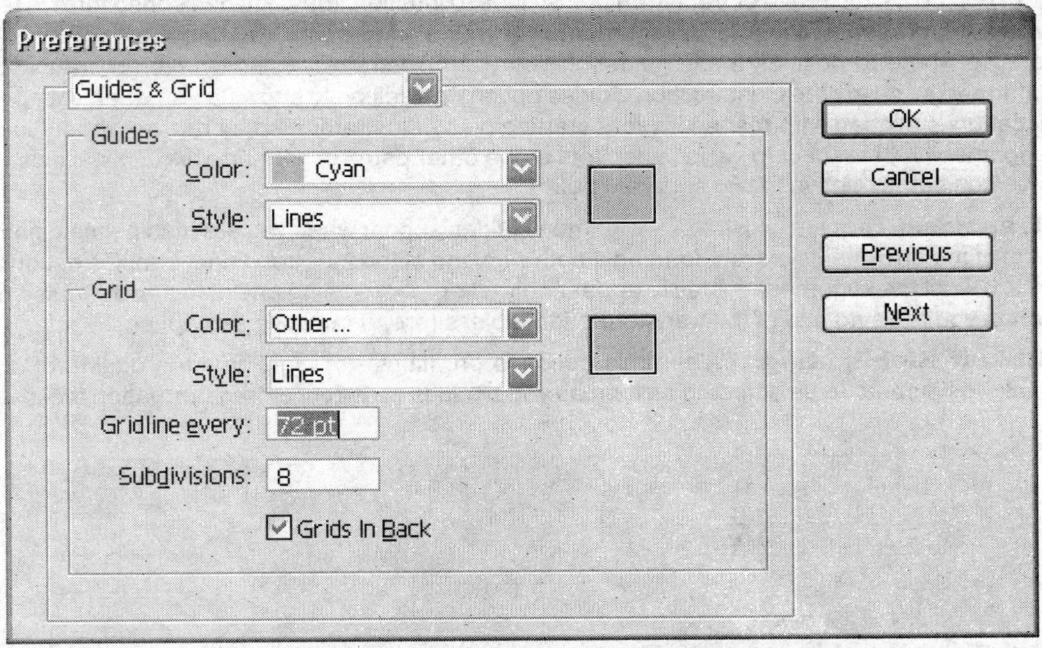

Gridlines every: Enter the size that you want your square grids to be. You can specify the units of this number of simply enter a number and have Illustrator use whatever units you set in the Units and Undo Preferences dialog box.

Subdivisions: Here you state the number of times you want to divide your grid both horizontally and vertically.

Grids in Back: When you're using a grid, you have the choice of having the grid overlaid on the pasteboard, partially obscuring parts of your artwork or having it appear in the background, giving your work the appearance of lying on top of graph paper. Simply select this option to place the grid in the background, where it's less intrusive.

Smart Guides & Slices

Provided you have selected this command, additional information and path outlines appear and disappear as you move your cursor over the different elements of your artwork. Smart guides are meant to help you align paths as you transform and move them by showing you where your transformation coincides with different intersection points within your artwork. Many people feel overloaded with information when they turn on the smart guides. The Smart Guides Preferences dialog box, as shown on the next page, lets you control what type of information is displayed when you turn on the smart guides as well as set the angles that the guides work along. Various options on this dialog box are:

Text Label Hints: With this option selected, several different labels (including path, anchor, align, intersect and page) may pop into view as you move your cursor or drag paths around the screen. They indicate that your cursor is over a special point of interest, aiding you in determining whether you have found the right spot. I suggest that you turn off this option. Artwork consisting of many paths is complex enough without the additional muddling these labels can add.

Construction Guides: One of the main functions of smart guides is the alignment guides that pop up as you move or transform paths. True to intuition, these guides spring forth to tell you when the present location is in alignment with your staring point. You use the Angles option to decide where to position these guides. If you want Illustrator to display even more alignment information, select the Construction Guides option. In addition to showing you when your present location is aligned with respect to your starting point, Illustrator also alerts you when you are in alignment with respect to various aspects of the other paths in your artwork. This allows you to position paths relative to two separate points.

Transform Tools: Illustrator's alignment guides appear when you are manipulating path with one of the arrow tools or transforming a path with one of the four traditional transformation tools. If you want the alignment guides to appear only when you're using one of the arrow tools and not when you're using one of the transformation tools, simply deactivate this option.

Object Highlighting: When this option is on, Illustrator highlights the outline of a path, making it appear to be selected as long as you position an arrow or transformation tool over the

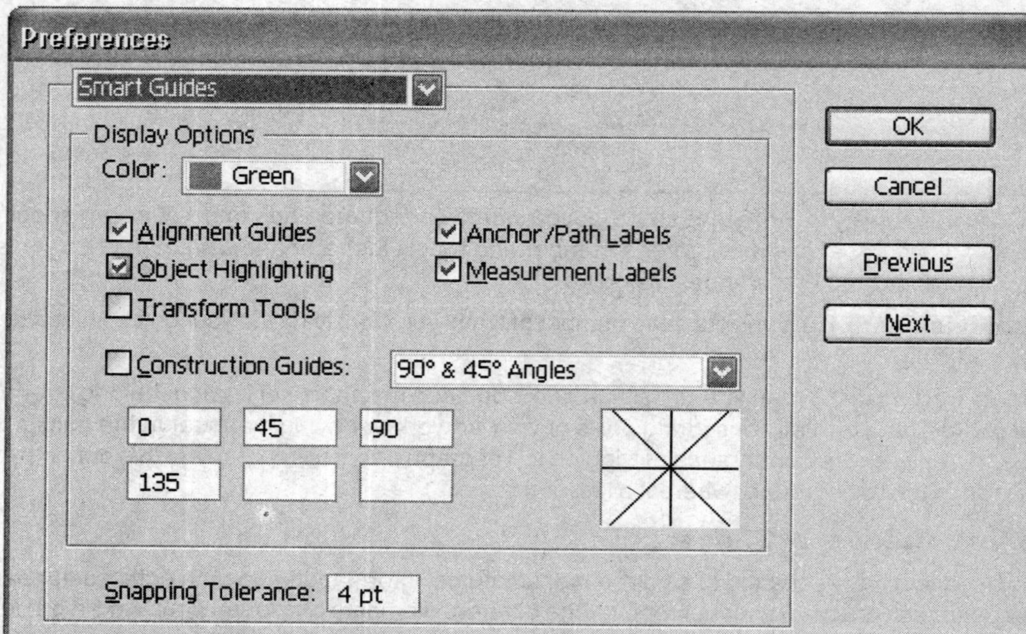

path. This is helpful when you're dealing with a number of overlapping paths, some of which are very small or just barely exposed. Otherwise, this option is better left off.

Angles: With these six option boxes, you decide at what angles Illustrator will inform you whether your present on-screen position aligns with either your initial position or one of the points of some other path in your artwork – that is, provided Construction Guides is selected. You can choose from one of seven predefined sets of angles or enter the angular values that best suit your needs. Package designers and others creating 3D perspectives may want to set their own angle here.

Snapping Tolerance: Here you decide within how many points (ranging from 0 to 10) you must position your cursor (that is, how close you must come to the various points of interest) before the alignment guides and text labels appear. The default value is 4 points. Higher numbers make the smart guides appear more readily; lower numbers mean you have to get closer to objects before the smart guides appear.

Slice: Web pages can contain many elements—HTML text, bitmap images, and vector graphics, to name a few. In Illustrator, you can use slices to define the boundaries of different web elements in your artwork. For example, if your artwork contains a bitmap image that needs to be optimized in JPEG format, while the rest of the image is better optimized as a GIF file, you can isolate the bitmap image using a slice. When you save the artwork as a web page using the Save For Web command, you can choose to save each slice as an independent file with its own format, settings, and color palette.

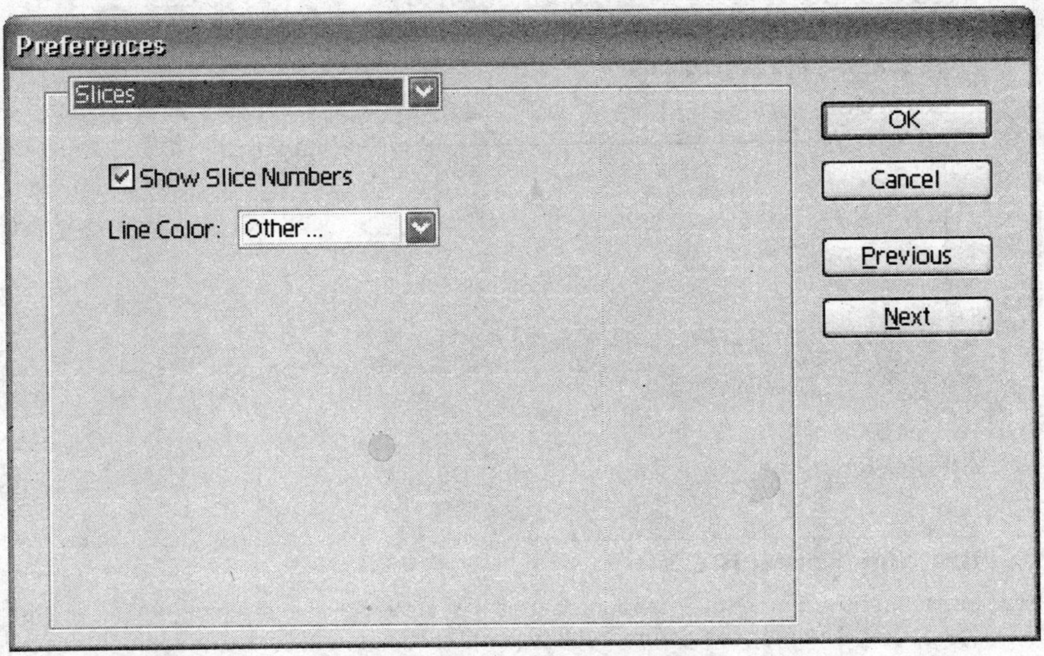

Hyphenation Options

Now we come to Hypenation options. This allows you to exclude words from Illustrator's automatic hyphenating capabilities. Though most Illustrator users go their entire careers without ever giving a second though to automatic hyphenation, you may feel compelled to rule out the occasional proper noun, so that Johnson never appears as John-son. Here's how:

1. Choose File >> Preferences >> Hyphenation Options to display the dialog box as shown on the next page.
2. Select a language from the Default Language pop-up menu to determine which set of rules Illustrator uses to hyphenate your words. For example, you wouldn't want Hungarian hyphenation if you were writing in Finnish.
3. Enter the word you want to protect from hyphenation harm into the New Entry option box. If you enter the word without any hyphens, it will never be hyphenated. If you place hyphens in the word, it will only be hyphenated at those places. So for example, if you enter the word therapist as thera-pist, it will only be hyphenated that way and never as the-rapist.
4. Click the Add button. The word appears in the scrolling list of Exceptions.
5. If you decide you've added a word in error, select it from the scrolling list and click the Delete button.
6. Click the OK button to exit the dialog box. Your hyphenation information is saved with the application that created the file. If you transfer the file to a different computer, the text may hyphenate differently. If you share files with others, it's a good idea to make sure everyone sets the some hyphenation exceptions.

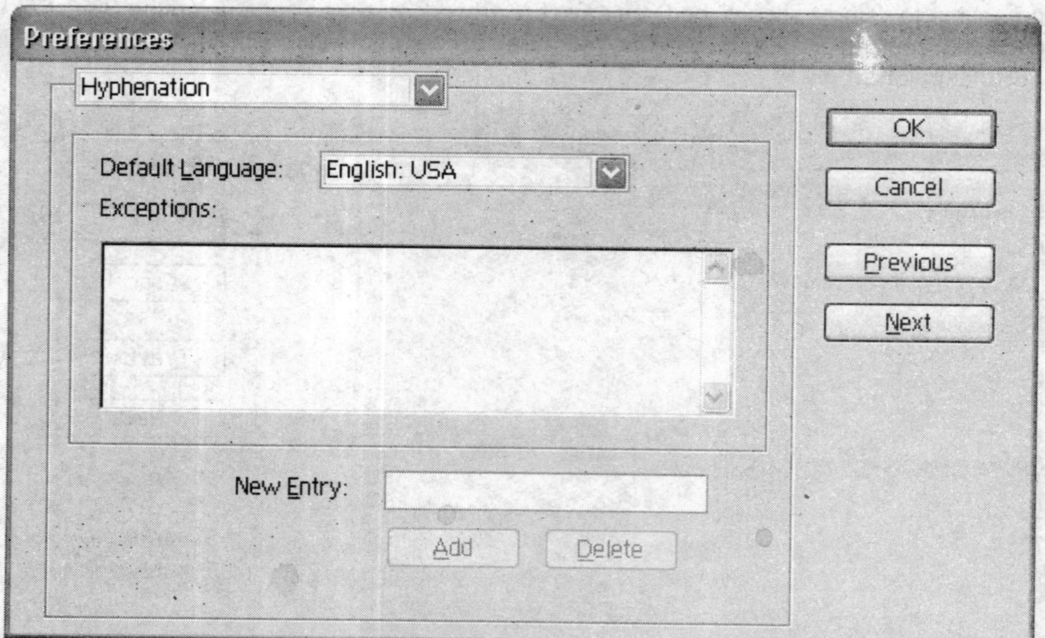

Plug-ins and Scratch Disk

These preferences are more maintenance issues that cover how Illustrator interacts with the rest of your computer. The plug-ins command lets you direct Illustrator or to the folder that contains the plug-ins you want to use. By default, all Illustrator plug-ins are installed in the Plug-ins folder inside the same folder that contains the Illustrator application. But because plug-ins consume a large amount of RAM, you may want to organize your plug-ins into a series of separate folders. This may make Illustrator perform faster or get it to work better with little memory. Then you can use the File>>Preferences >>Plug-ins command to tell Illustrator which set of filters you want to use the next time you start the program.

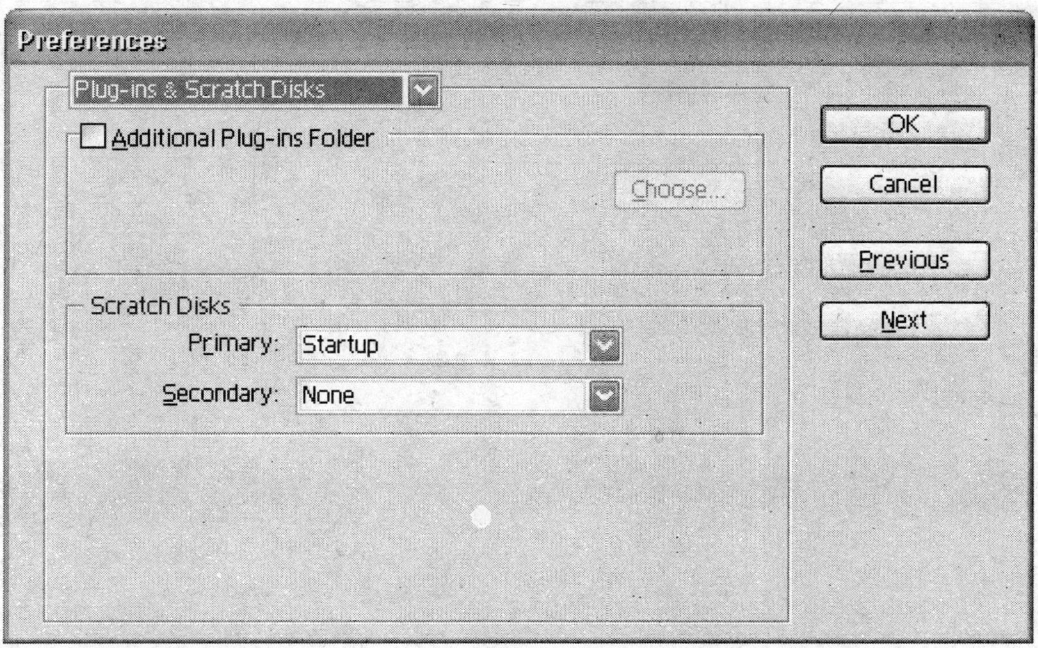

1. Choose File>>Preferences>>Plug-ins and Scratch Disks. The dialog box as shown above will appear.
2. Click the Choose button and locate the folder that contains the set of plug-ins you want to use next.
3. Click the OK button.
4. Quit Illustrator by pressing Ctrl+Q.
5. Launch Illustrator again to load the program as well as the new set of plug-ins.

You also have the option of specifying the location of a primary and secondary scratch disk–the virtual memory that Illustrator uses when your RAM is full. Because virtual memory resides on your hard drive, reading and writing to virtual memory will slow Illustrator considerably. Choose the location of the first place that you want Illustrator to use for virtual memory from the Primary pop-up menu. From the Secondary pop-up menu you select the location of the scratch disk that supplements Illustrator's memory when the first scratch disk is full. If you have a second hard drive or another form of storage media, you can use this as your secondary scratch disk.

User Interface

These preferences are based on the brightness of the icons, as shown below.

File Handling & Clipboard

The final entry in the Files>>Preferences submenu is the Files Handling & Clipboard command. This command opens the Files and Clipboard dialog box, as shown below, that controls how files are named, how links are updated and the format for items copied to the clipboard.

Version Cue and Files: Version Cue projects and files reside in the Version Cue Workspace on the host computer. The master copies of files added to the project, including file versions and other file data, such as comments, version dates, and user IDs, are saved on this host computer.

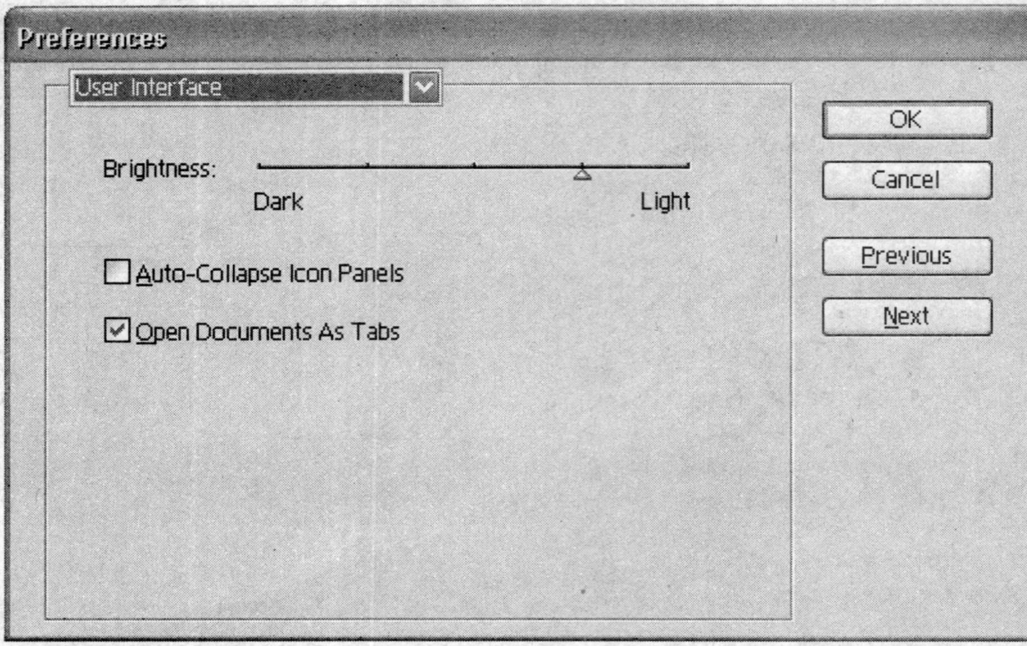

When you work in files from a Version Cue project, you're editing a working copy of the master file on your computer, not the master file on the Version Cue Workspace, which remains protected and untouched.

Update Links: When you place images from other programs in Illustrator, they keep a link to the original file. If you modify the original file, the linked needs to be updated in Illustratcr. This

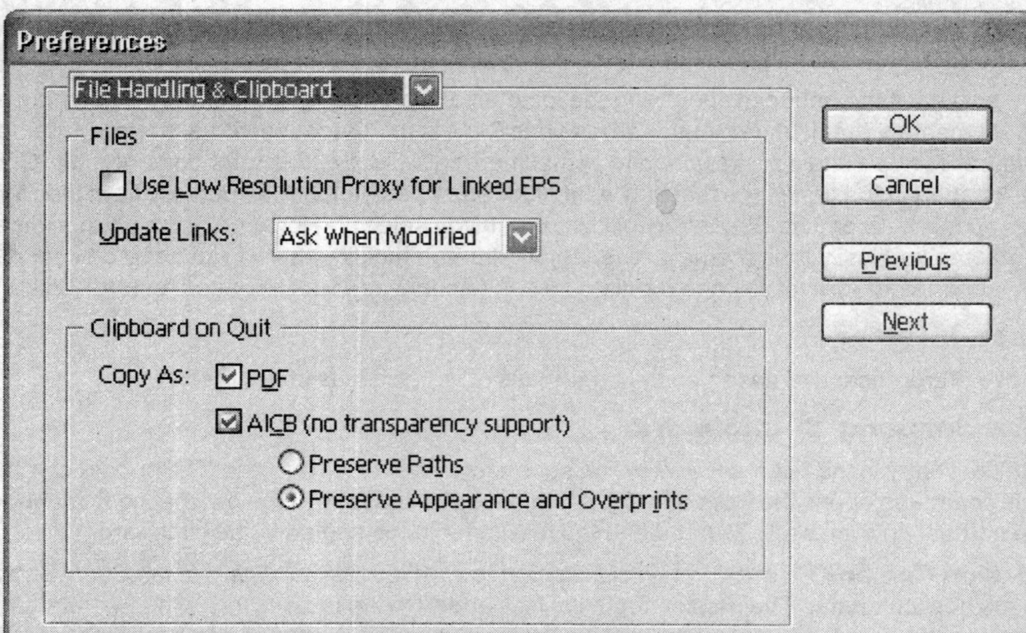

option controls how the updates happen: automatically, manually or with a dialog box that asks if you want to update the modified links.

Clipboard on Quit: This option controls how much information gets sent to the clipboard. This doesn't do anything if you copy from one Illustrator document to another. But if you copy from Illustrator and then paste into other programs, you may need to set these options. For instance, older programs may not be able to handle PDF information or transparency. Changing your options here can help you copy and paste.

Appearance of Black

In Illustrator pure CMYK black (K=100) appears jet black (or rich black) when viewed on-screen, printed to a non-Postscript desktop printer, or exported to an RGB file format. If you prefer to see the difference between pure black and rich black as it will appear when printed on a commercial press, you can change the Appearance Of Black preferences. These preferences do not change the color values in a document.

1. Choose Edit > Preferences > Appearance Of Black.
2. Choose an option for On Screen:
3. Display All Blacks Accurately Displays pure CMYK black as dark gray. This setting allows you to see the difference between pure black and rich black.
4. Display All Blacks As Rich Black Displays pure CMYK black as jet black (RGB=000). This setting makes pure black and rich black appear the same on-screen.
5. Choose an option for Printing/Exporting:
6. Output All Blacks Accurately When printing to a non-Postscript desktop printer or exporting to an RGB file format, outputs pure CMYK black as using the color numbers in the document. This setting allows you to see the difference between pure black and rich black.

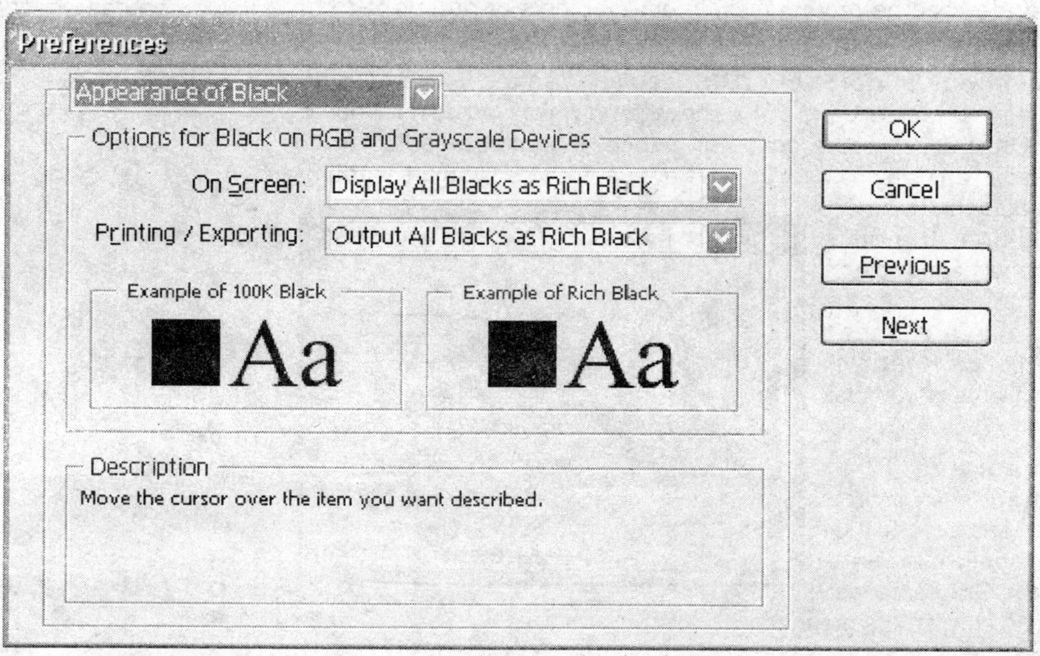

7. Output All Blacks As Rich Black When printing to a non-Postscript desktop printer or exporting to an RGB file format, outputs pure CMYK black as jet black (RGB=000). This setting makes pure black and rich black appear the same.

Object menu

Transform: You can transform selected objects—that is, change their size, shape, and orientation by selecting one or more objects and then applying various transformation actions on them. For example, you can change the angle of an object by rotating it, or add perspective to an object by shearing it. Various options under this are shown here.

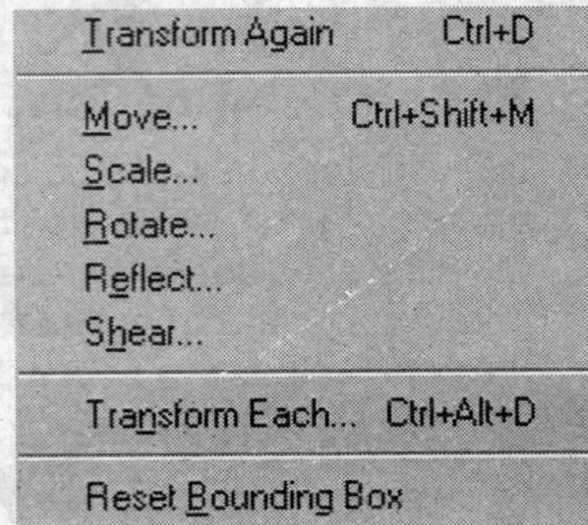

Arrange: This command is used for the followings:

- Bring to Front to make the layer the topmost layer.
- Bring Forward to move the layer one level up in the stacking order.
- Send Backward to move the layer one level down in the stacking order.
- Send to Back to make the layer the bottommost layer in the image (except for the background).

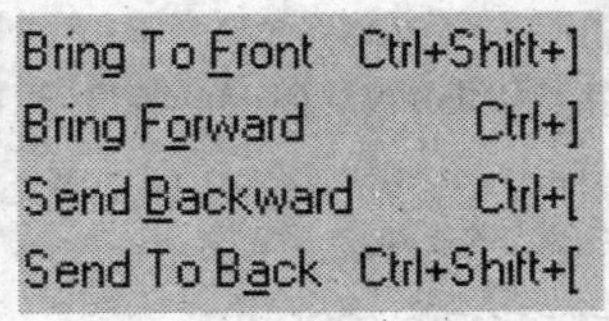

Group/Ungroup: You can combine several objects into a group so that the objects are treated as a single unit. You can then move or transform a number of objects without affecting their individual positions or attributes. For example, you might group the objects in a logo design so that you can move and scale the logo as one unit. Groups can also be nested—that is, they can be grouped within other objects or groups to form larger groups.

Lock/Unlock/Hide/Show All: You can use the Lock and Hide commands to isolate parts of your artwork on which you do not want to work. Once an object is locked or hidden, it cannot be selected or modified in any way. These features are useful when you are working on objects that overlap. In addition, the Hide command makes objects temporarily invisible, and so may speed performance when you work on large or complex artwork.

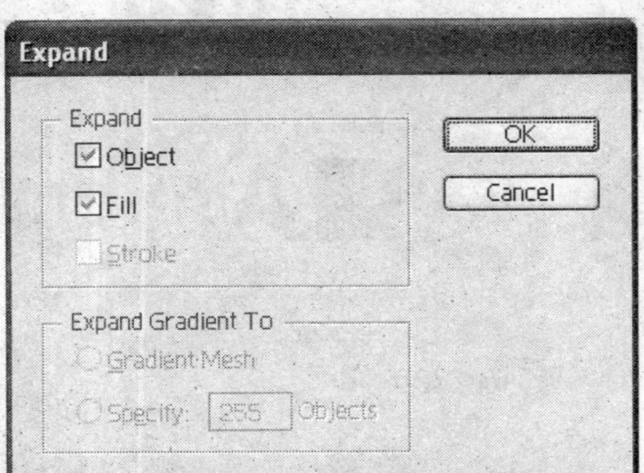

Expand: This command converts strokes and fills into their more basic elements. Click the Gradient Mesh option to convert the mesh object.

Expand Appearance: This command turns the objects used to define the brush into discrete objects that are no longer attached to the brush definition.

Flatten Transparency: This command is used to convert transparency effects into ordinary objects.

Rasterize: This command allows you to rasterize the image.

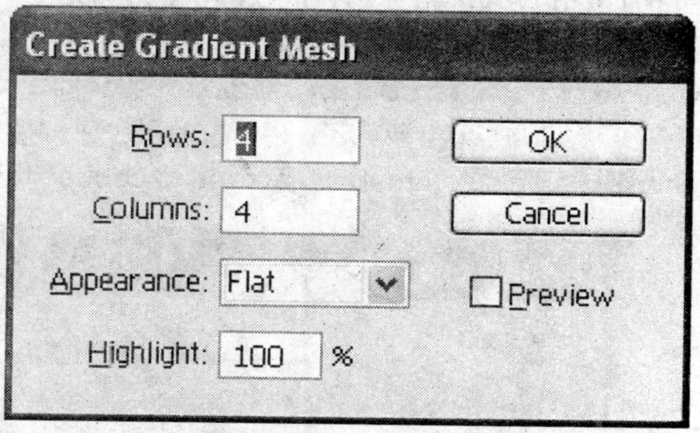

Create Gradient Mesh: This command allows you to create a gradient mesh around the object.

Slice: When you create a slice, Illustrator generates automatic slices to create a valid HTML table if you save artwork as a Web page. There are two types of automatic slices: auto slices and subslices. Auto slices account for the areas of your artwork that are not already defined by slices. Illustrator regenerates auto slices every time you add or edit slices. Subslices indicate how overlapping slices will be divided. Although subslices are numbered and display a slice symbol, you cannot select them separately from the underlying slice. Illustrator regenerates subslices every time you arrange the stacking order of slices.

Path: It allows you to select one of the commands given under its sub-menu.

Blend: Using this command you can blend one object with a stroke to another object without a stroke. Various options are shown here.

Envelope Distort: You can create an envelope from three sources: the topmost selected object, a preset warp shape, or a mesh. You can edit any of these envelopes at any time.

Live Paint: Live Paint is an intuitive way to create colored drawings. A common way for graphic artists to create a colored drawing on canvas or paper is to first draw some strokes, using a tool such as a pen or pencil, and then color in the areas between those strokes, without worrying about how many different strokes were used to surround each area, what order they were drawn in, or how they are connected.

Live Paint translates this natural way of drawing into Illustrator. It lets you use the full range of Illustrator's vector drawing tools, but treats all the paths you draw as being on the same flat surface. That is, none of the paths is behind or in front of any other. Instead, the paths divide the drawing surface up into areas, any of which can be colored, regardless of whether the area is bounded by a single path, or by segments of multiple paths. The result is that painting objects is like filling in a coloring book or using watercolors to paint a pencil sketch.

Live Trace: It allows you the various options of tracing.

Text wrap: You can wrap text around any object, including type objects, imported images, and objects you draw in Illustrator. If the wrap object is a bitmap image, Illustrator wraps the text around opaque or partially opaque pixels and ignores fully transparent pixels. Wrapping is determined by the stacking order of objects, which you can view in the Layers palette. In order for Illustrator to wrap text around an object, the wrap object must be directly above it. Illustrator does not wrap text that is above the wrap object in the stacking order or in a separate sublayer or group from the wrap object.

Clipping Mask: Clipping masks crop part of the artwork so that only a portion of the artwork appears through the shape or shapes you create. In Adobe Illustrator, you mask objects by using the Clipping Mask command.

Compound Path: If you are printing Adobe Illustrator files containing overly long or complicated paths, the file may not print and you may receive limit-check error messages from your printer. To simplify paths, you can split long, complex paths into two or more separate paths using Split Long Paths in the Printing & Export panel of the Document Setup dialog box. This command allows you to then compound them.

Convert to Artboards: Crop area define where the artwork is trimmed after it is printed. You can mark crop area directly into your artwork using the this command.

Graph: This command allow you to choose the various options of Graph.

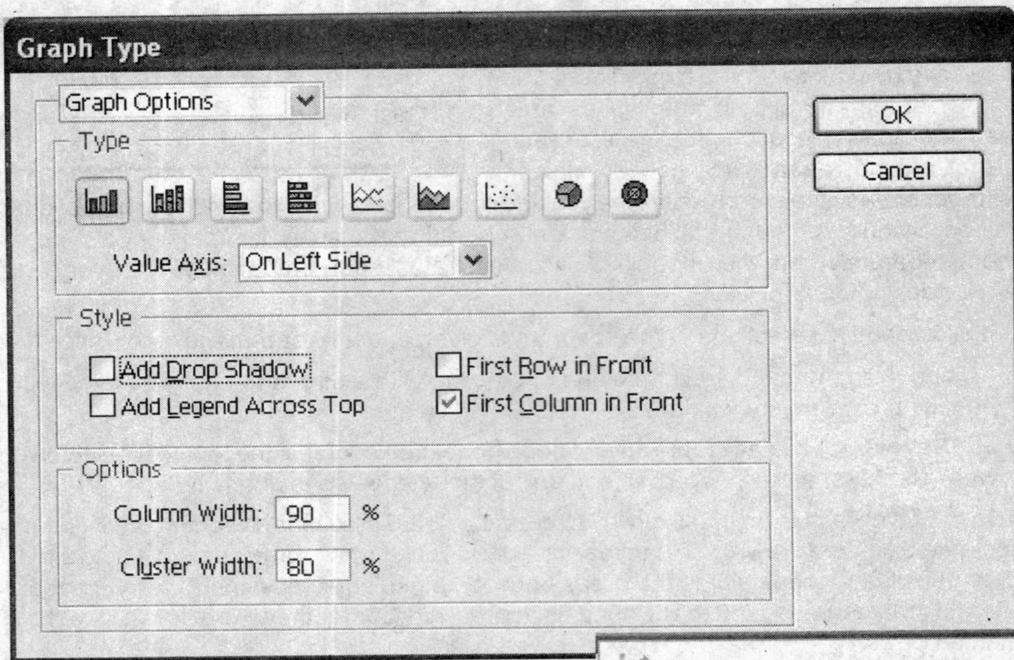

Type menu

Font: This command is used to define the type design used to print selected text or the next text you type. When you choose Font, Illustrator displays a list of fonts installed on your computer, as well as any additional font that may have been used in your publication.

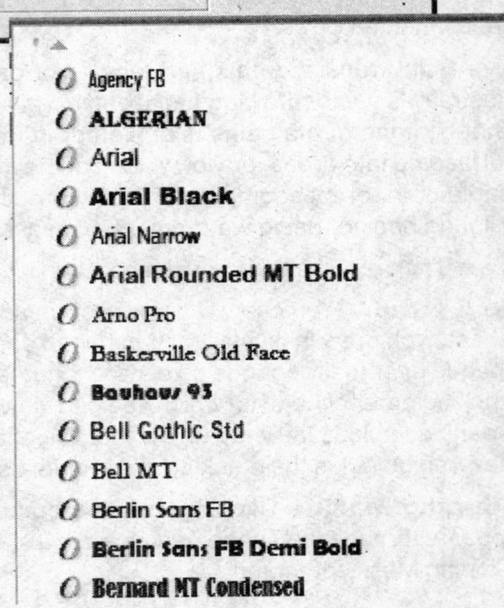

Recent Fonts: This command shows you the fonts which have been used recently.

Size: This command is used to specify printed point size of selected text or of the next text you type.

Glyphs: Typefaces include many characters in addition to the ones you see on your keyboard. Depending on the font, these characters can include ligatures, fractions, swashes, ornaments, ordinals, titling and stylistic alternates, superior and inferior characters, old-

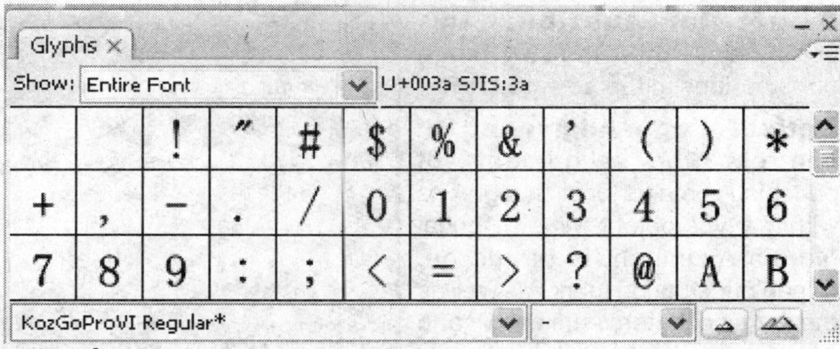

style figures, and lining figures. A glyph is a specific form of a character. For example, in certain fonts, the capital letter A is available in several forms, such as swash and small cap.

There are two ways to insert alternate glyphs:

The **Glyphs** palette lets you view and insert glyphs from any typeface.

The **OpenType** palette lets you set up rules for using glyphs. For example, you can specify that you want to use ligatures, titling characters, and fractions in a given text block. Using the OpenType palette is easier than inserting glyphs one at a time and ensures a more consistent result. However, the palette works only with OpenType fonts.

Area Type Options/Type on a Path/Threaded Text: In Illustrator, there are three methods for creating type: at a point, inside an area, and along a path.

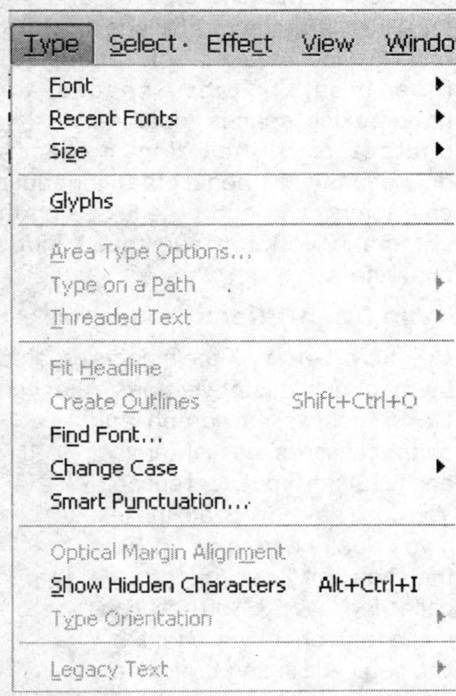

Point type is a horizontal or vertical line of text that begins where you click on the artboard and expands as you enter characters. Entering text this way is useful for adding a few words to your artwork.

Area type uses the boundaries of an object to control the flow of characters, either horizontally or vertically. When the text reaches a boundary, it automatically wraps to fit inside the defined area. Entering text this way is useful when you want to create one or more paragraphs, such as for a brochure.

Type on a path flows along the edge of an open or a closed path. When you enter text horizontally, the characters are parallel to the baseline. When you enter text vertically, the characters that are perpendicular to the baseline. In either case, the text flows in the direction in which points were added to the path.

If you enter more text than can fit within an area or along a path, a small box containing a plus symbol (+) appears near the bottom of the bounding area.

Fit Headline: Illustrator lets you fit type across the full width of a type path in an object by using the Fit Headline command. The Fit Headline command was designed to work with Adobe Multiple Master fonts by adjusting the weight of the font and the tracking value when distributing type along a path. However, the Fit Headline command also works with other fonts by adjusting only the tracking value.

Create Outlines: This command allows you to create outlines.

Find Font: This command allows you to find a particular font in the text.

Change Case: With this command you can change the case of the selected text.

Smart Punctuation: This command allows you to change punctuations in the selected text.

Optical Margin Alignment: It controls the alignment of punctuation marks for all paragraphs within a type object. When Optical Margin Alignment is turned on, roman punctuation marks as well as the edges of letters (such as W and A) hang outside the text margins so that the type looks aligned.

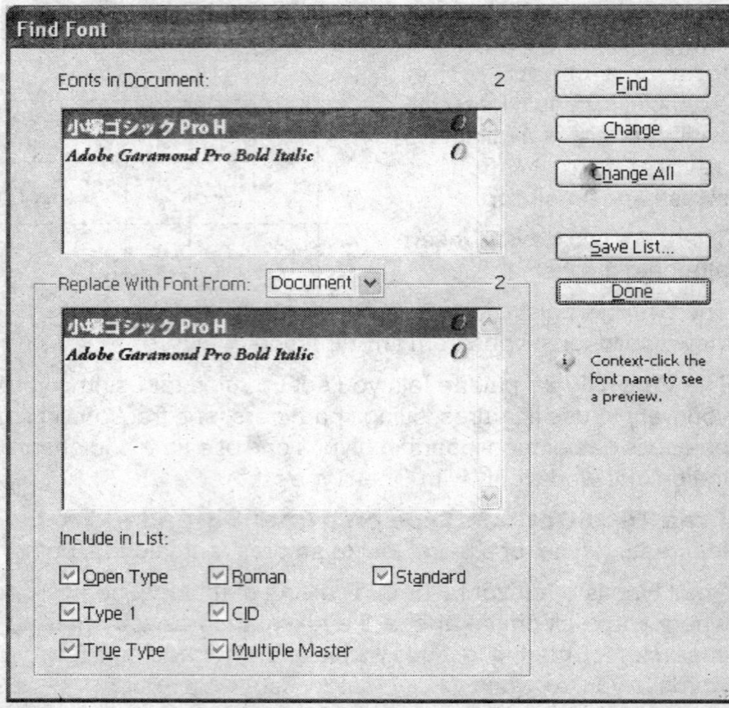

Show Hidden Characters: As you work with type, nonprinting characters are embedded into the file to indicate keyboard actions or states, such as spaces, returns (line breaks), and tabs. These characters include hard returns (line breaks), soft returns (line breaks), tabs, spaces, nonbreaking spaces, double-byte characters (including spaces), discretionary hyphens, other nonprinting characters, and end of text. Using this command you can see these hidden characters.

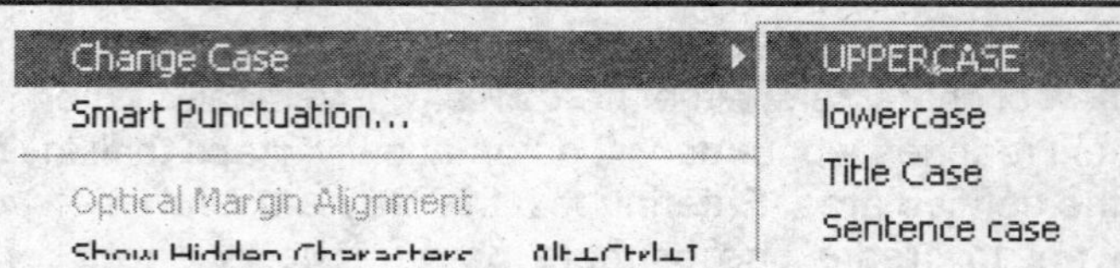

Type Orientation: You can make the typed text in different orientation like Horizontal or Vertical.

Legacy Text: Type objects created in Illustrator CS4 and earlier are uneditable until you update them for use in later versions. After you update you have access to all the text features in Illustrator CS4, such as paragraph and character styles, optical kerning, and full OpenType® font support. You don't have to update the text if you don't need to edit it. Text that has not been updated is called legacy text. You can view, move, and print legacy text, but you can't edit it. Legacy text has an x through its bounding box when selected.

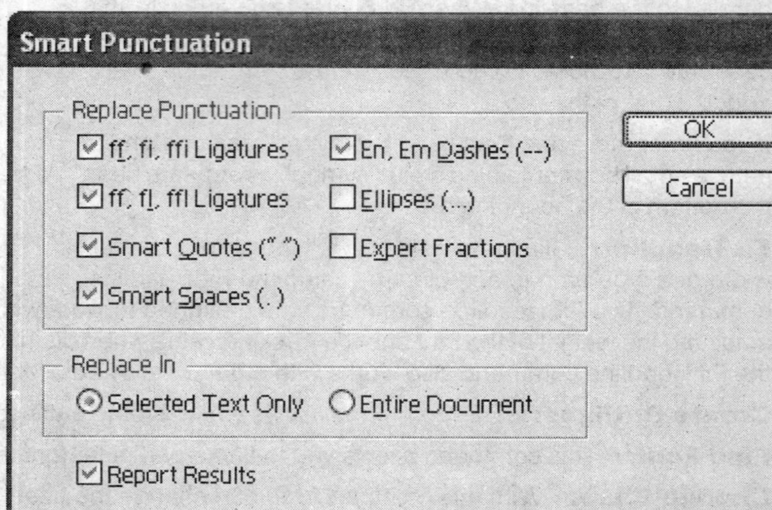

After updating legacy text, you may notice some minor reflow changes. You can easily readjust the text on your own, or you can use a copy of the original text for reference. By default, Illustrator appends the word "[Converted]" to the filename when you update the text in a file, effectively making a copy of your document to preserve the integrity of your original file. If you don't want Illustrator to append the filename, choose Edit > Preferences > General, and deselect Append [Converted] Upon Opening Legacy Files.

Select menu

All: This command is used to select all the items on the screen.

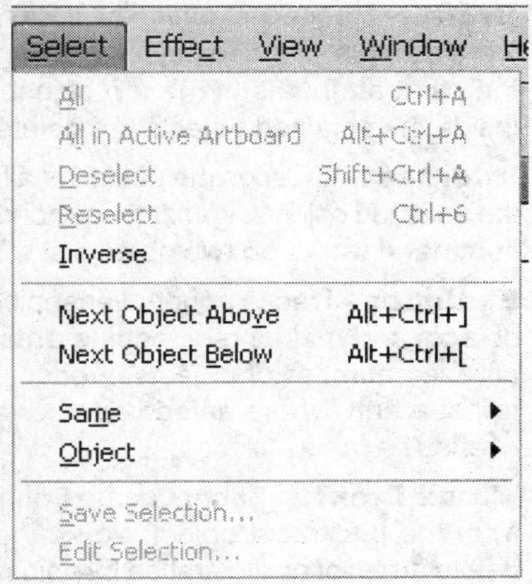

All in Active Artboard: This command is used to select all the items on the screen.

Deselect: Reverse of the above command, deselects the selected items.

Reselect: You can again select the above deselected items.

Inverse: This command is used to inverse the selected item.

Next Object Above: You can select the item immediately above the selected item.

Next Object Below: You can select the item immediately below the selected item.

Same/Object: Using this command you can also select objects based on their paint style, stroke color, stroke weight, style, blending mode, opacity, and whether they are masks, stray points, or brush strokes.

Save/Edit Selection: Using the commands in the Select menu, you can save, edit, and load selections for reuse in your artwork.

Effect menu

Apply Last Effect/Last Effect: This command allows you to call or apply the last effect used.

Document Raster Effects Setting: Illustrator uses a document's raster effects settings whenever you apply a filter to a bitmap image or apply a raster effect to a vector graphic. These settings can have a large impact on the resulting artwork; therefore, it's important to check the Document Raster Effects Settings dialog box before you start working with filters and effects.

Illustrator Effects: Following is the list of effects which can be used in Illustrator CS4.

3D: It has 3 main settings mainly, Exrude & Bevel Options, Revolve and Rotate.

Convert to Shape: This command allows you to choose from rectangle, ellipse, or rounded rectangle.

Crop Marks: This command allows you to put crop marks.

Distort & Transform: The distortion commands are found in both the Filters and Effects menus. The transform command, found under the Effect menu, is more powerful version of the Free Transform tool.

Path: This command has the following options.

Offset Path: This command creates a new shape that follows the outline of the original path.

Stroke Path: This command turns the Stroke of a path into a closed shape.

Outline Object: This command creates a vector outline for objects that ordinarily would not have one such as the gradient mesh, placed raster images, and text.

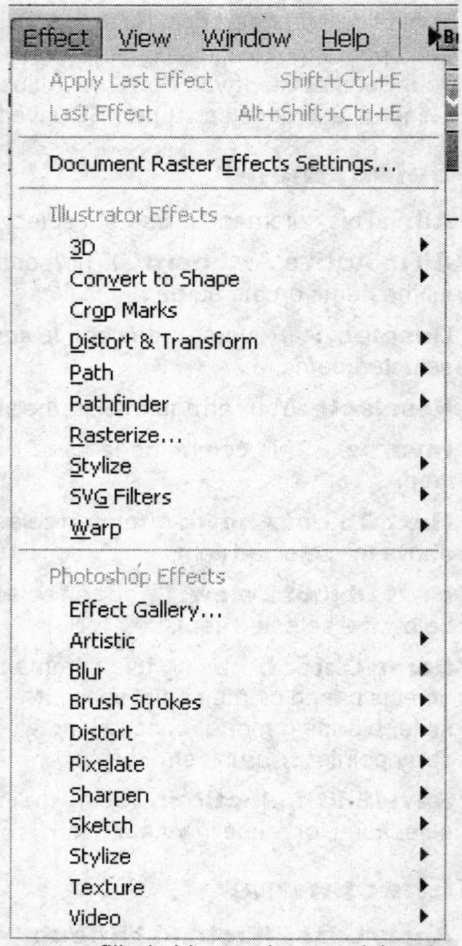

Pathfinder: The Pathfinder command in the Effect menu combines, isolates, and subdivides objects, and they build new objects formed by the intersections of objects. It has the following options.

Unite: Traces the outline of all selected objects as if they were a single, merged object. The resulting shape takes on the paint attributes of the top object selected. Any objects inside the selected objects are deleted.

Intersect: Traces the outline of all overlapping shapes in the selected objects, ignoring any nonoverlapping areas. This command works on two objects at a time.

Exclude: Traces all nonoverlapping areas of the selected objects and makes overlapping areas transparent. Where an even number of objects overlap, the overlap becomes transparent. Where an odd number of objects overlap, the overlap becomes filled.

Minus Front: Subtracts the frontmost selected objects from the backmost object. You can use this command to delete areas of an illustration by adjusting the stacking order.

Minus Back: Subtracts the backmost selected objects from the frontmost object. You can use this command to delete areas of an illustration by adjusting the stacking order.

Divide: Divides a piece of artwork into its component filled faces (a face is an area undivided by a line segment). The resulting faces can then be ungrouped and manipulated independently of each other. You can choose to delete or preserve unfilled objects when applying the Divide command.

Trim: Removes the part of a filled object that is hidden. It removes any strokes and does not merge objects of the same color.

Merge: Removes the part of a filled object that is hidden. It removes any strokes and merges any adjoining or overlapping objects filled with the same color.

Crop: Divides artwork into its component filled faces and then deletes all the parts of the artwork that fall outside the boundary of the topmost object. It also removes any strokes.

Outline: Divides an object into its component line segments, or edges. Each edge can be ungrouped and independently manipulated. This command is useful for preparing artwork that needs a trap for overprinting objects.

Rasterize: This command converts all Illustrator objects into grayscale.

Stylize: This command has the following options.

Add Arrowheads: This command adds an arrowhead to the end of an open path. Illustrator bases the size of the arrowhead on the thickness of the stroke.

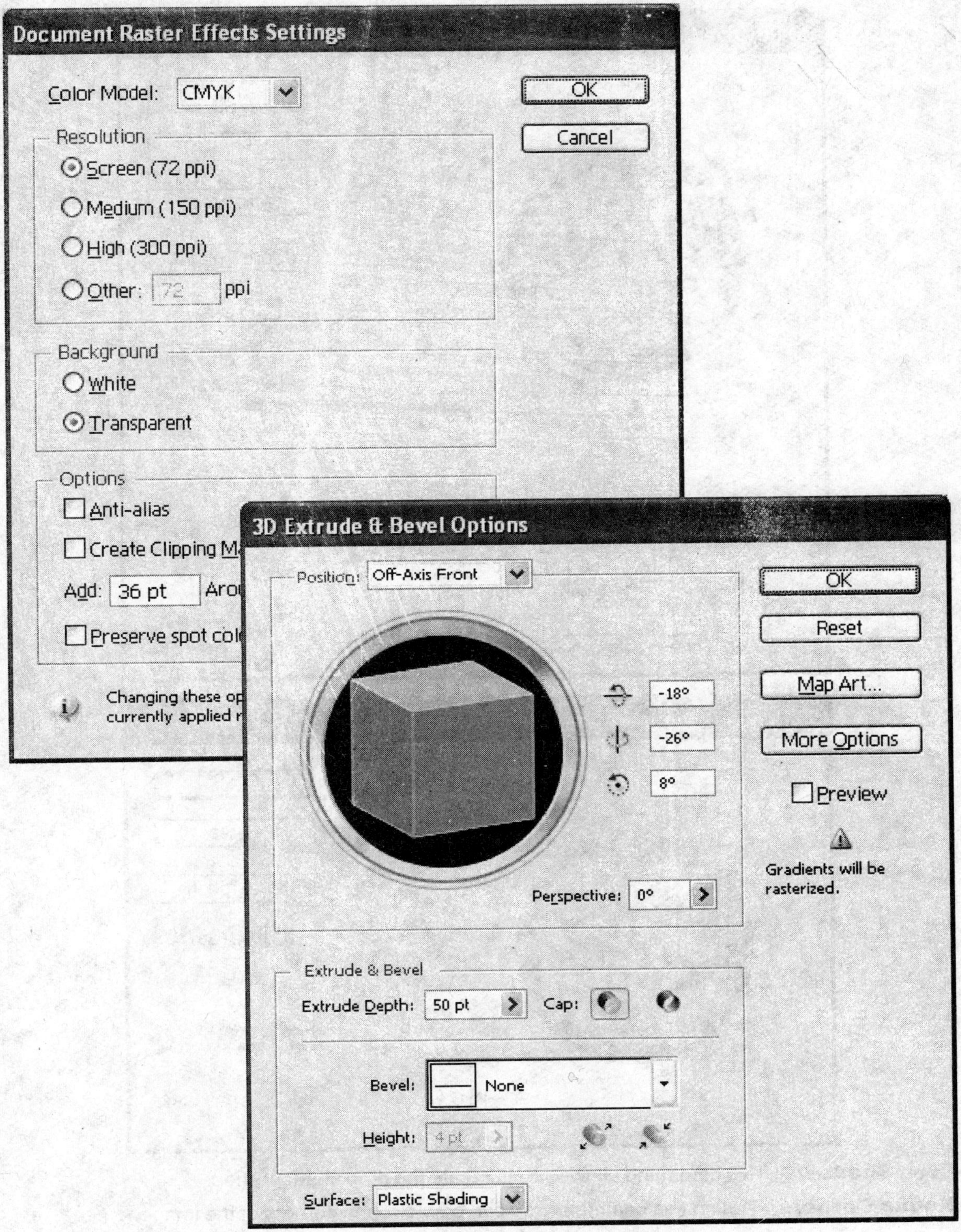
Document Raster Effects Settings
Color Model:
CMYK
OK
Cancel
Resolution
Screen (72 ppi)
Medium (150 ppi)
High (300 ppi)
Other:
72
ppi
Background
White
Transparent
Options
Anti-alias
Create Clipping Ma
Add:
36 pt
Aro
Preserve spot col
Changing these op
currently applied r
3D Extrude & Bevel Options
Position:
Off-Axis Front
OK
Reset
Map Art...
More Options
Preview
-18°
-26°
8°
Gradients will be rasterized.
Perspective:
0°
Extrude & Bevel
Extrude Depth:
50 pt
Cap:
Bevel:
None
Height:
4 pt
Surface:
Plastic Shading

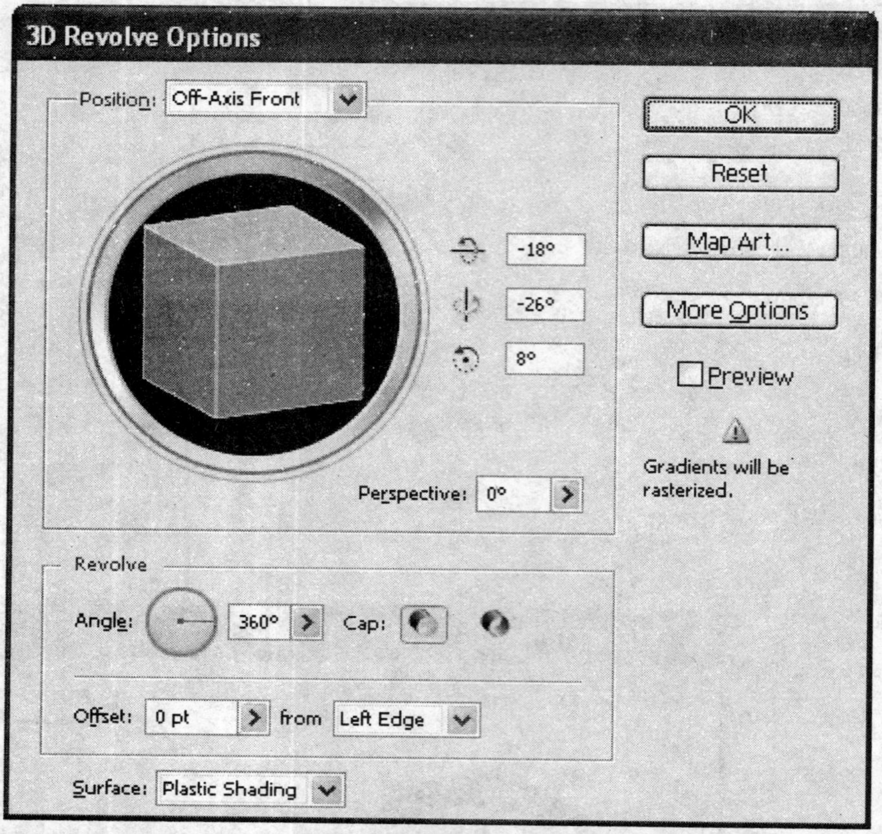

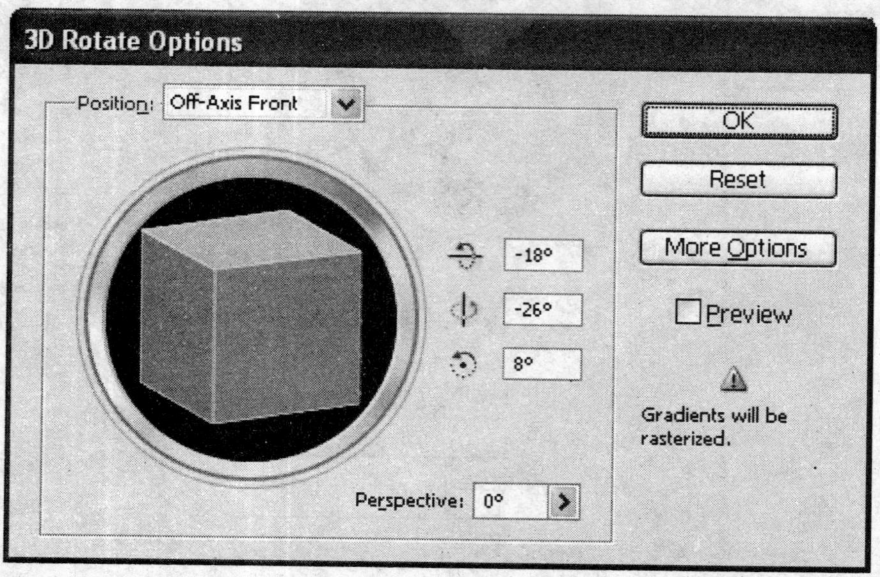

Drop Shadow: This command allows you to create the drop shadow effect.

Round Corners: Using this command you can create round corners of the image.

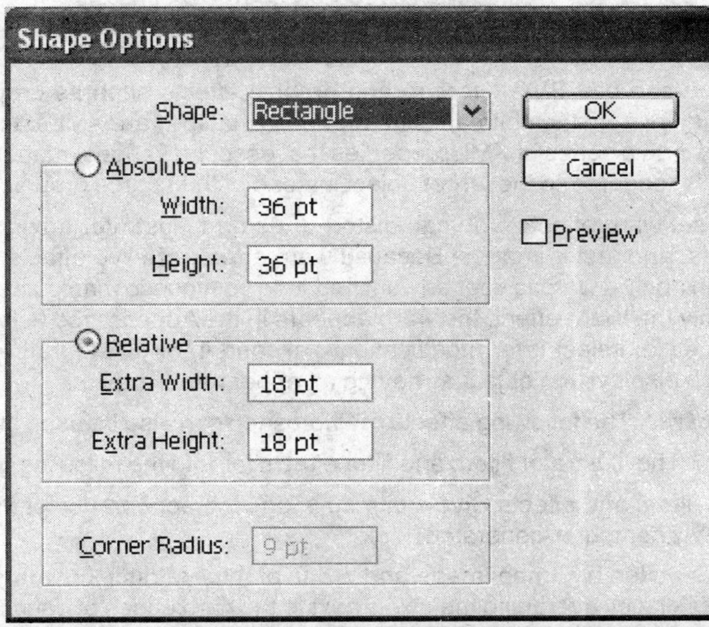
Shape Options
Shape:
Rectangle
OK
Cancel
Absolute
Width:
36 pt
Height:
36 pt
Preview
Relative
Extra Width:
18 pt
Extra Height:
18 pt
Corner Radius:
9 pt

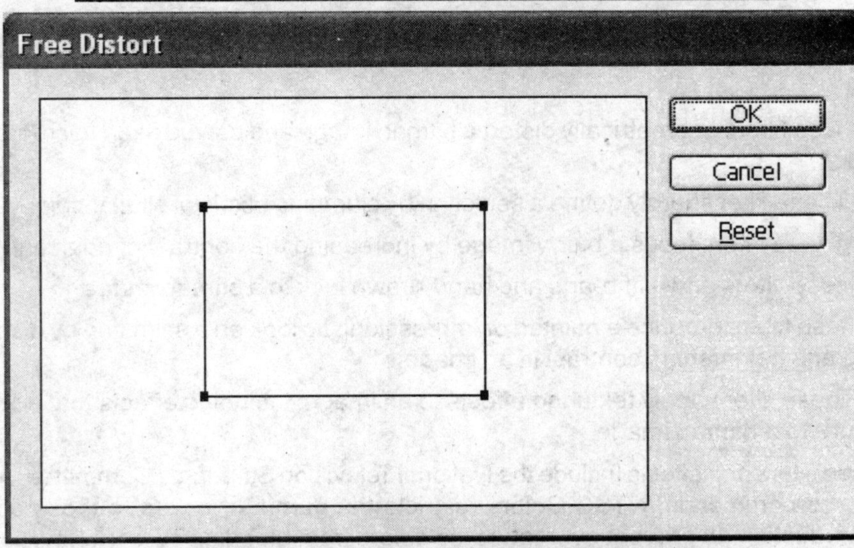
Free Distort
OK
Cancel
Reset

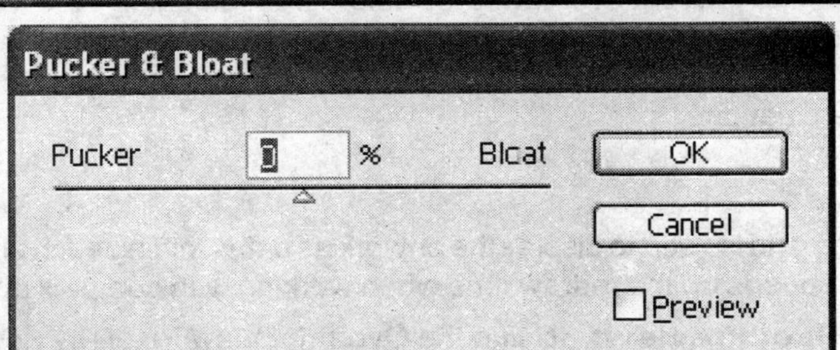
Pucker & Bloat
Pucker
%
Bloat
OK
Cancel
Preview

Inner Glow: This command creates the effect of inner glow on the image.

Outer Glow: Similar to above this creates the outer glow on the image.

SVG Filters: You can use SVG filters to add graphic effects such as drop shadows to your artwork. SVG filters differ from their bitmap counterparts in that they are XML-based. In fact, an SVG filter is nothing more than a series of XML properties that describe various mathematical operations. The resulting effect is rendered to the target object instead of the source graphic.

Warp: Using preset warp effects, you can distort or deform Illustrator artwork, including paths, text, meshes, blends, and raster images. Because warp effects are live effects, available from the Effect menu, you can apply a warp to your artwork and then continue to manipulate the artwork at any time. Once you apply the Warp effect, the warp appears in the Appearance palette, where you can save it as part of a style, select it for modifications, expand it, or delete it. It also appears in the Layers palette, which displays the object as having an appearance applied.

Photoshop Effects: The following effects of Photoshop can also be used in Illustrator CS4.

Effects Gallery: The Illustrator filters and filter effects fall into the following general categories.

Artistic: Artistic filters and effects Give a bitmap image the appearance of different media for a more organic (and less computer-generated) look.

Blur: These filters soften a bitmap image and are useful for retouching images. Blur filters and effects smooth transitions by averaging the pixels next to the hard edges of defined lines and shaded areas where significant color transitions occur in a bitmap image.

Brush Strokes: This filter gives a bitmap image a fine-arts look by using different brush and ink stroke effects.

Distort: These filters geometrically distort a bitmap image and can be used to create 3-D or other plastic effects.

Pixelate: These filter sharply define a selection by clumping pixels of similar color values in cells.

Sharpen: These filters focus a blurry image by increasing the contrast of adjacent pixels.

Sketch: These filters add a fine-arts and hand-drawn look to a bitmap image.

Stylize: These filters produce a painted or impressionistic look on a selection by displacing pixels and by finding and heightening contrast in an image.

Texture: These filters apply texturing effects to an image, including effects that add grain, paint, glass, or texture to a bitmap image.

Video: Video filters and effects Include the National Television Standards Committee (NTSC) Colors and De-Interlace commands. NTSC Colors restricts the gamut of colors to those acceptable for television reproduction, to prevent oversaturated colors from bleeding across television scan lines. De-Interlace smooths moving bitmap images captured on video by removing either the odd or the even interlaced lines in a video image. The command gives you the option of replacing the discarded lines by duplication or interpolation.

View menu

Outline: This command is used to display the artwork as paths, hiding each object's paint attributes. Working in this view speeds up the redraw time when working with complex artwork.

Overprint View/Pixel Preview: Using the Overprint View/Pixel Preview command, you can view the artwork as if it had already been rasterized, preview anti-aliased edges, and adjust the edges

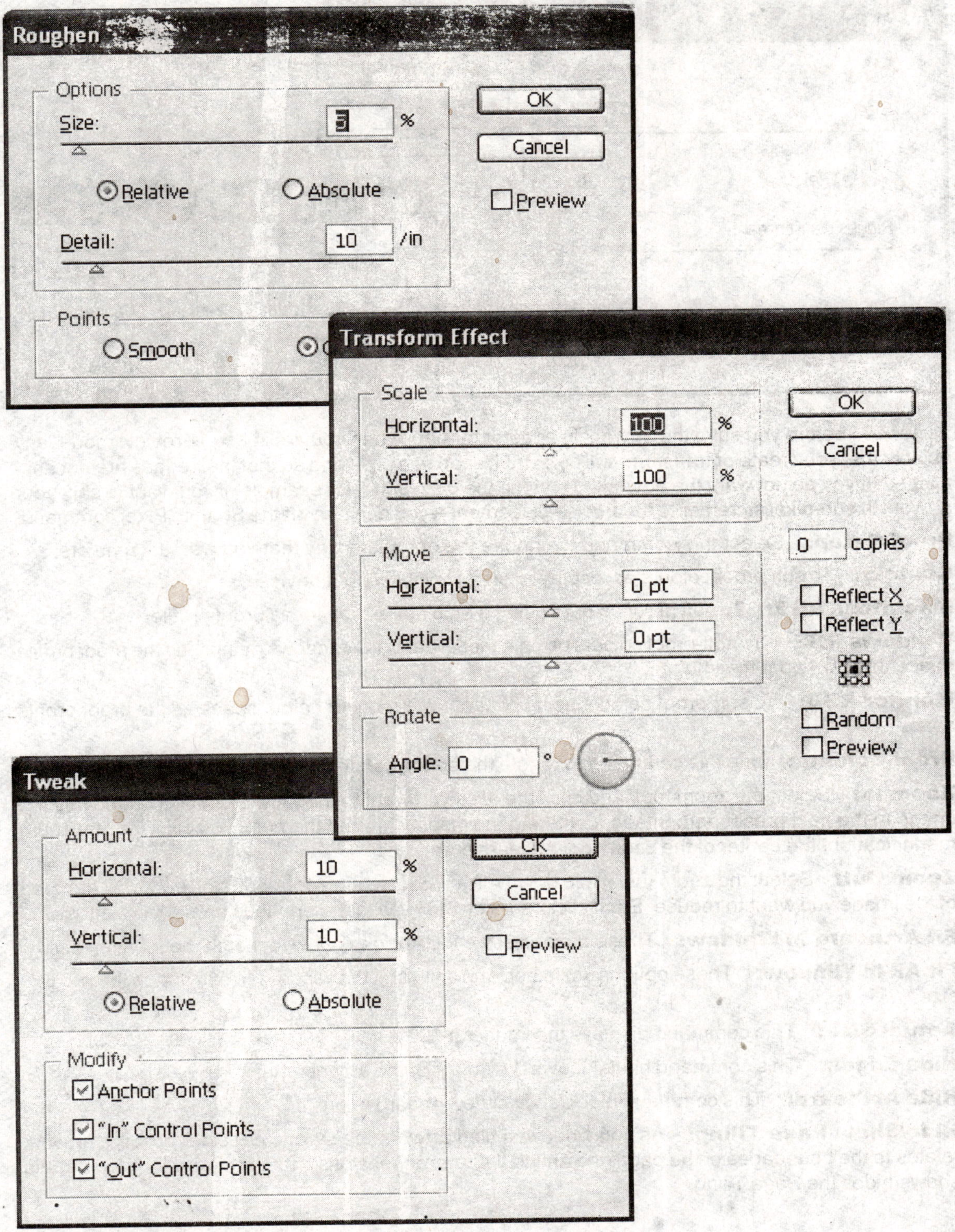
Roughen
Options
Size:
%
Relative
Absolute
Detail:
10
/in
Points
Smooth
OK
Cancel
Preview
Transform Effect
Scale
Horizontal:
100
%
Vertical:
100
%
Move
Horizontal:
0 pt
Vertical:
0 pt
Rotate
Angle:
0
OK
Cancel
0
copies
Reflect X
Reflect Y
Random
Preview
Tweak
Amount
Horizontal:
10
%
Vertical:
10
%
Relative
Absolute
Modify
Anchor Points
"In" Control Points
"Out" Control Points
OK
Cancel
Preview

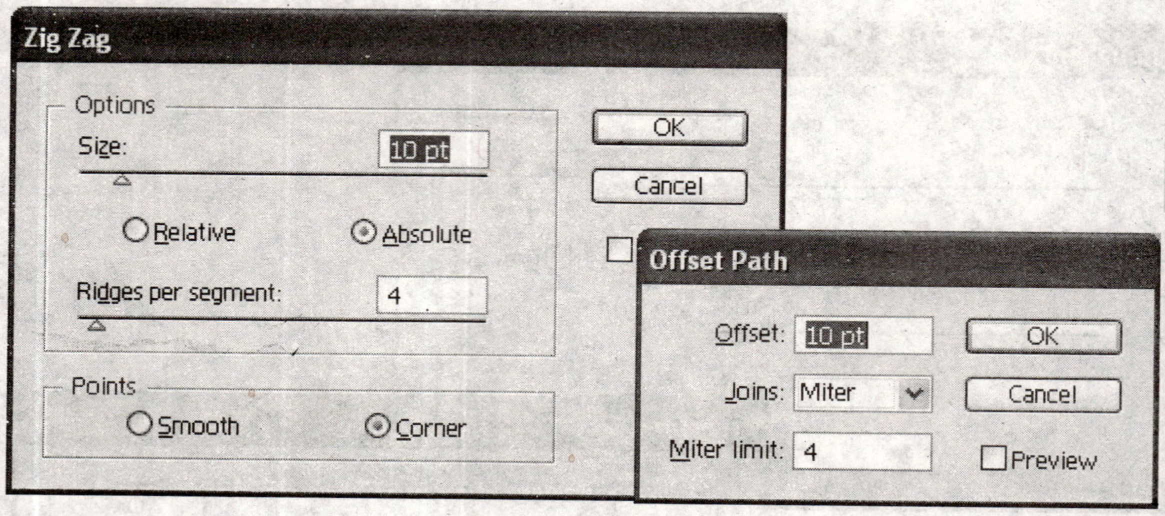

as needed before you save the artwork in a raster format. When you are in Pixel Preview mode, any objects that you create or transform will by default snap to a pixel grid so that their edges are not anti-aliased. If you do not want the artwork to snap to the pixel grid—for example, if you want to shift your artwork in sub-pixel increments for precise placement—you can turn off the Snap to Pixel command.

Proof Setup: Select this command to choose the output display that you want to simulate:

Custom: To soft proof colours as displayed on a specific output device.

Macintosh RGB: To soft proof colours using a Macintosh monitor as proof profile.

Windows RGB: To soft-proof colours using either a standard Windows monitor as the proof profile space that you want to simulate.

Monitor RGB: To soft-proof colours using your current monitor colour space as the proof profile space.

Proof Colours: Use this command to toggle the soft-proof display on or off.

Zoom In: Select the zoom tool, and click the area you want to magnify. Each click magnifies the image to the next preset percentage, centering the display around the point you click. At maximum magnification, the center of the zoom tool appears empty.

Zoom Out: Select the zoom tool. Hold down Alt to activate the zoom-out tool, and click the area of the image you want to reduce. Each click reduces the view to the previous preset percentage.

Fit Artboard In Window: These options scale the Artboard view to match the monitor size.

Fit All In Window: These options scale both the view and the window size to match the monitor size.

Actual Size: This command displays the image at 100%.

Hide Edges: This command hides/shows the edges of the artwork.

Hide Artboard: This command hides/shows the Artboard or not.

Hide/Show Page Tiling: As you work with tiled artwork, be sure to consider how the artwork relates to the boundaries of the page grid and to the total dimensions of the artboard. This command shows/hides the Page Tiling.

Show Slices: This command hides/shows the slices.

Lock Slices: This command locks/unlocks the slices.

Hide Template: This command toggles between hiding/showing the Templates.

Hide/Show Rules: Shows or hides rulers on the screen.

Show Artboard Rulers: Show or hide rulers of the artboard.

Hide Bounding Box: Shows or hides bounding box of the artwork.

Show Transparency Grid: Shows or hides Transparency Grid on the screen.

Hide Text Threads: This command hides/shows the text threads.

Show Live Paint Gaps: This command hides/shows the Artboard or not.

Guides: This command has the following sub-command.

Hide Guides: This command hides all the guides from the screen.

Make Guides: This command allows you to make a new guide on the screen.

Lock Guides: This command locks all the column and ruler guides so that you cannot move them accidentally.

Release Guide: This command allows you to release the guides of the graphics turning it into an regular graphics object.

Clear Guides: This command clears all guides from the screen.

Smart Guides: Smart Guides are temporary, "snap to" guides that help you create, align, edit, and transform objects relative to other objects. You can also use Smart Guides when rotating, scaling, and shearing objects. Objects can snap to locked objects and objects on locked layers.

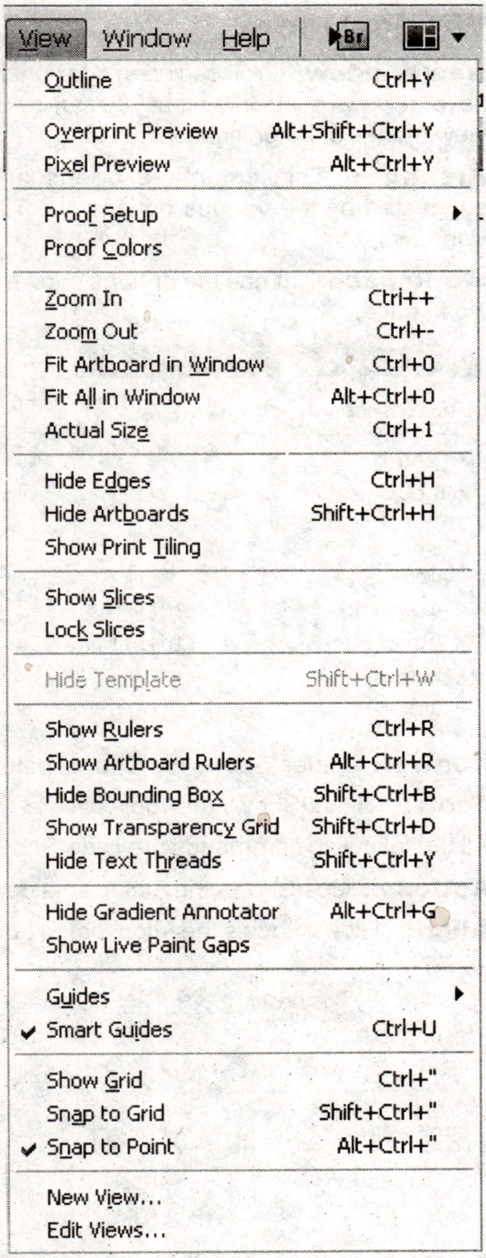

Show Grid: This command allows you to show all the grids on the screen.

Snap To Grid: Using this command you can select the various guides which you want to snap to.

Snap to Point: This command snaps the various guides on the screen to a point.

New Views: Using this command you can open additional windows to display several views at once, so that you can quickly switch between view modes or magnifications.

Edit Views: You can delete/edit a different view created as above.

Window menu

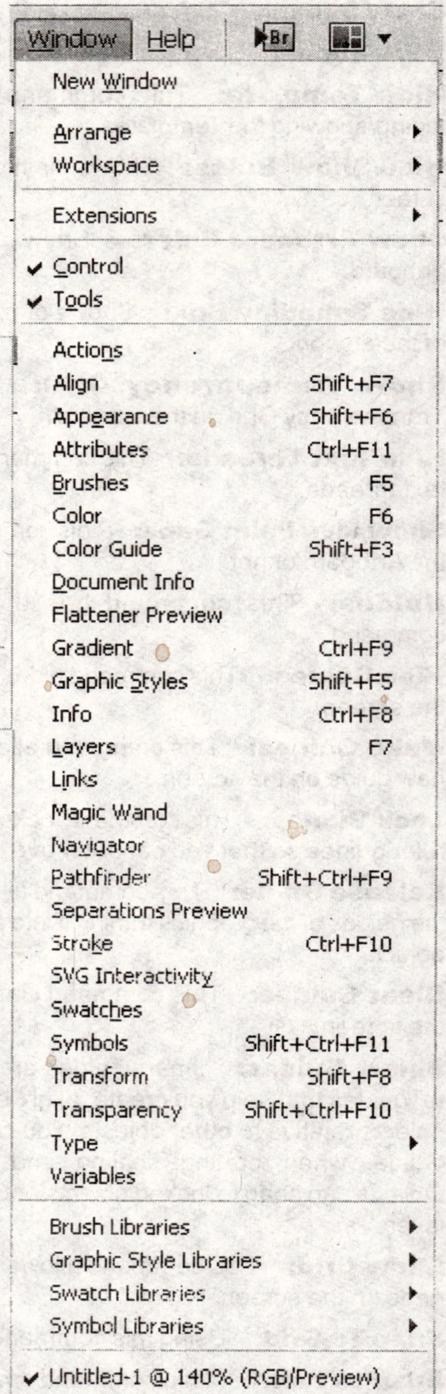

New Window: You can open additional windows to display several views at once, so that you can quickly switch between view modes or magnifications.

Arrange: This command opens another window as suggested by the various options like Tile, Cascade, Fit in Windows, etc.

Workspace: It has the options shown here for working in workspace.

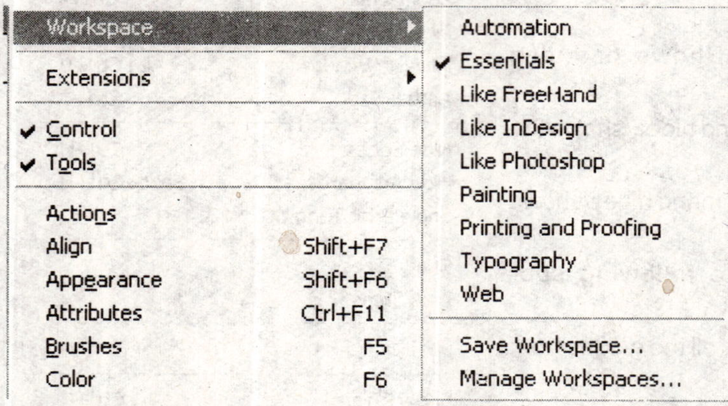

Control: Hides/Shows the Control palette.

Tools: Hides/Shows the Tools palette.

All the following commands are Hide/Show toggles.

Actions: Hides/Shows the Actions dialog box on the screen.

Align: Hides/Shows the Align dialog box on the screen.

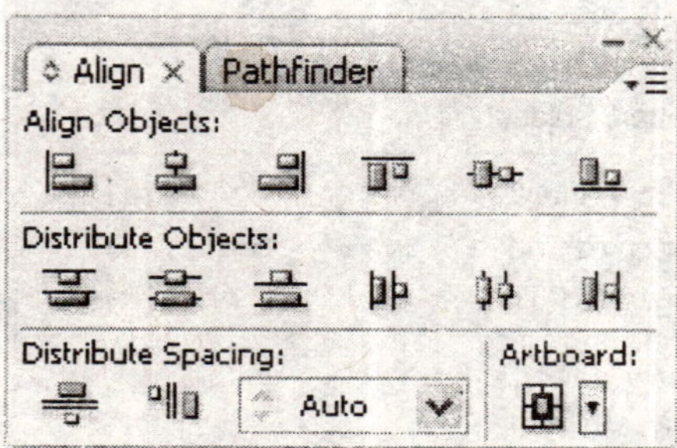

Appearance: Hides/Shows the Appearance dialog box on the screen.

Attributes: Hides/Shows the Attributes dialog box on the screen.

Brushes: Hides/Shows the Brushes dialog box on the screen.

Colour: Hides/Shows the Color dialog box on the screen.

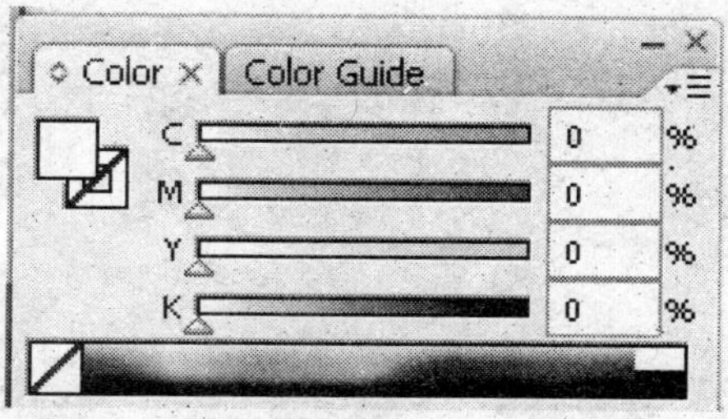

Document Info: Hides/Shows the Document Info dialog box on the screen.

Gradient: Hides/Shows the Gradient dialog box on the screen.

Info: Hides/Shows the Info dialog box on the screen.

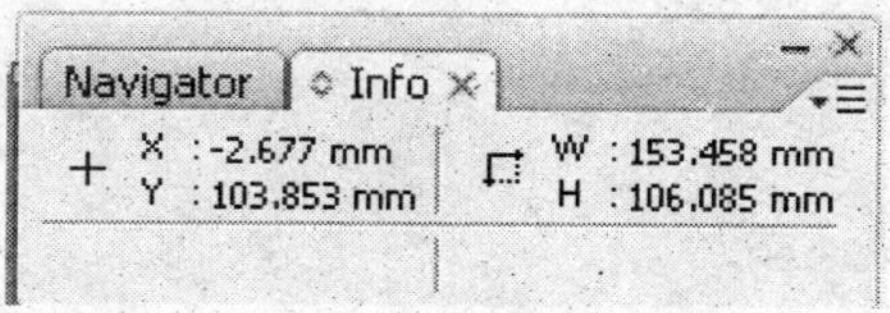

Layers: Hides/Shows the Layers dialog box on the screen.

Links: Hides/Shows the Links dialog box on the screen.

Magic Wand: Hides/Shows the Magic Wand dialog box on the screen.

Navigator: Hides/Shows the Navigator dialog box on the screen.

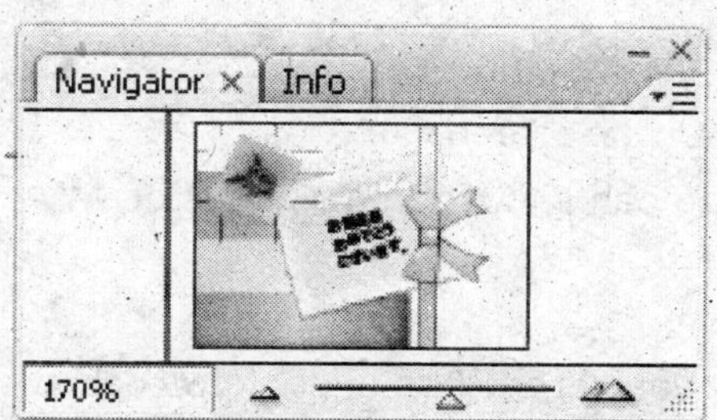

Pathfinder: Hides/Shows the Pathfinder dialog box on the screen.

Stroke: Hides/Shows the Stroke dialog box on the screen.

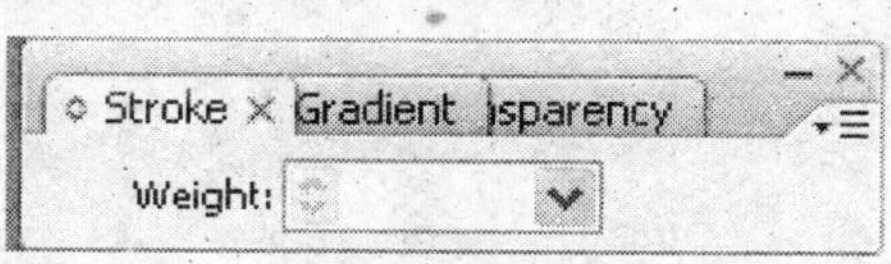

Styles: Hides/Shows the Styles dialog box on the screen.

SVG Interactivity: Hides/Shows the SVG Interactivity dialog box on the screen.

Swatches: Hides/Shows the Swatches dialog box on the screen.

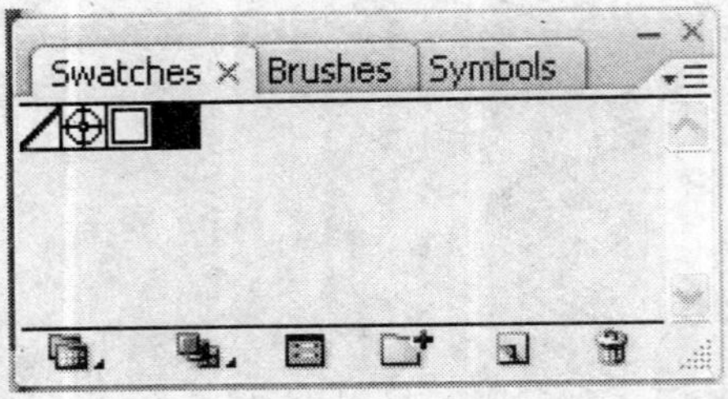

Symbols: Hides/Shows the Symbols dialog box on the screen.

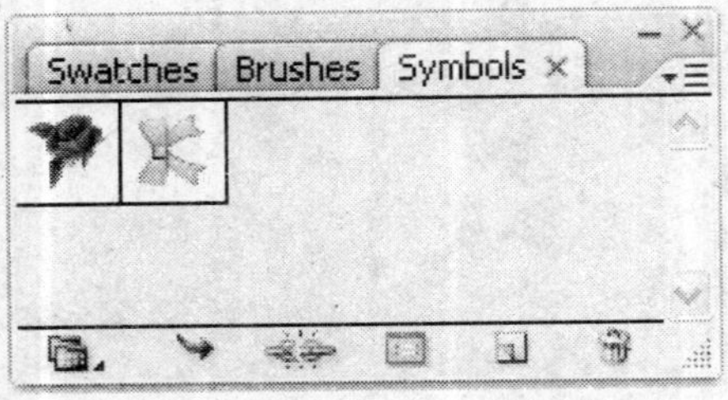

Tools: Hides/Shows the tools dialog box on the screen.

Transform: Hides/Shows the Transform dialog box on the screen.

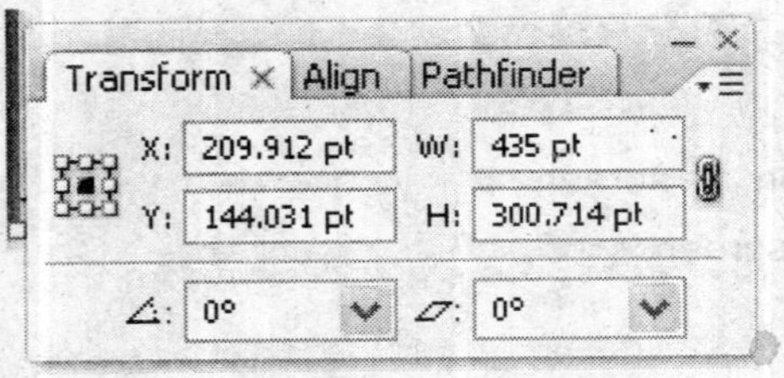

Transparency: Hides/Shows the Transparency dialog box on the screen.

Type: Hides/Shows the Type dialog box on the screen. You can choose from Character, MM Design, Paragraph or Tab Ruler.

Variable: Hides/Shows the Variable dialog box on the screen.

Brush Libraries: It shows the option of calling on screen the various brush libraries shown below. One of them Arrow_Special is shown here.

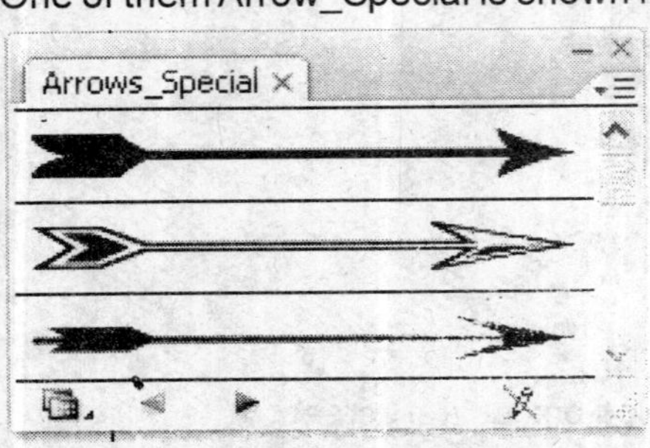

Graphic Style Libraries: It shows the option calling on screen the various libraries shown below. One of them Image Effects is shown here.

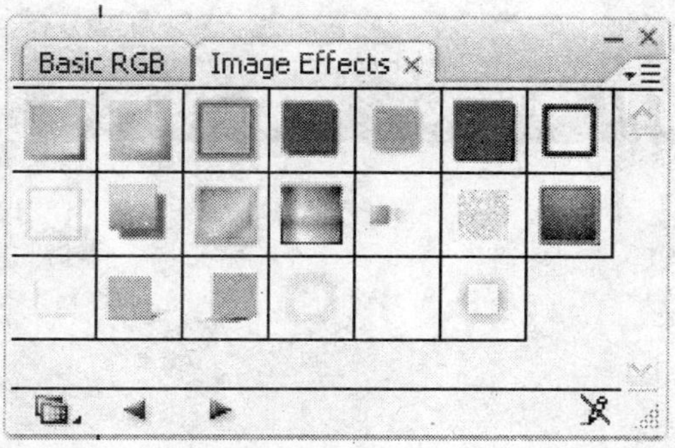

Swatches Libraries: It shows the option of calling on screen the various swatches on screen from the library shown here. One of them Kid Stuff is shown here.

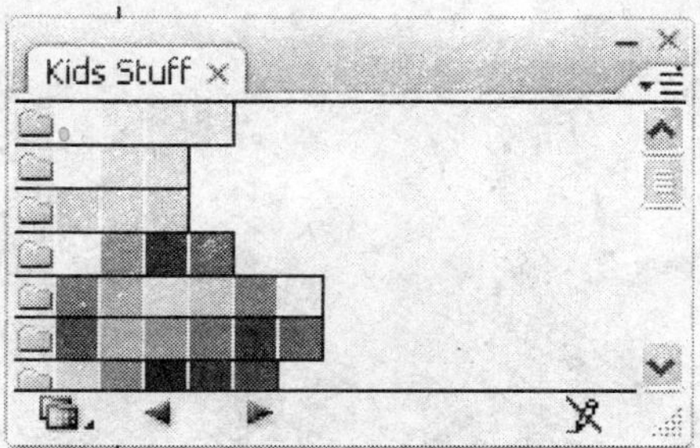

Symbol Libraries: It shows the option of calling on screen the various symbols on screen from the library shown here. One of them Charts is shown here.

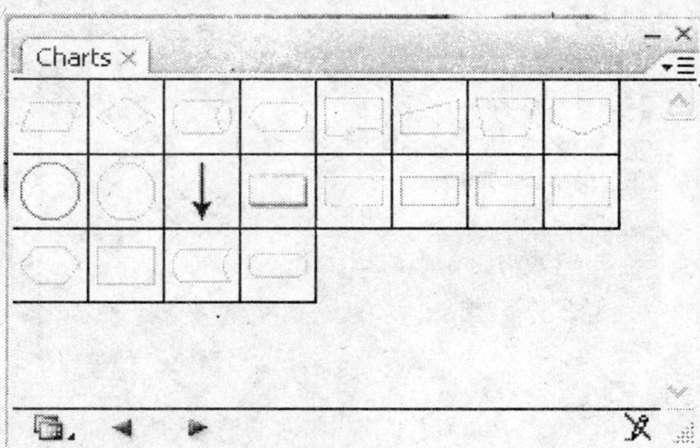

Help menu

This menu has the various options which help you in case you want to know more about any command.

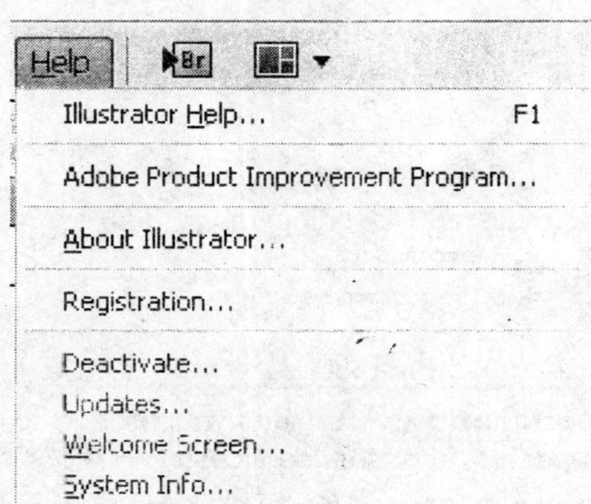

Illustrator Help: It takes you to the complete help of Illustrator which can be accessed through Index or Search.

About Product Improvement Program: Read about it in the beginning of the chapter.

About Illustrator: Shows the Illustrator copyright screen.

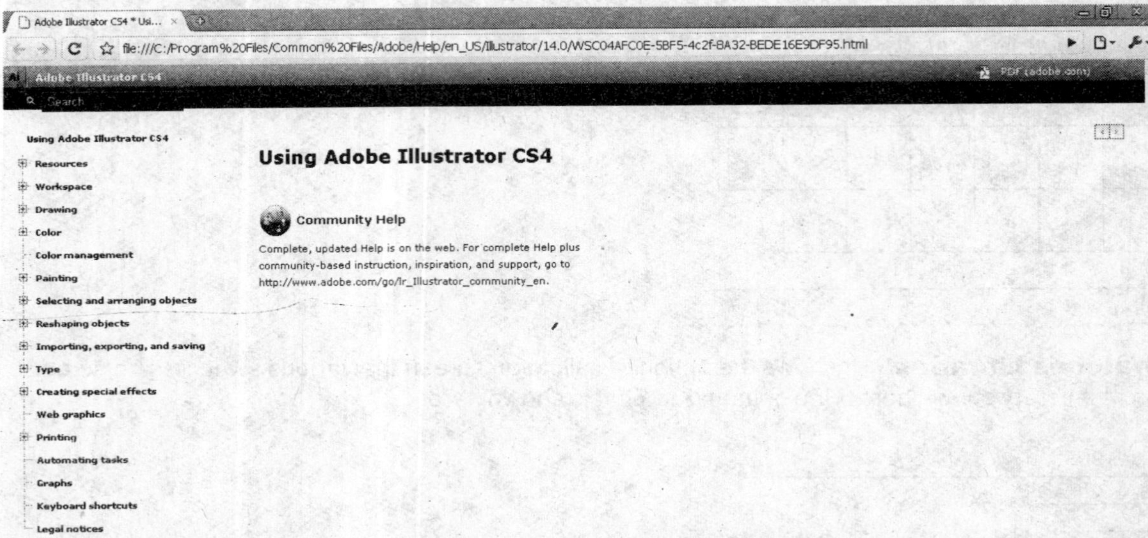

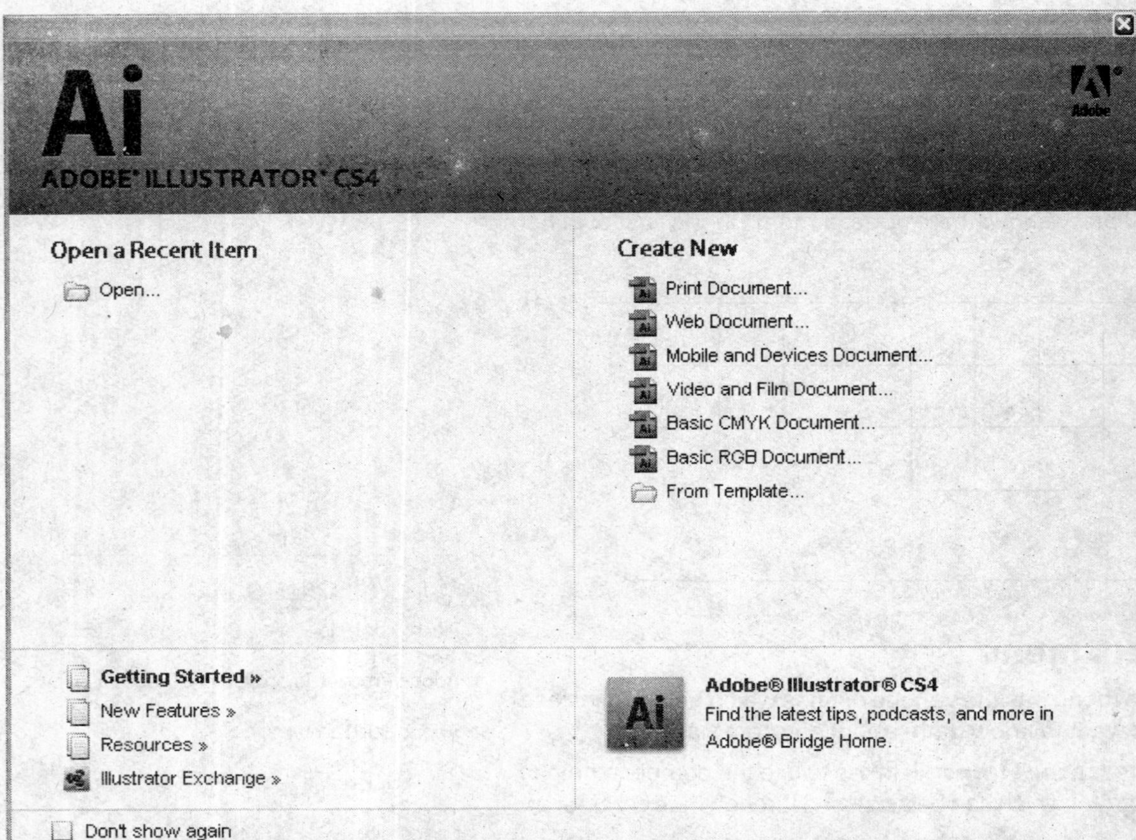

Registration: Register your product to receive complimentary installation support, notifications of updates, and other services.

Adobe Online: It takes you to the Website of the software company called Adobe and there you

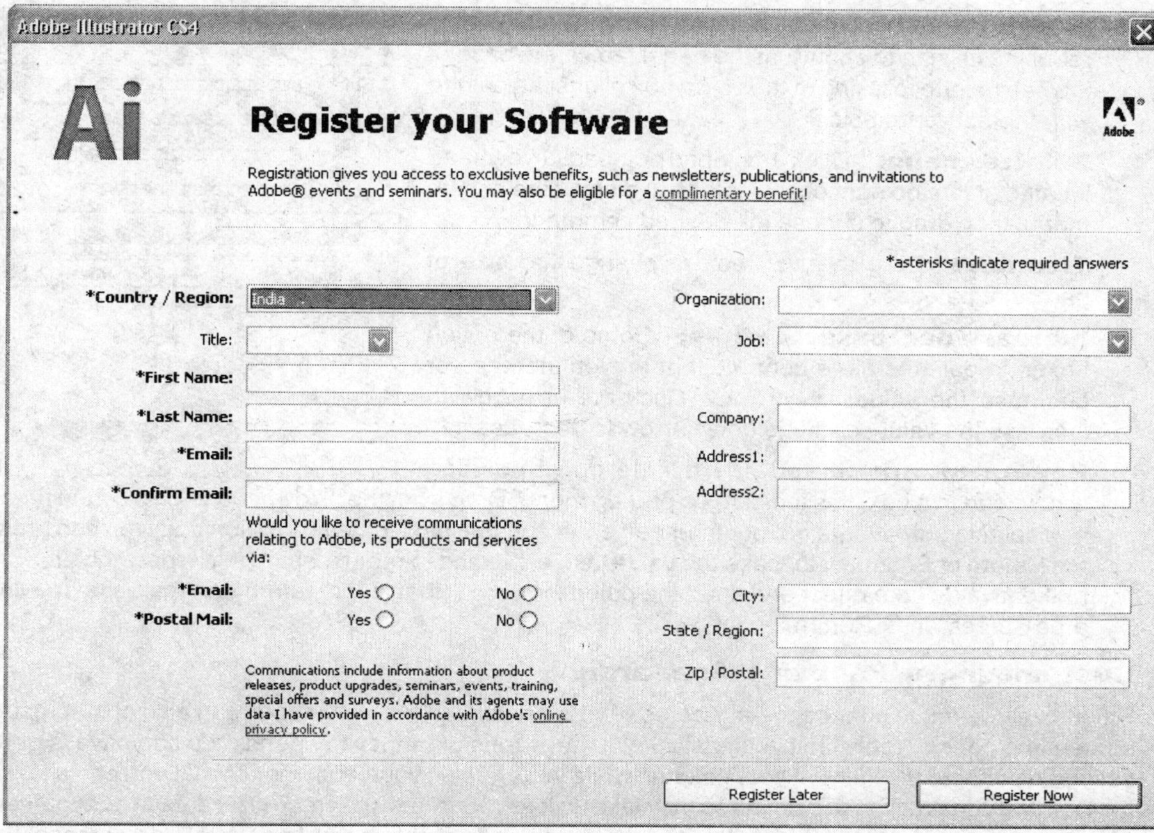

can see the information about Activate, Deactivate, Updates, Welcome Screen, System Information, etc.

Using Palettes

A palette is nothing more than a dialog box that can remain open while you fiddle about inside the software. You can show or hide all of Illustrator's numerous palettes (including the toolbox) by choosing the appropriate command. To hide all palettes, including the toolbox, press Tab. To redisplay them, press Tab again. Illustrator displays only those palettes that were on screen before you pressed Tab the first time. If you press Shift+Tab, you hide all the palettes except the toolbox.

A typical palette is shown on the next page. As you can see palettes offer many of the same kinds of options that you find inside dialog box including check boxes, scrolling lists and the like. A bar tops of each palette. Drag the bar to move the palette on screen Illustrator's palettes snap into alignment with other palettes; they also snap into alignment with the edges of the screen.

Options vary more widely in palettes than they do in dialog boxes. Some are so specific to the function of the palette, there's no point in explaining them here. So for now, we'll just cover the ones that you see quite a bit in Illustrator and other applications

Close box: Windows uses will find their close boxes in the right corner.

Zoom box: Palettes offer zoom boxes, known as minimize buttons in windows, on the right sides of their title bars. When you click in the zoom box, Illustrator changes the size of the palettes, either making it larger to show the options or reducing its size to show just the panel tab. In the case of the Tab palette, clicking in the zoom box aligns the palette with the active text block.

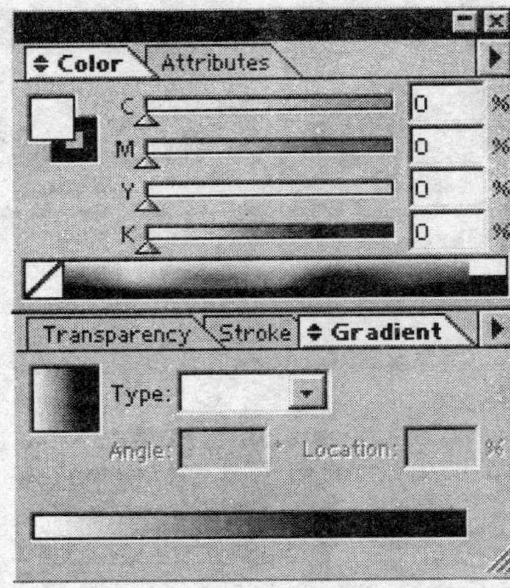

Palette menu: Click the right-pointing arrowhead located at the top right of any palette to display the palette menu, then drag to choose the desired command.

Size box: Drag the size box to change the size of particular palettes.

Increase/decrease controls: Some of the option boxes in palettes have controls that let you increase or decrease the values in the box. Click the up arrow to increase the value; click the down arrow to decrease it.

Pop-up menu: If you see a little down-pointing arrowhead in a box, this indicates a pop-up menu. Drag from the arrowhead to display the menu and select your favorite option. After you enter a value into a palette's option box, you can press the Return or Enter key to make the value take effect and to return control to the drawing area. To make a value take effect and keep the palette in focus (that is, not return control to the drawing area), press Shift+Return.

Customizing a Palette's Appearance

Palettes allow you to change the attributes of your artwork on the fly, but they can also clutter up the screen and considerably limit your view. If you have tons of money to spend, you can always get a second monitor to display just your palettes while you work on your main monitor. Or you can change the look and construction of palettes so they take up less room on your screen. The default arrangement of the palettes groups certain palettes together, as panels within a single palette. For instance, the color panel is grouped with the attributes panel. To change a panels group, click and drag on the panel's tab and move the pane to its new location. One of three things happens. *First*, if you end your drag on an area free of palettes, you separate the panel from its original group. *Second*, if you move the tap onto another panel in a different palette, the panel you move will join the new group as the newest and rightmost member of that group. When you drag a panel onto a new palette, Illustrator will indicate that is ready to let the panel join the destination palettes little family by ringing the palette with a strip of black. So if you really need to free up some screen real estate, you can group all your palettes into one humongous group.

The *Third* result of dragging a panel is that you will dock the panel below a palette. Docking a palette results in a meta-palette. Once you have formed a meta-palette, you have the option of adding palettes to either group, as described above or even of making an ultra-meta-palette by dragging another palette onto the bottom of the meta-palette.

Color Settings

Not all preference settings reside with Preferences command. In fact, some of the most complex and compelling lurk next door within the dark recesses of Edit>>Color Settings. The Color Settings command specifies hoe Illustrator manages colors inside any currently open or future illustrations. Very likely, you've heard of color management, which sometimes goes by the acronym CMS (short for color management system).

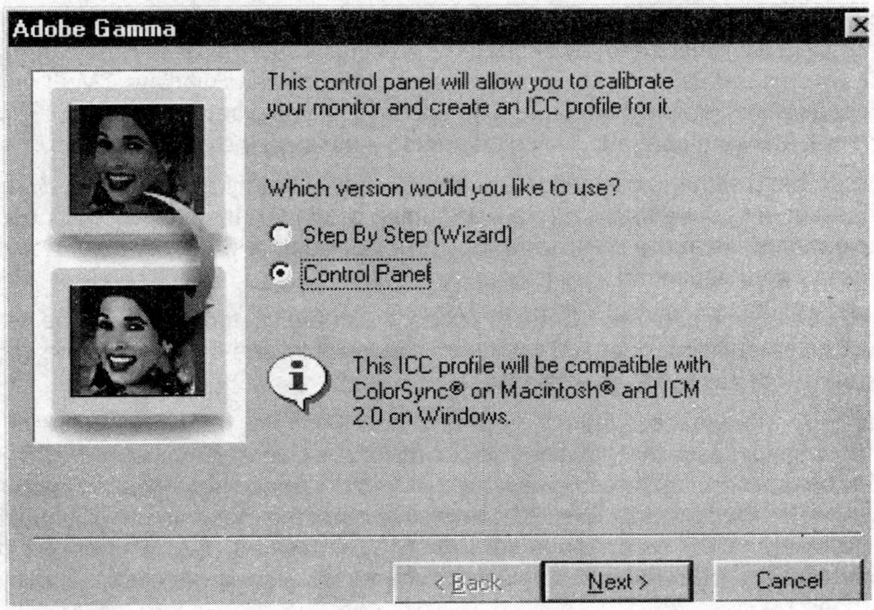

First, the Color Settings command determines whether Illustrator modifies the colors in a graphic when opening or importing the artwork. *Second*, it determine how those colors are modifies, with the ostensible goal of making sure that what you see on screen is more or les indicative of what you'll get on the Web or in print. And third, it tells Illustrator whether or not to append a few lines of code at the end of each file that explains the environment in which the illustraton was last viewed and edited.

What Color Settings does not do is calibrate your monitor, your printer or any other piece of hardware in your office. You can calibrate your monitor in a number of ways, including using a hardware puck or a piece of software such as Adobe Gamma. Calibrating a printer is typically the domain of the printer manufacturer or a commercial prepress technician. Illustrator can make use of this calibration data, but it cannot – nor should it – generate such data.

Of course, it's one thing to know what a command can and can't do; it's quite another to actually put it to use. Here's blow-by-blow account of how to achieve accurate color in Illustrator CS4:

1. Like Photoshop, InDesign and other Adobe applications, Illustrator contains Adobe Gamma, which you can use to adjust the color on your monitor. We recommend you use it. Choose Settings from the Start menu, then choose Control Panel. Then double-click on the Adobe Gamma icon. From that point on, it's just a matter of reading the instructions and responding as directed. Our single suggestion – when you get to the screen with the View Single Gamma Only check box, turn it off. Then you can adjust the red, green and blue settings independently, which is essential for getting the color just right.

   In the end, Gamma asks you to save characterization, settings as either a ColorSync file on the Mac or an ICM file on the PC. Both formats are understood by most major graphics applications. This file defines your monitor's color space so that Illustrator can properly translate CMYK and even Web-based RGB colors so they look great on your particular screen.

2. Now that you've characterized your monitor, it's time to return to Illustrator and choose the Color Settings command from the Edit menu. Illustrator displays the Color Settings dialog

box as shown earlier. The dialog box is filled with a million options, nearly all of which are dimmed. This is because, by default, the Settings option is set to Emulate Adobe Illustrator 6.0, which deactivates the color management functions and displays CMYK values on screen according to a generic color table. The upshot is that Illustrator leaves your colors absolutely unmodified when opening or placing artwork, just as in the good old days.

3. The problem with the good old days is they really weren't all that good. Selecting no color management is like forgoing the vegetables at dinner. It's all well and good to avoid the unpleasantness in the short term, but your poor diet and lack of color activism will come back to haunt you in the long run.
4. At this point, you can press Enter to accept the default setting or tweak the settings to make them better suit your needs. If you figure Illustrator knows best, skip to the end of the steps. If you choose to tweak, keep reading.
5. The 2 Working Spaces settings determine how Illustrator translates RGB and CMTK colors to the monitor space that you specified using Adobe Gamma. Adobe RGB [1998] is a fantastic RGB space for print professionals; the sRGB color space is well suited to on-line designers because it emulates a generic PC screen, typical of the monitors used by most Web surfers. State-side, the CMYK option is set to U.S. Web Coated (SWOP) both for print and Web professionals. If you print to a different commercial standard, select the appropriate option from the list.
6. The next set of options, named Color Management Policies, controls how illustrator interprets graphics that contain embedded profiles. A profile explains where a file came from so that Illustrator can make the required changes to display the artwork property on your screen.
7. Last but not last are the Profile Mismatches options, which ask you what to do when opening or importing artwork that is profiled in a way that doesn't exactly match the settings you selected in Step 5. When turned on, Ask When Opening displays a message anytime you open an illustration with a non-matching profile; Ask When Pasting affects any artwork pasted, dragged and dropped or imported using the File>>Place command.
8. If you like pain, you can select the Advanced Mode check box of the top of the dialog box and make more work for yourself. This option lets you fine tune the exact manner in which Illustrator converts colors. If you're a color scientist, go nuts. Otherwise, leave well enough alone. Adobe's default color engine and relative Colorimetric rendering intent are better suited to vector artwork than any of the alternatives.
9. That's it. When you're done, click the OK button.

2 Tools of Illustrator CS 4

Understanding Tools

The toolbox, like any other palette, is entirely independent of all other desktop elements, so if you reduce the size of a drawing window the toolbox remains unchanged, with 26 tools visible and easily accessible. The toolbox serves and is positioned in front of any and all open illustrations. You can move the toolbox by dragging its tittle bar and hide it by choosing the Window>>Hide Tools command. To redisplay the toolbox, choose Window >> Show Tools. You can hide the toolbox and all other palettes by pressing the Tab key. Press Tab again to bring all the palettes back. To get rid of all palettes except the toolbox, press Shift+Tab (that is, hold the Shift key and then tap the tab key).

As with other graphics and publishing programs, you select a tool in Illustrator by clicking on its icon in the toolbox. Illustrator highlights the active tool so it stands out prominently. The toolbox contains 24 tool slots. In addition to the default tools occupying these slots, Illustrators offers 36 alternate tools that are initially hidden. For example, Illustrator hides the polygon, star and spiral tools under the ellipse tool slot. To use one of these hidden tools, you have to click the and hold the ellipse icon to display a pop-up menu of alternates. Select the desired tool as you would a command – that is, by highlighting the tool and releasing the mouse button. Slots that offer alternate tools have tiny right-facing arrowheads in their lower right corners.

Tear off

Slots have an added benefit of letting you tear off the tools so they appear in their own little row. Just drag your cursor over to the tearoff icon (indicated by the small arrowhead) at the end of the slot. Release the mouse. That slot appears in its own little toolbar. You can then position the slot anywhere on your window. You can even have multiple slots for the same tools.

The following paragraphs explain how to use each of Illustrator's tools in the illustration window. For example, if an item instructs you to drag, click the tool icon to select it and then drag inside the drawing area; don't drag on the icon itself. These are intended as introductory descriptions only.

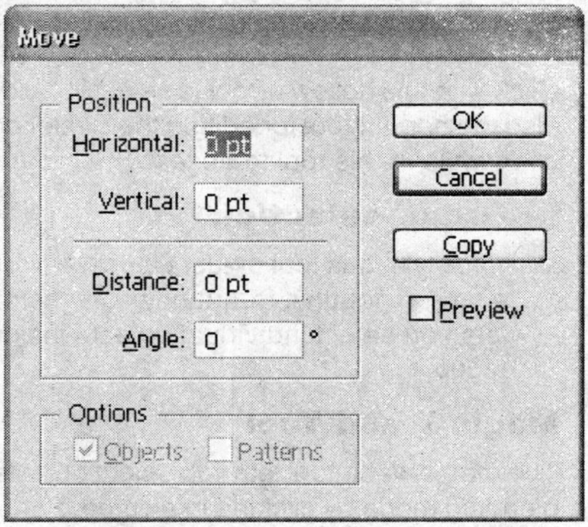

Selection Tool

The selection tool – which is usually called the "arrow tool" in deference to its appearance – is active when you first start illustrator. Use this tool to select object that you've created so you can manipulate them. Click an object to select the entire object. Drag an object to move it. You can also use the selection tool to select text blocks.

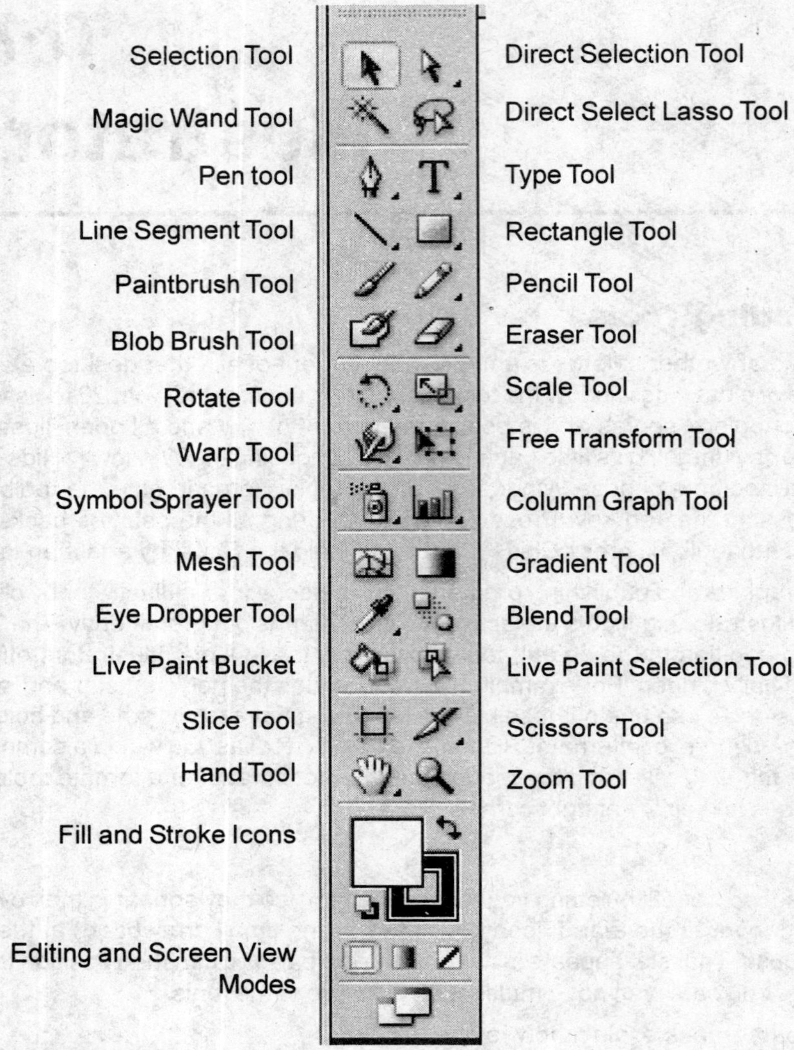

Direct Selection Tool

Click with this hollow arrow to select individual anchor points and segments in a line or shape. This is also the perfect tool for editing the Bezier control handles that govern the curvature of segments. Alt-click while in this tool to access the group selection tool.

Group selection

Click with this tool or just Option/Alt-click with the direct selection tool to select whole objects at a time. Though it frequently acts the same as the standard arrow tool, the group selection tool lets you select individual objects inside groups, whereas the arrow tool selects all objects in a group.

Magic Wand Tool

The magic wand tool lets you select objects of the same color, stroke weight, stroke color, opacity, or blending mode by clicking in a colored area.

Direct Select Lasso Tool

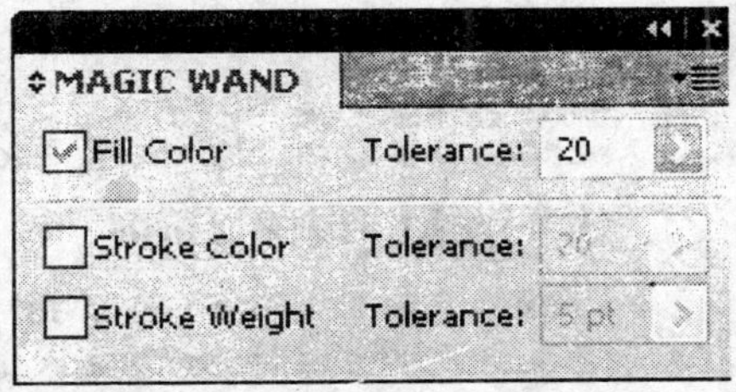

Drag with this tool to select the individual points within a non-rectangular area. When you release the mouse, any points or paths within the lasso area will be selected.

Pen Tool

This is Illustrator's most powerful drawing tool. Use the pen tool to draw a line as a series of individual points. Click to add the corners to a line, drag to add arcs. You can also Option/Alt-drag on an arc to change it to a cusp. Illustrator automatically connects your points with straight or curved segments. Option/alt-click while in this tool to access the convert direction tool.

Add point

Click a segment with the add point tool to insert a new point into a line. Option/Art-click to access the delete anchor point tool.

Delete point

Click a point with this tool to remove the point while leaving the line intact. That's why we'd rather call this the remove point tool – "deleting" a point would create a hole. Option/Alt-click to access the add anchor point tool.

Convert point

Use this tool to change a corner in a line to an arc or vice versa. Click an arc to make it a corner, drag on a corner to make it an arc.

Type Tool

Click with this tool and then enter text from the keyboard to create a line of type in the standard left-to-right format. To create a text block with type that automatically wraps from one line downs to the next, drag with the type tool and then start from one line downs to the next, drag with the type tool and then start banging away at the keyboard. You can also use this tool or one of the other five type tools to highlight characters in a text block – allowing you to edit or format them. Shift-click while in this tool to access the vertical type tool.

Area type

Click a line or shape to create text that wrap inside an irregular boundary. Option/Art-click to access the path type tool. Shift-click to access the vertical area type tool.

Path type

Click a line or shape to create text that follow the contours to the object, better known as text on a curve. Option/Alt-click to access the area type tool. Shift-click to access the vertical path type tool.

Vertical type

Very similar to the type tool, this tool arranges text vertically, the way Japanese script appears. Click with this tool and then enter text from the keyboard to create an ascending column of type. To create a text block with type that automatically wraps from one column to the next (from right to left), drag with the vertical type tool and then start them magic fingers fluttering. Option/Alt-click to access the vertical path type tool. Shift-click to access the type tool.

Vertical area type

Click a line or shape to create text that fills an irregular boundary column. Option/Alt-click to access the vertical path type tool. Shift-click to access the area type tool.

Vertical path type

Click a line or shape to create text that follows the contours of the object. As you probably guessed, one letter will stack upon the next to form a column that follows the curve. Option/alt-click to access the vertical area type tool. Shift-click to access the path type tool.

Line Segment Tool

Use the line and arc segment tools to quickly and easily create individual lines and arcs by dragging. The Line and Arc Segment dialog boxes display the values of the last segment created.

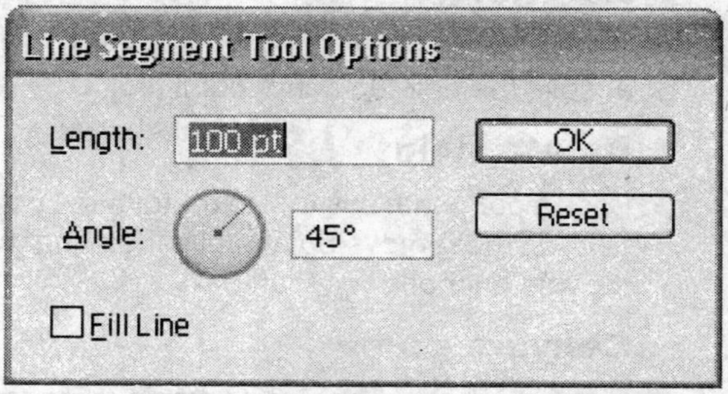

Arc Tool

The Arc tool allows you to create an arc.

Spiral Tool

The spiral tool creates a spiral-shaped object of a given radius and number of winds; that is, the number of turns that the spiral completes from start to finish.

Rectangular Grid Tool

Use the grid tools to quickly draw rectangular or polar grids. Specify the grid size and the number of dividers, and then drag to create the grid anywhere on the artboard. The rectangular grid tool creates rectangular grids of a specified size with a specified number of dividers.

Polar Grid Tool

Use the grid tools to quickly draw rectangular or polar grids. Specify the grid size and the number of dividers, and then drag to create the grid anywhere on the artboard. The polar grid tool creates concentric circles of a specified size and a specified number of dividers.

Rectangle Tool

This tool works just like the ellipse tool, except that it makes rectangles and squares. Shift-drag to draw a square or Alt-drag to create a rectangle from center outward.

Rounded rectangle

If you want your rectangles to have rounded corners, use this tool. To adjust the roundness of the corners of future shapes, click with the tool in the drawing area. Shift-drag to draw a rounded square. As you may have guessed, you can Option/Alt-drag to create a rounded rectangle from the center outward.

Ellipse Tool

Drag with this tool, previously called the oval tool to draw an ellipse. You can also Shift-drag to draw a circle or Alt-drag to draw an ellipse from the center outward. Click with the tool to enter numerical dimensions for your ellipse.

Polygon

When you drag with this too, you draw a regular polygon, like a triangle or pentagon. Click with the tool to change the number of sides.

Star

Drag with this tool to draw a star with symmetrical points. Option-drag to constrain the star so opposite arms are perfectly aligned, as for a five-pointed American star or a Star of David. Click with the tool to change the number of points.

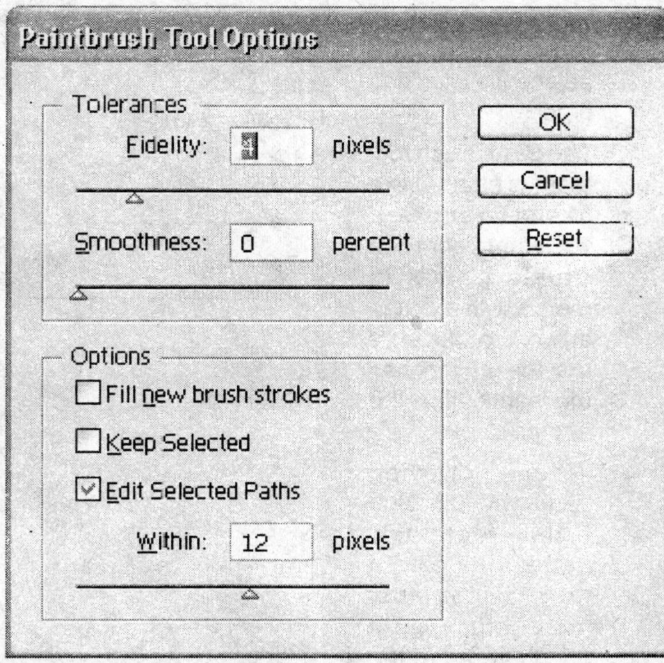

Flare

The flare tool creates flare objects with a bright center, a halo, and rays and rings. Use this tool to create an effect similar to a lens flare in a photograph.

Paintbrush Tool

This tool creates an open path that is automatically styled with one of the calligraphy, artistic, scatter or pattern brushes. Double-click the icon to set the sensitivity of the paintbrush. Like the pencil tool, the paintbrush can also be used to modify a previously drawn brushstroke.

Pencil Tool

Formally known as the freehand tool, the pencil tool makes a freeform line when you drag with it, much as if you were drawing with a pencil. If you are not satisfied with the final result, simply drag over the part of your path you wish to correct and the offending snippet toes the line.

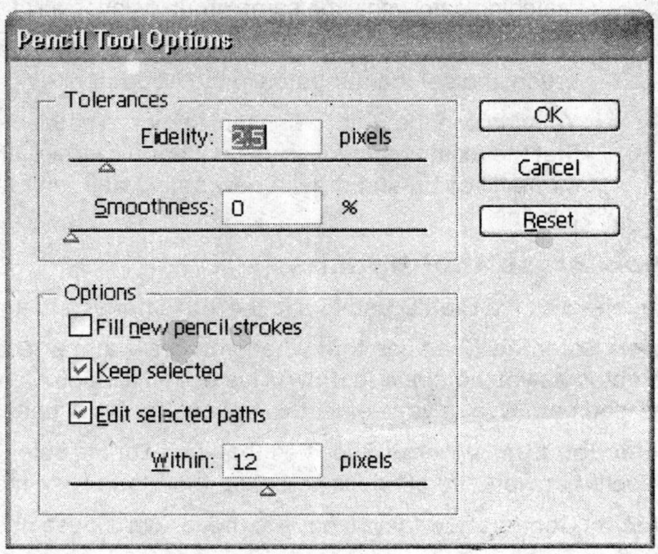

Smooth

Use the smooth tool to reposition points and reshape paths quickly. After you drag with this tool, Illustrator will add or remove points (or even more points) in an attempt to streamline the path and smooth it out.

Erase

With the erase tool, you drag over a segment of an entire path to remove it. This allows you to open closed paths and delete unnecessary paths easily.

Blob Brush Tool

Use the Blob Brush tool to paint filled shapes that you can intersect and merge with other shapes of the same color.

Blob Brush tool guidelines

- When using the Blob Brush tool, keep the following guidelines in mind:
- To merge paths, they must be adjacent in stacking order.

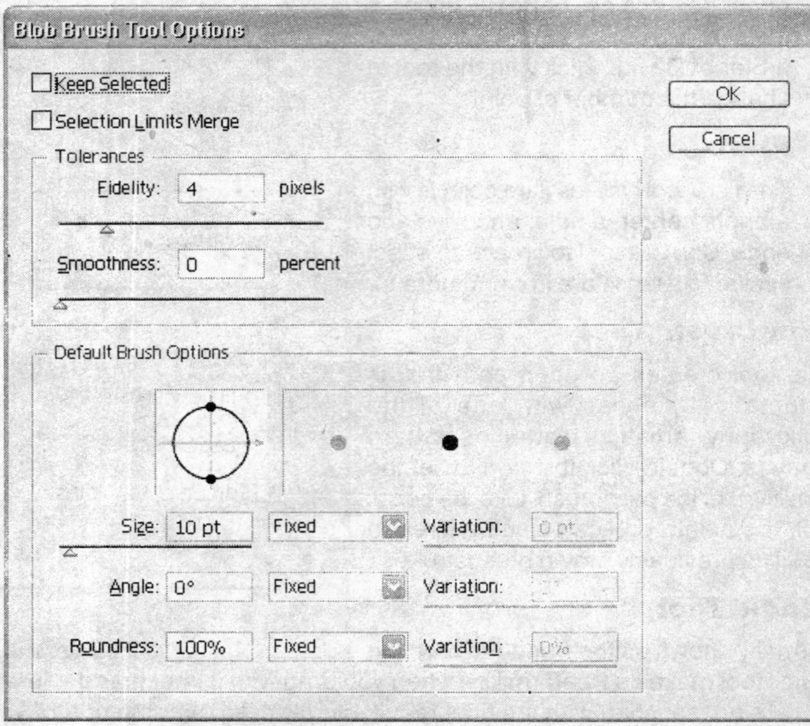

- The Blob Brush tool creates paths with a fill and no stroke. If you want your Blob Brush paths to merge with existing artwork, make sure that the artwork has the same fill color and no stroke.
- When drawing paths with the Blob Brush tool, new paths merge with the topmost matching path encountered. If the new path touches more than one matching path within the same group or layer, all of the intersecting paths are merged together.
- To apply paint attributes (such as effects or transparency) to the Blob Brush tool, select the brush and set the attributes in the Appearances panel before you start drawing.
- You can use the Blob Brush tool to merge paths created by other tools. To do this make sure that the existing artwork does not have a stroke; then set up the Blob Brush tool to have the same fill color, and draw a new path that intersects all of the paths that you want to merge together.

Blob Brush tool options

Double-click the Blob Brush tool in the Tools panel and set any of the following options:

Keep Selected Specifies that when you draw a merged path, all paths are selected and remain selected as you continue to draw. This option is useful for viewing all paths that are included in the merged path. When you select this option, the Selection Limits Merge option is disabled.

Selection Limits Merge Specifies that if artwork is selected, the Blob Brush merges only with the selected artwork. If nothing is selected, the Blob Brush merges with any matching artwork.

Fidelity Controls how far you have to move your mouse or stylus before Illustrator adds a new anchor point to the path. For example, a Fidelity value of 2.5 means that tool movements of less than 2.5 pixels aren't registered. Fidelity can range from 0.5 to 20 pixels; the higher the value, the smoother and less complex the path.

Smoothness Controls the amount of smoothing that Illustrator applies when you use the tool. Smoothness can range from 0% to 100%; the higher the percentage, the smoother the path.

Size Determines the size of the brush.

Angle Determines the angle of rotation for the brush. Drag the arrowhead in the preview, or enter a value in the Angle text box.

Roundness Determines roundness of the brush. Drag a black dot in the preview away from or toward the center, or enter a value in the Roundness text box. The higher the value, the greater the roundness.

Eraser Tool

You can erase portions of your artwork using the Path Eraser tool, the Eraser tool, or the eraser on a Wacom stylus pen. The Path Eraser tool lets you erase parts of a path by drawing along the path. This tool is useful when you want to limit what you erase to a path segment, such as one edge of a triangle. The Eraser tool and the eraser on a Wacom stylus pen let you erase any area of your artwork, regardless of structure. You can use the Eraser tool on paths, compound paths, paths inside Live Paint groups, and clipping paths.

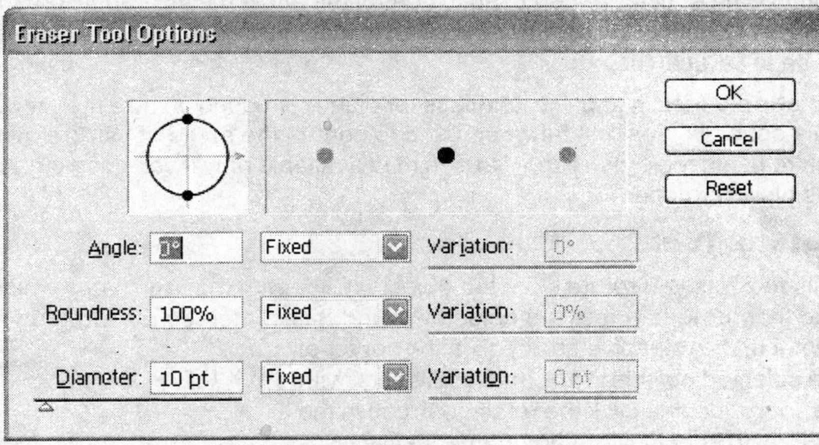

Eraser tool options

You can change the Eraser tool options by double-clicking the tool in the Tools panel.

Note: You can change the diameter at any time by pressing] to enlarge or [to reduce.

Angle Determines the angle of rotation for the tool. Drag the arrowhead in the preview, or enter a value in the Angle text box.

Roundness Determines roundness of the tool. Drag a black dot in the preview away from or toward the center, or enter a value in the Roundness text box. The higher the value, the greater the roundness.

Diameter Determines the diameter of the tool. Use the Diameter slider, or enter a value in the Diameter text box.

The pop-up list to the right of each option lets you control variations in the shape of the tool. Select one of the following options:

Fixed Uses a fixed angle, roundness, or diameter.

Random Uses random variations in angle, roundness, or diameter. Enter a value in the Variation text box to specify the range within which the brush characteristic can vary. For example, when the

Diameter value is 15 and the Variation value is 5, the diameter can be 10, or 20, or any value in between.

Pressure Varies in angle, roundness, or diameter based on the pressure of a drawing stylus. This option is most useful when used with Diameter. It is available only if you have a graphics tablet. Enter a value in the Variation text box to specify how much more or less the original value the brush characteristic will vary. For example, when the Roundness value is 75% and the Variation value is 25%, the lightest stroke is 50% and the heaviest stroke is 100%. The lighter the pressure, the more angular the brush stroke.

Stylus Wheel Varies in diameter based on manipulation of the stylus wheel.

Tilt Varies in angle, roundness, or diameter based on the tilt of a drawing stylus. This option is most useful when used with Roundness. It is available only if you have a graphics tablet that can detect the direction in which the pen is tilted.

Bearing Varies in angle, roundness, or diameter based on the pressure of a drawing stylus. This option is most useful when used to control the angle of calligraphic brushes, especially when you're using the brush like a paintbrush. It is available only if you have a graphics tablet that can detect how close to vertical the pen is.

Rotation Varies in angle, roundness, or diameter based on how the drawing stylus pen tip is rotated. This option is most useful when used to control the angle of calligraphic brushes, especially when you're using the brush like a flat pen. It is available only if you have a graphics tablet that can detect this type of rotation.

Rotate Tool

This tool lets you rotate selected objects. Click with the tool to determine the center of the rotation and then drag to rotate the objects around this center. Or just drag right off the bat to position the center of the rotation smack dab in the center of the selected objects. You can also Alt-click with the tool or double click the rotate tool icon in the toolbox to specify a rotation numerically.

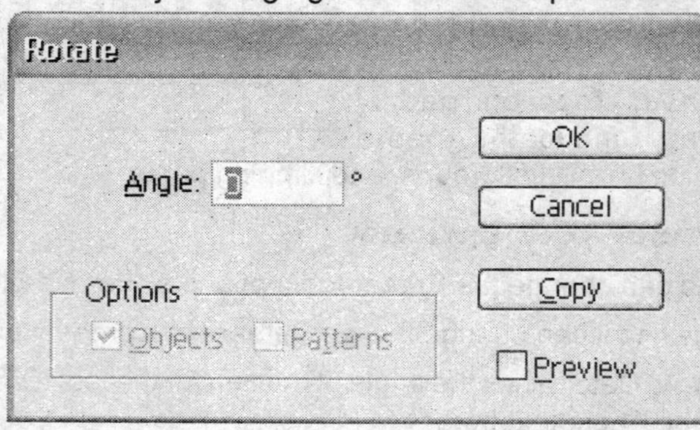

Reflect

Reflecting an object flips the object across an invisible axis that you specify. Copy while reflecting to create a mirror image of an object.

Twist

The Twist command and the twist tool rotate a selection more sharply in the center than at the edges.

Scale Tool

This tool and the two other transformation tools, reflect and shear, work just like the rotate tool. The only difference is that the scale tool enlarges and reduces selected objects.

Shear

Drag with the oddly named shear tool to slant or skew selected objects. The effects of Shift-dragging are generally easier to predict; when the Shift key is down, the shear tool slants objects horizontally or vertically.

Reshape

Click and drag with this tool on an open path to deform the path in a freeform manner. The result of the deformation is entirely dependent on which points of the object were selected.

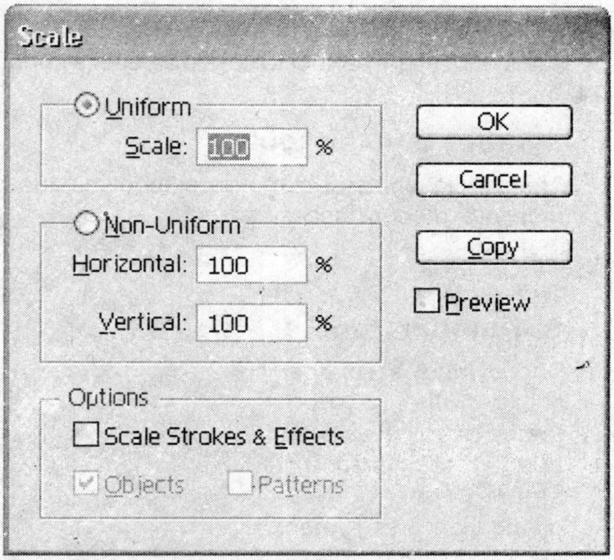

WarpTool

Stretches objects as if they were made of clay. When you drag or pull portions of an object using this tool, the pulled areas attenuate.

The twirl tool

Creates swirling distortions of an object.

The pucker tool

Deflates an object by moving control points toward the cursor.

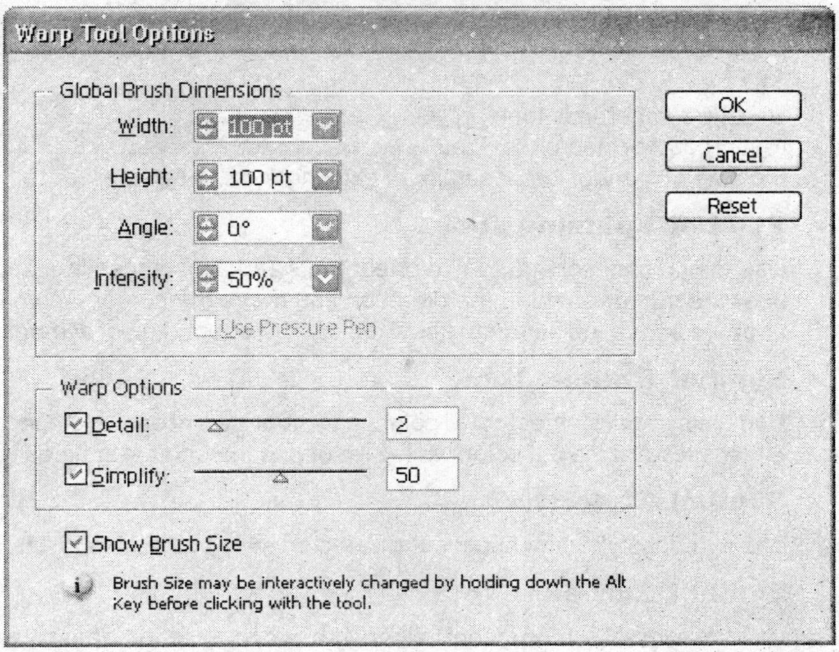

The bloat tool

Inflates an object by moving control points away from the cursor.

The scallop tool

Adds random, smooth, arc-shaped details to the outline of an object.

The crystallize tool

Adds random spike, arc-shaped details to the outline of an object.

The wrinkle tool

Adds random arc and spike-shaped details to the outline of an object.

Free Transform Tool

The free transform tool allows you to scale, rotate, reflect and shear as well as properly four-point distort selected paths, all right on screen. A lame version of this tool that uses a dialog box is found under Filter >> Distort >> Free Distort. A live version of the Free Distort filter is found under Effect >> Distortion and Transform >> Free Distort. This allows you to transform an object without permanently changing its shape.

Symbol Spray Tool

Use the symbol sprayer tool to create a set of symbol instances or add more instances to an existing set.

Symbol Shifter tool

The symbol shifter tool moves symbol instances around. It can also change the relative paint order of symbol instances in a set.

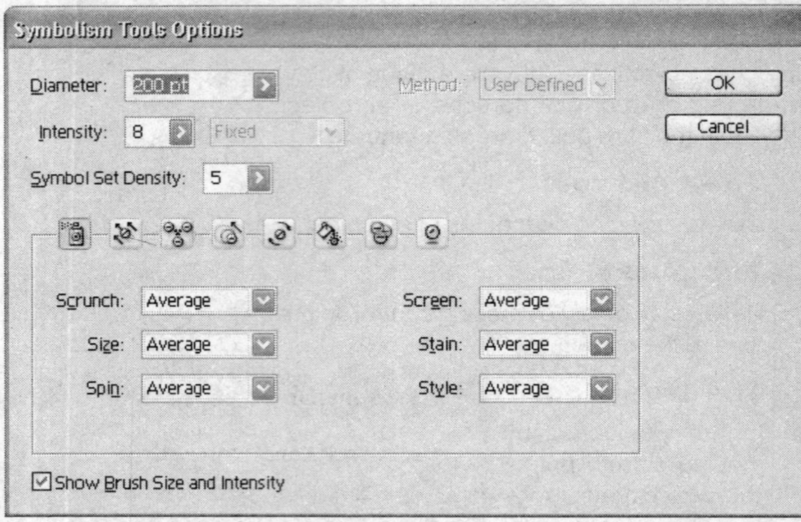

Symbol Scruncher tool

The symbol scruncher tool pulls symbol instances together or apart. Use this tool to shape the density distribution of a symbol set

Symbol Sizer tool

Use the symbol sizer tool to increase or decrease the size of symbol instances in an existing symbol set

Symbol Spinning tool

Use the symbol spinner tool to orient the symbol instances in a set. Symbol instances located near the cursor orient in the direction you move the cursor. As you drag the mouse, an arrow appears above the cursor to show the current orientation of symbol instances

Symbol Stainer tool

Use the symbol stainer tool to colorize symbol instances. Colorizing a symbol instance changes the hue toward the tint color, while preserving the original luminosity.

Symbol Styler tool

The symbol styler tool applies the selected style to the symbol instance

Symbol Screener tool

Use the symbol screener tool to increase or decrease the transparency of the symbol instances in a set.

Column Graph Tool

Drag with this tool to specify the rectangular boundaries of a standard column graph. Shift-dragging constraints the boundary to a square and Option/Alt-dragging forms rectangular boundaries from the center out. Illustrator then presents you with a spreadsheet in which you can enter your data. Double-click the graph tool icon in the toolbox to specify the options for the graphs you want to create.

Stacked column

This tool and the seven other graph tools that follow work just like the column graph tool, except that dragging with this tool specifies the boundaries of a stacked column graph.

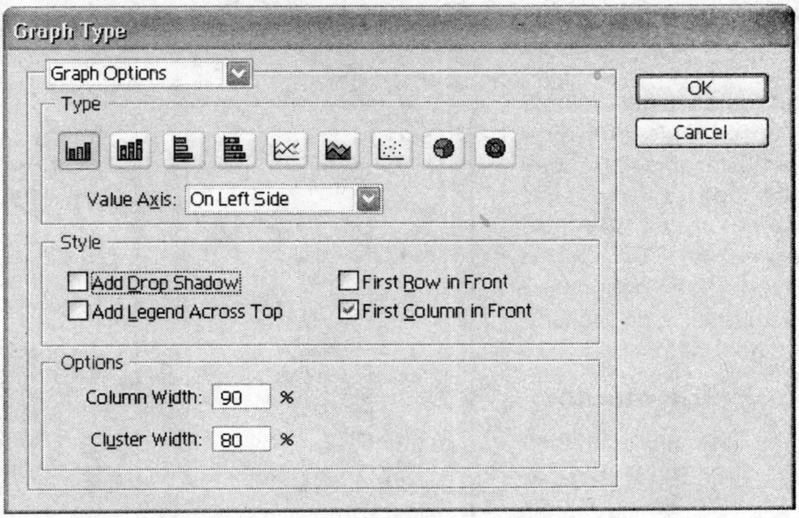

Bar

Drag with this tool to specify the boundaries of a stacked horizontal bar graph in which each entity appears farther to the right.

Line

Drag with this tool to specify the boundaries of a line graph – you know, your basic dot-to-dot with a few labels to make it look official.

Area

Drag with this tool to specify the boundaries of an area graph. It's the color-within-the-lines evolution of the line graph.

Scatter

Drag with this tool to specify the boundaries of a pie graph. Enough said.

Radar

Drag with this tool to specify the boundaries of a radar graph. This is the ideal graph for confusing anyone attending your presentation.

Mesh Tool

The mesh tool, the Create Mesh command, and the Expand command can all be used to transform an object into a mesh object. A mesh object is a single, multicolored object on which colors can flow in different directions, and transition smoothly from one point to another. By creating a fine mesh on an object and manipulating the color characteristics at each point in the mesh, you can precisely manipulate the coloring of the mesh object. You can also apply color to four mesh points at the same time by clicking the patch between them, to create broad color changes on part of the object.

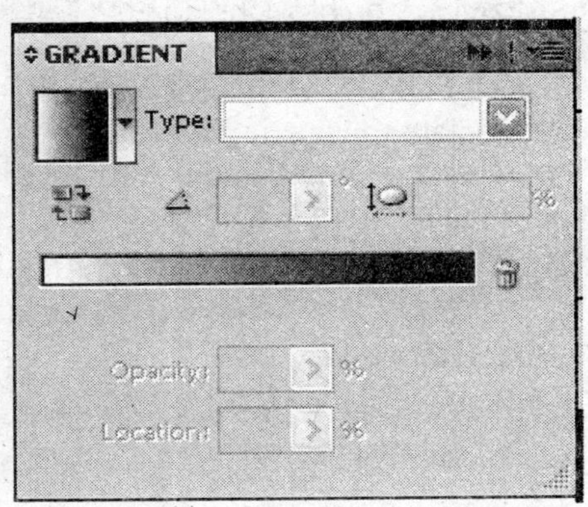

Gradient Tool

Drag inside a selected object that's filled with a gradation to change the angle of the gradations, as well as the location of the first and last colors. Shift-drag to constrain your drag to 45-degree increments.

Eyedropper Tool

Click or drag across text to copy the text attributes. These attributes can then be applied to other text using the paint bucket. Click an object to copy its fill and stroke attributes to the toolbox. You can also double-click an object to copy the colors from that object to all selected objects. Set the eyedropper options by double-clicking the icon in the toolbox.

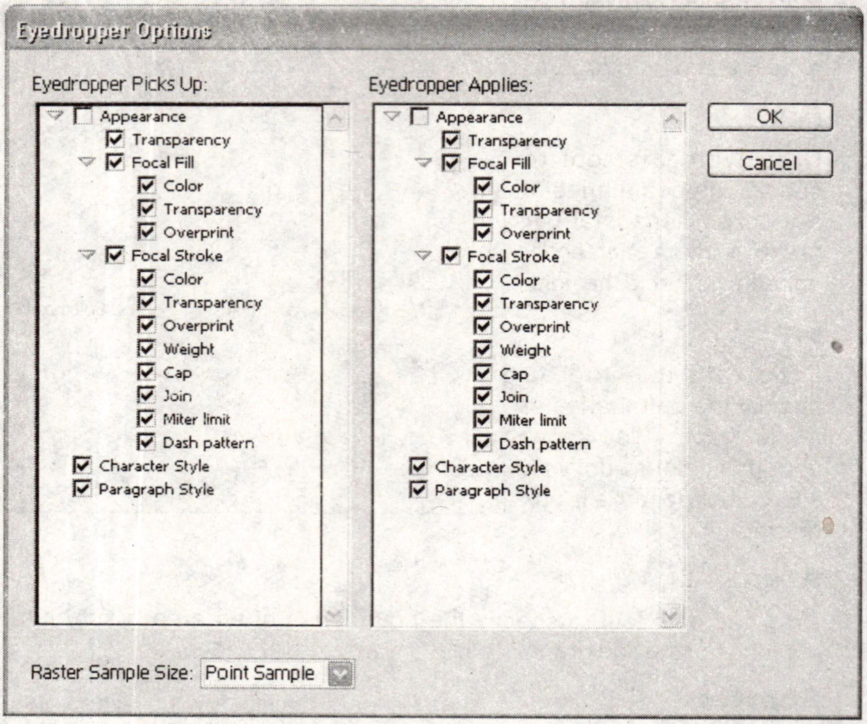

Paint bucket

Click or drag across text to apply the attributes copied by the eyedropper. Click an object with the paint bucket tool to apply the fill and stroke from the toolbox to the object. Set the paint bucket options by double-clicking the icon in the toolbox.

Measure

Drag with this tool to measure the distance between tow points. Alternatively, you can click in one spot and then click in another. Illustrator displays the measurements in the Info palette.

Blend Tool

The blend tool allows you to create custom gradations. After selecting two or more objects with one of the arrow tools, use the blend tool to click a point in one object, then click a point in the others. Illustrator creates a collection of intermediate shapes between the two objects and fills these with intermediate colors. Blends can also be created using the blend command.

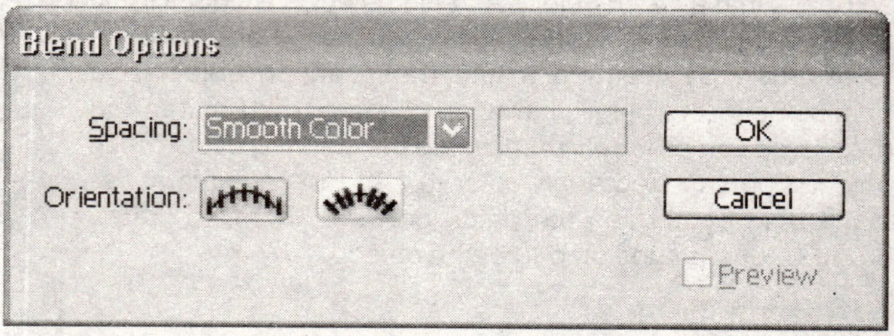

Autotrace

Click or drag within 6 screen pixels of a raster image to trace a line around the image. This tool is easily Illustrator's worst; you're almost always better off tracing images with the pen or pencil.

Live Paint Bucket Tool/Live Paint Selection Tool

The Live Paint Selection tool acts on the faces and edges of a Live Paint group, the Select tool acts on the entire Live Paint group, and the Direct Select tool acts on the individual paths inside a Live Paint group. For instance, clicking once with the Selection tool selects the entire Live Paint group, and clicking once with the Direct Selection tool or the Group Selection tool selects individual paths that make up the Live Paint group.

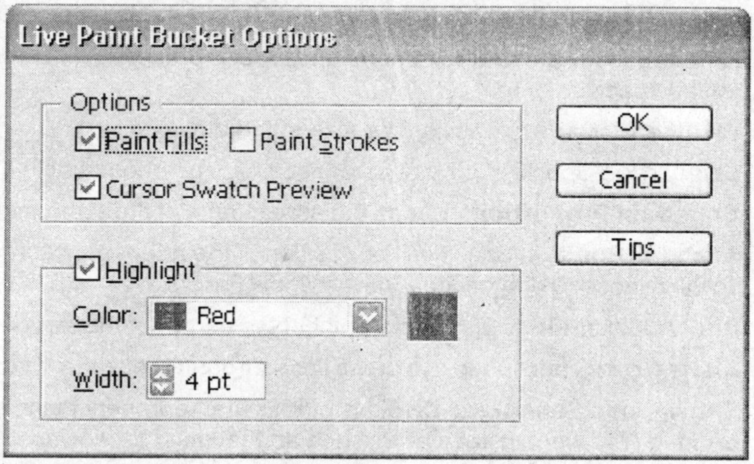

Artboard Tool

Artboards represent the regions that can contain printable artwork. You can use artboards as crop areas for printing or placement purposes—they work the same way as crop areas work in Illustrator CS3. Multiple artboards are useful for creating a variety of things such as multiple page PDFs, printed pages with different sizes or different elements, independent elements for websites, video storyboards, or individual items for animation in Adobe Flash or After Effects.

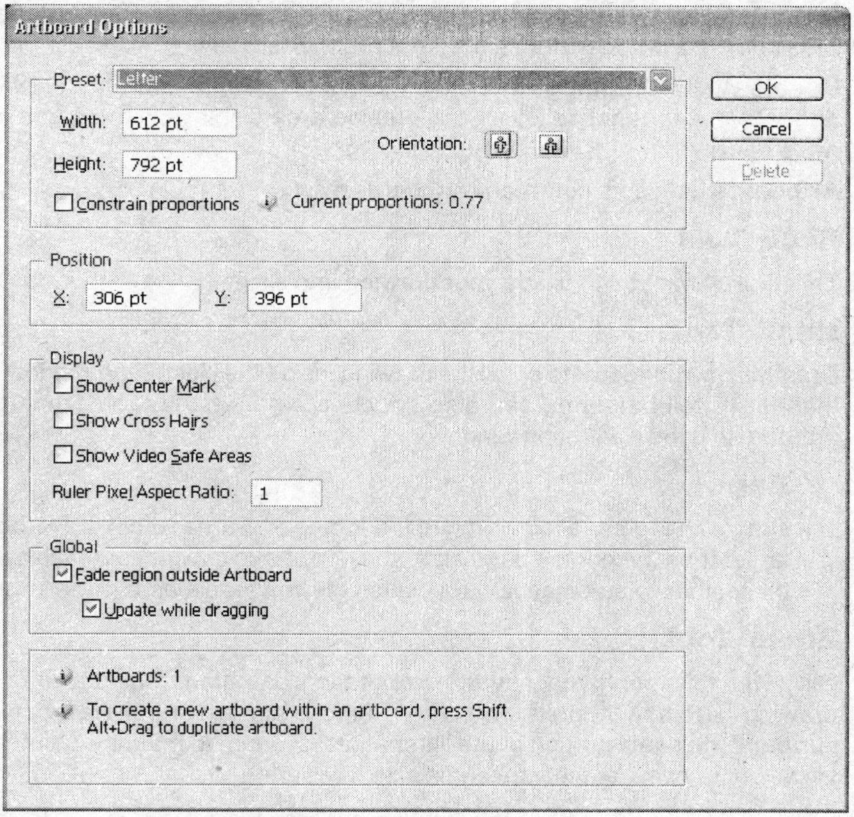

Note: If you created crop areas in a Illustrator CS3 document, the crop areas will be converted to artboards in CS4. You may be prompted to specify how you want the crop areas to convert.

You can have 1 to 100 artboards per document depending on size. You can specify the number of artboards for a document when you first create it, and you can add and remove artboards at any time while working in a document. You can create artboards in different sizes, resize them by using the Artboard tool , and position them anywhere on the screen—even overlapping one another.

Artboard options

You open the Artboard Options dialog box by double-clicking the Artboard tool , or clicking the Artboard tool and then clicking Artboard Options button in the Control panel.

Preset Specifies artboard dimensions. These presets set the ruler Pixel Aspect Ratio appropriately for the specified output.

Width and Height Specifies the size of the artboard.

Orientation Specifies portrait or landscape page orientation.

Constrain Proportions Keeps the aspect ratio of the artboard intact if you manually resize it.

X: and Y: Position Specifies the position of the artboard according to Illustrator's workspace rulers. To view these rulers, choose View > Show Rulers.

Show Center Mark Displays a point in the center of the artboard.

Show Cross Hairs Displays cross lines through the center of each side of the artboard.

Show Video Safe Areas Displays guides that represent the areas that fall inside the viewable area of video. You want to keep all text and art that must be viewable to users inside the video safe areas.

Ruler Pixel Aspect Ratio Specifies the pixel aspect ratio used for the rulers.

Fade Region Outside Artboard Displays the area outside of the artboard a darker shade than the area inside the artboard when the Artboard tool is active.

Update While Dragging Keeps the area outside of the artboard darker as you drag to resize the artboard. If this is not selected, the outside area displays in the same color as inside the artboard while resizing.

Artboards Indicates how many artboards exist.

Slice Tool

This tool allows you to divide your drawing into slices.

Hand Tool

Drag with the hand tool to scroll the drawing inside the illustration window. It is much more convenient than the scroll bars. You can also double-click the hand tool icon in the toolbox to fit the entire artboard into the illustration window.

Page

Drag with the page tool to move the imageable area within the artboard. Unless the artboard is larger than the printed page size, you don't have to worry about this tool. Double-click the icon in the toolbox to automatically reposition the imageable area to the lower left corner of the artboard.

Zoom Tool

Click with this tool to magnify the size of the illustration. This doesn't affect the printed size of the drawing, just how it looks on screen. Alt-click to zoom out. You can also draw with the tool to surround the exact portion of the illustration you want to magnify. Double-click the zoom tool icon to view your drawing at the very same size it will print.

Using Drawing Tools

Now we come to the serious business of using the drawing tools to draw the various items on the screen. In fact, drawing in Illustrator is actually a three-part process. You draw lines and shapes, you manipulate these objects and apply special effects and you stack the objects one in front of another like pieces of paper in a collage.

But before we go any further and start drawing, we must understand few points.

Points and Segments

Points are those which are required to create a line. The bits of line between points are called segments. A segment can be straight, as if it were drawn against the edge of a ruler. A straight segment flows directly from one point to another in any direction. A segment may also curve, like the outline of an ellipse. Curved segments connect two points in an indirect manner, ending inward or outward along the way.

Strokes and Fills

If you draw a line on the paper with 2 different pencils, one with thick lead and another with thin lead, the lines would look different. But, you can achieve the same by using the same pencil too. Although a line drawn with a dull pencil is heavier than a line drawn with a sharpened one, the thickness of any line fluctuates depending on how hard you press the pencil tip to the page.

In Illustrator, the thickness (or weight) of an outline is absolutely consistent throughout the course of a path. In other words, different paths can have different weights, but the weights of each path is constant.

The thickness of an outline is called the stroke. In addition to change weight of the stroke, you can change its color. Strokes can be black, white, gay or any of several million colorful variations.

You can also color the interior of a path by assigning it a fill. Like a stroke, a fill may be black, white or any color.

Now we can start with the drawings.

Drawing a Rectangle

To draw a rectangle, select the rectangle tool and then click and drag inside the drawing area. The point at which you start dragging sets one corner of the rectangle; the point at which you release sets the opposite corner as shown in the figure on the next page. The two remaining corners line up vertically or horizontally with their neighbors. You can also use the rectangle tool as follows:

1. If you press the Alt key while drawing with the rectangle tool, the start point of your drag marks the center of the rectangle. As before, the release point becomes a corner point.
2. Shift-drag with the rectangle tool to draw a perfect rectangle – also called a square. You can press and release the Shift key in mid-drag to switch between drawing a rectangle or a square.
3. Alt+Shift+drag with the rectangle tool to create a square from center to corner.
4. Press the tilde (~) key while dragging with the rectangle tool to create a series of rectangles, all of which border on a common point. Press Alt+~ while you drag to create a series of concentric rectangles.
5. Press the spacebar while dragging to move the rectangle rather than change its size. When you get it positioned properly, release the spacebar and continue dragging or release.

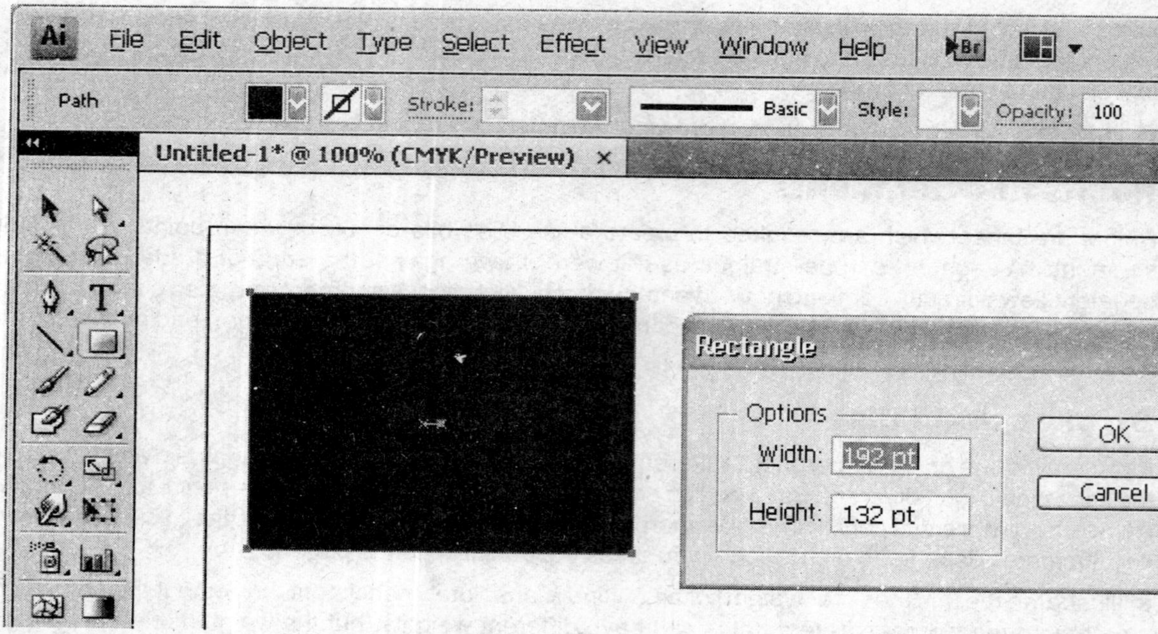

Using Numbers

You can also enter the dimensions of a rectangle numerically. Click with the rectangle tool – that's right, just click inside the drawing area – to display the dialog box as shown in the figure above. Here you can enter values for the Width and Height options.

After you press Enter or click OK, Illustrator creates a rectangle to your exact specifications. Well, for square you will give the same width and height. Here the numbers are given in terms of points where a point is 1/72 of an inch.

Rounding off a Rectangle's Corners

To draw a rectangle with rounded corners, select the rounded rectangle tool from the rectangle tool slot and drag away. Illustrator creates a shape with eight points – two along each side with a curved segment around each corner – as shown below. You control the roundness of the corners by changing the Corner Radius value in the General Preferences dialog box.

You can also click with the rounded rectangle tool and enter a value into the Corner Radius option box. Once you draw with the rounded rectangle tool, there is no way to change the roundness of the corners. Illustrator now lets you add live rounded corner's to rectangles.

Creating a Live Rounded Rectangle

First draw a regular rectangle. With the rectangle still selected, choose Effect>>Stylize>>Round Corners. This opens the Round Corners dialog box, as shown above, which has but one simple field in which to enter the radius amount. The plain rectangle is transformed into a rounded rectangle. Of course creating a rounded rectangle is easy; the hard part is making changes to the amount of rounding.

To change the size of the corner radius, you need to open the Appearance palette. With the object selected, you will see a listing for Round Corners. Double-click the entry and the Round corners dialog box appears again.

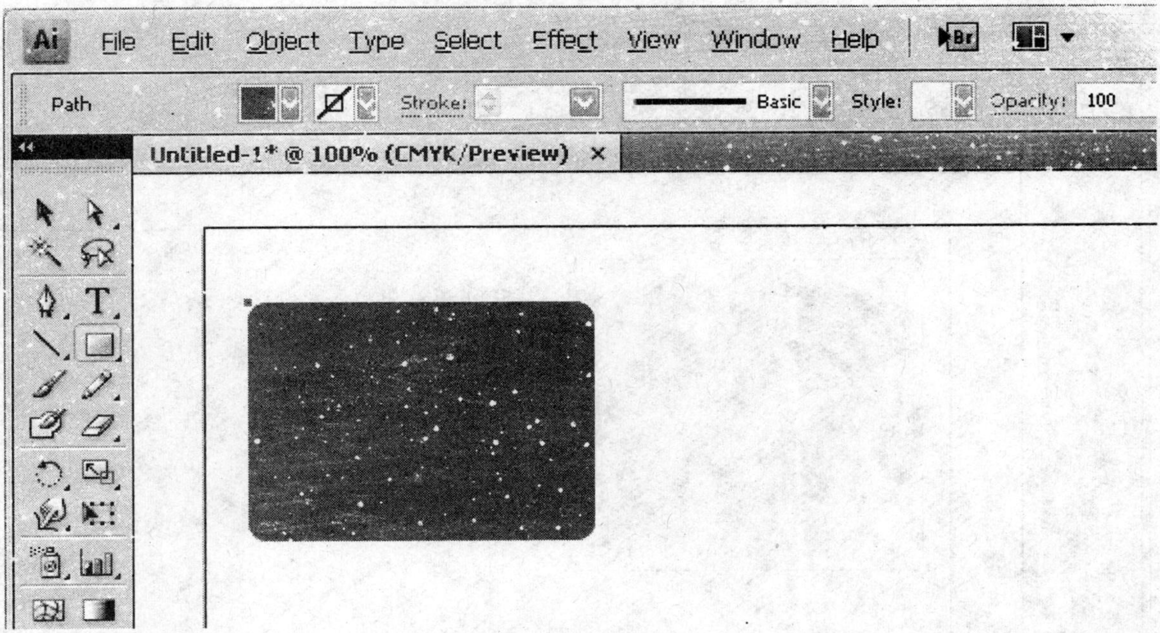

Make whatever changes you want to the corner radius. If you get totally tired of the rounded corners, drag the Round Corners listing into the Appearance palette's trash – instantly you've got your regular rectangle again.

Drawing an Ellipse

Ellipse and circle belong to the circle family. When it comes to drawing ellipse and circles, the ellipse tool is the one for the job. Simply click and drag along a diagonal line to form your ellipse. It fills the imaginary rectangle you create as you drag.

In most other respects, the ellipse tool works much like the rectangle tool:

1. Alt+drag with the ellipse tool to create an ellipse outward from the center. As always, the release point becomes the middle of an arc, determining the size and shape of the ellipse.
2. Shift+drag to draw a perfect ellipse (also called a circle). Alt+Shift+drag to draw a circle from the center point outward.
3. Press the tilde (~) key while dragging with the ellipse tool to create a series of ellipses. Press Opt/Alt-~while you drag to create a series of concentric ellipses.
4. Press the spacebar while dragging to move the ellipse rather than change its size. When you get it positioned properly, release the spacebar and continue dragging or release.
5. Click in the drawing area to bring up the Ellipse dialog box. It contains Width and Height options for specifying the width and height of the shape. The shape aligns to your click point by the middle of the upper left arc. If you press Alt+click with the ellipse tool, the ellipse align by its center.
6. Use the W and H values in the Transform palette to change the width and height of an ellipse that you've already drawn.

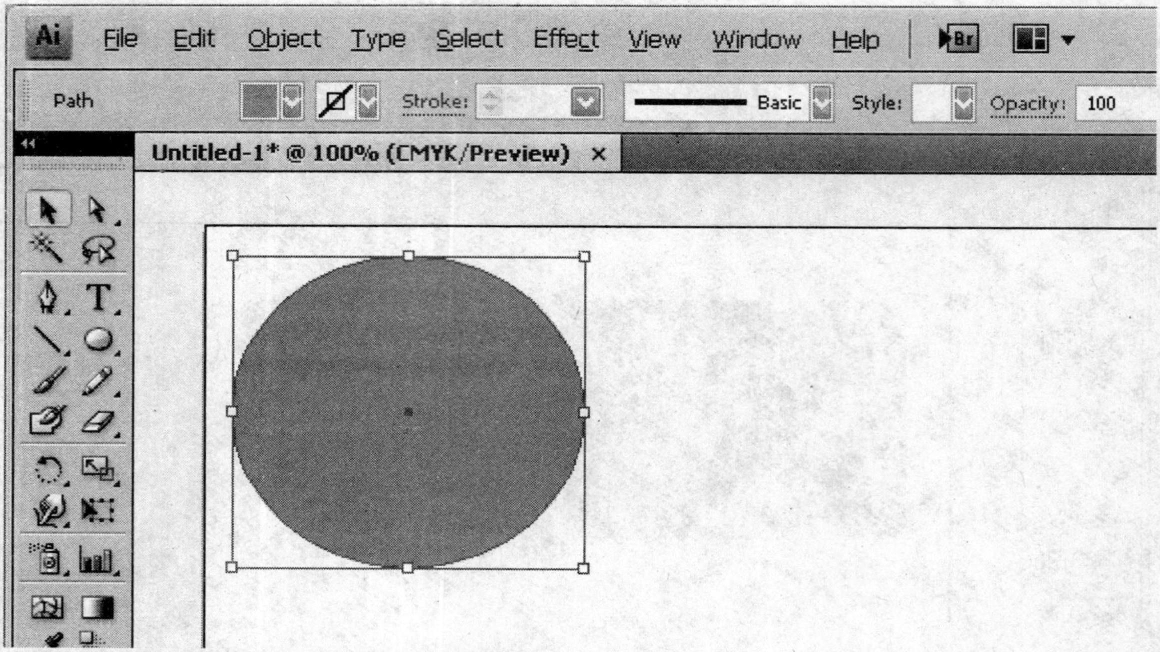

Simple Shapes at an Angle

If you change Constrain Angle value in the General Preferences dialog box to say 20, all the rectangles that you create will be slanted at an angle of 20 degrees as shown on the next page. The constraint axes control the angles at which you move and transform objects when pressing the Shift key. But they also control the creation of rectangles, ellipses and text blocks.

The Constrain Angle value has no impact on the creation of stars, polygons or spirals whatsoever – even if you hold down the Shift key while drawing one of these shapes, they will still align to the horizontal despite the option box's value. If someone has indeed reset your Constrain Angle, press Ctrl-K or choose File>>Preferences >>General. Enter 0 into the Constrain Angle option box and press Enter.

Polygons, Stars and Spirals

Illustrator offers three tools that let you draw polygons, stars and spirals by dragging in the drawing area. These were discussed in the earlier chapter. The new functions still leave a thing or two to be desired, particularly when it comes time to edit the paths, for example, you can't automatically change the number of points in a star after you create it.

Drawing a Regular Polygon

A regular polygon is a shape with multiple straight sides – each side is identical in length and meets its neighbors at the same angle. An equilateral triangle is a regular polygon, as a square. Other examples include pentagons, hexagons, octagons and just about any other shape with a gon in its name, as shown in the figure below.

To draw a polygon, select the polygon tool and drag in the drawing in the drawing area. You always draw a polygon from the middle outward, whether you press the Alt key or not. The direction of your drag determines the orientation of the shape. By default, Illustrator draws hexagons (six-sided shapes)

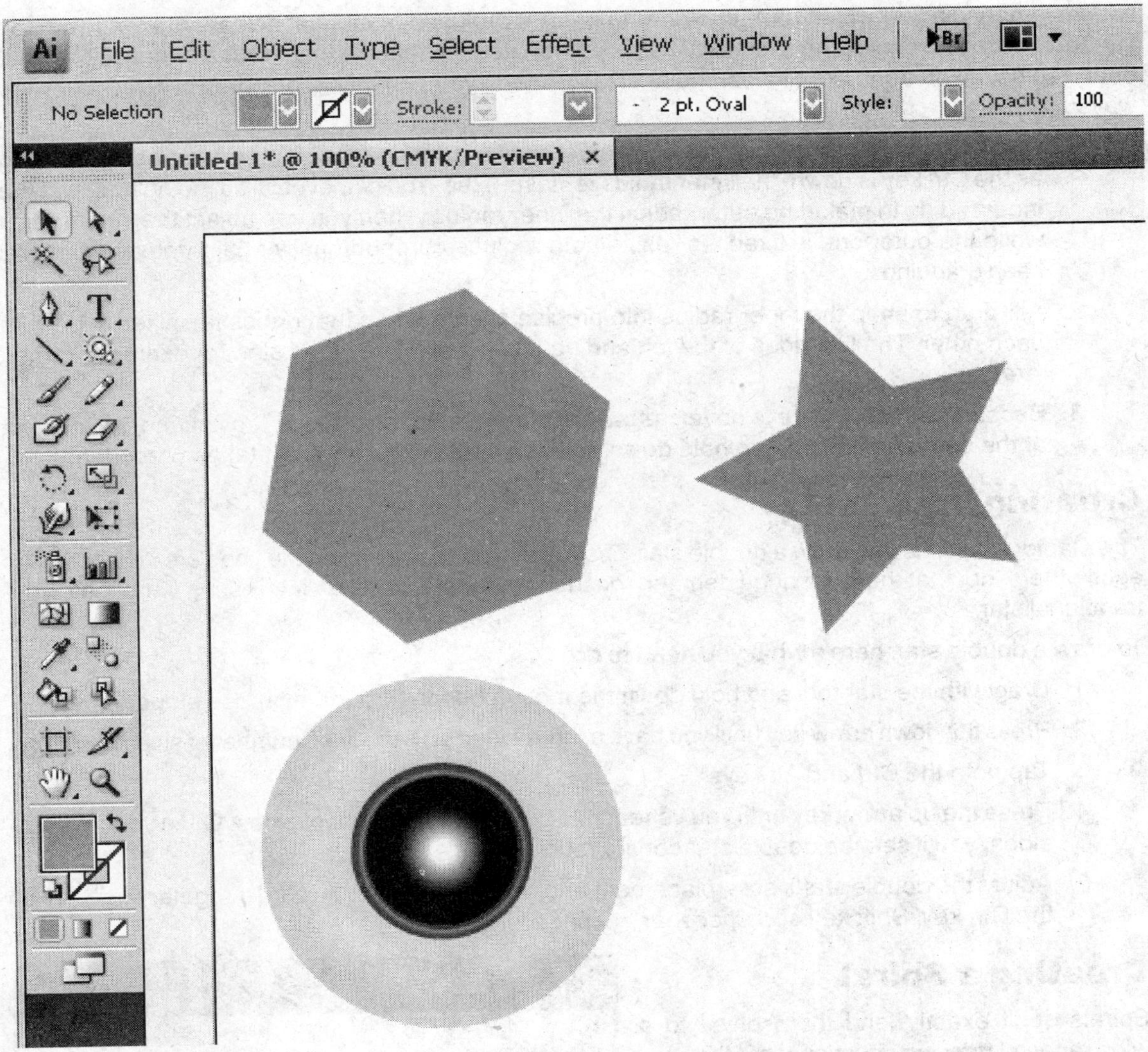

with the polygon tool. You can change the number of sides while dragging with the polygon tool by pressing the up and down arrow keys. The up arrow key adds a side: the down arrow key deletes one.

Another way to change the number of sides is to click with the Polygon tool in the drawing area. Illustrator displays the Polygon dialog box, as shown next, which lets you specify a Radius value and a number of sides. The Radius value is the distance from the center of the shape to any corner point in the shape. Therefore, a regular polygon with a radius of 100 points would fit entirely inside a circle with a radius the tilde (~) key while dragging to create a series of concentric polygon.

Drawing a Star

Illustrator lets you draw regular stars, in which each spike looks just like its neighbors. To draw a star, drag with the star tool, which is the second alternative tool in the ellipse tool slot. Illustrator of the star tool by pressing the Ctrl and Alt keys as you drag. A star is made up of two sets of points, one at the points where the spikes meet and one at the tips of the spikes. These points revolve around one of two imaginary circles, which form the inner and outer radiuses of the star. When you drag with the star tool, Illustrator scales the two radiuses proportionately, so that the inner radius is exactly half the outer radius. If you don't like this particular arrangement, you can gain more control in the following ways:

1. Press Ctrl while dragging to scale the outer radius independently of the inner radius. So long as the Ctrl key is down, the inner radius remains fixed. You can even drag the outer inside the inner radius to make the outer radius the inner radius. Then you can adjust the inner radius while the outer one is fixed. To resize both radiuses proportionally again, release Ctrl and keep dragging.
2. Alt+drag to snap the inner radius into precise alignment so that opposite spikes align with each other. The top sides of the left and right sides of a five-sided star, for example, from a straight line.
3. Because Ctrl and Alt keys have mutually exclusive effects on a star, they cannot be in effect at the same time. If you do hold down both the Ctrl and Alt keys, Alt takes precedent.

Creating Double Star

The star tool also lets you draw a double star. That's the type of star where the lines are visible across each other – not that there's a huge demand for such a shape, but it is an interesting variation on the traditional star.

To draw a double star, here's what you need to do:

1. Drag with the star tool and hold down the mouse button throughout these steps.
2. Press the down arrow key until you have a three-sided star, the least number of sides permitted.
3. Tap both the Ctrl and Alt keys.
4. Press the up arrow key until you've reached the desired number of sides. Once you're at four sides, you'll see the double star configuration.
5. Adjust the double star's size, placement and orientation as you would a regular star's – with the Ctrl key, Shift key and spacebar, respectively.

Creating a Spiral

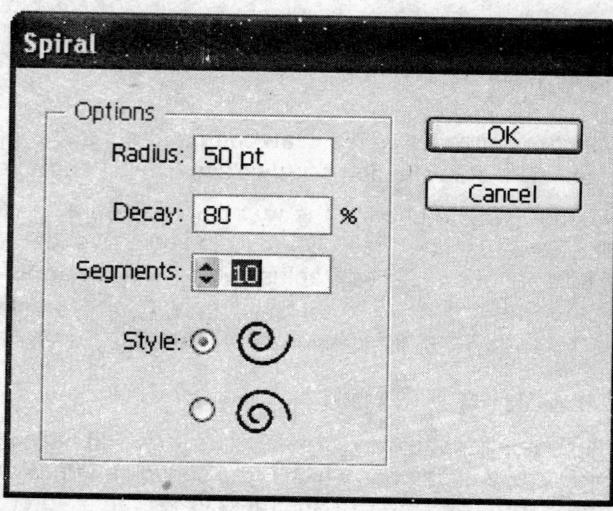

Spirals don't exactly lend themselves to a wide range of drawing situations, but they are great to look at. Spirals are one of the most difficult things to create in Illustrator. To draw, just drag with the spiral and the spiral grows outward from its center. The Spiral dialog box, as shown here has the following options.

Radius: Enter a Radius value to specify the size of the spiral. This represents the distance from the center of the shape to the last point on the spiral.

Decay: The decay value determines how quickly the spiral loops in on itself. Small values result in short loops. Larger values – up to 99.99 percent – result in more tightly packed spirals.

Segments: Enter the number of curved segments between points into the Segments option box. Each segment represents a quarter coil in the spiral.

Style: Select a radio button to coil the spiral counterclockwise or clockwise. (This assumes a Decay value of less than 100 percent. If the Decay is higher than 100, the spiral coils in the opposite direction.)

By itself, an increased Segments value may not result in more coils. You have to raise both the Decay and Segments values to wind the coils more tightly This is because Illustrator drops segments when Decay is too low to accommodate them. Once you're set the spiral dialog box, you can drag new spirals directly on the page. However, you might want to make your spiral experience more interactive. Fortunately Illustrator lets you control spirals as you drag.

Controlling Spirals

You an modify coils without resorting to the Spiral dialog box. It takes a little getting used to, but it works. Here's how:

1. When you drag with the spiral tool, you're changing the radius and rotating the spiral around. We just want to get that straight before we go for any farther.
2. Press the Ctrl key while dragging to modify the decay. Drag outward to lower the decy; drag inward to raise it. If you drag inward past one of the coils, the spiral flips on itself, indicating a decay of more than 100 percent.
3. Don't press the Ctrl key the moment you start dragging or you'll pop the Decay value to some ridiculously low number such as 7 percent. Start dragging and then press Ctrl in mid-drag. Release the key to modify the radius again.
4. Press the up and down arrow keys while dragging with the spiral tool to raise and lower the number of segments in a spiral.
5. You can also change the number of segments by pressing the Alt key. Alt-drag toward the center of the spiral to delete segments and reduce the radius. Drag outward to both add segments and increase the radius, thus better accommodating the new coils.
6. If you press both Ctrl and Alt simultaneously, Ctrl takes precedence.

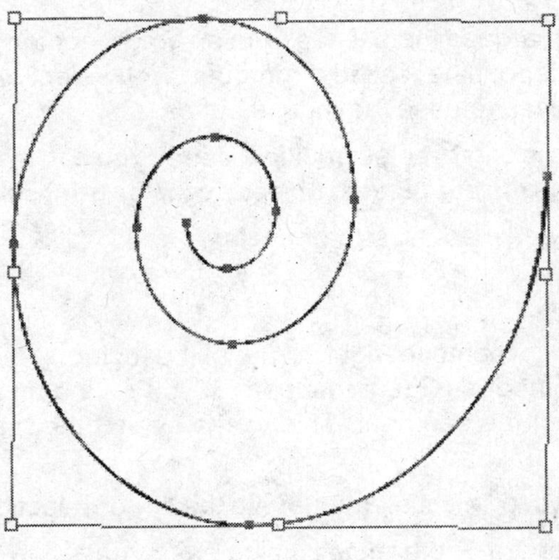

7. You can also press the spacebar while dragging with the spiral tool to reposition the path. Shift-drag to constrain the spiral to some 45-degree angle.
8. You can create a series of spirals by pressing the tilde (~) key as you drag.

Using Selection and Curves

Whether you use Illustrator's pencil, paintbrush or autotrace tool, you still get the same thing – paths divided by anchor points. A drawing tablet helps, but only to communicate smoother lines to Illustrator; it doesn't helps Illustrator better interpret your beautiful work.

Arrows and Lassos

The arrows, also known as the selection, direct selection and group selection tools, are the most powerful of selection tools. Not only can they select objects and points, but if you drag with them they move things around. Lassos (also known as the lasso and direct selection lasso) aren't as powerful the arrow tools. They can only select things; if you want to move the selection around, you have to switch to an arrow.

The Plain Black Arrow Tool

The selection tool – which we call the arrow tool to distinguish it from its selection friends – is the most straightforward of them. When the arrow tool is active, you can click anywhere along the outline of a path to select the path in its entirety. If the Use Area Select check box to turned on inside the General Preferences dialog box, you can also click inside the path to select it, provided the path has a fill. After selecting a path with the arrow tool, you can move it, apply a transformation or perform any other manipulation that affects the path as a whole. You cannot move points or bend segments. If the path has been grouped with other paths, the arrow tool selects the entire group, prohibiting you from altering the grouped path independently of another.

Here are few other ways to select paths with the arrow tool:

- ❑ When you click a path, you not only select the path you click, you also deselect any previously-selected path. To select multiple paths, click the first path and then hold the Shift key as you click each additional path you want to select (this is called a Shift-click). The Shift key prevents Illustrator from deselecting paths as you click new ones.
- ❑ Another way to select multiple paths is to marquee them. Drag from an empty portion of your drawing area to create a dotted rectangular outline, called a marquee. You select all paths that even slightly inside this outline when you release the mouse button.
- ❑ You can combine marqueeing with Shift-clicking to select multiple paths. You can also drag a marquee while pressing Shift, which adds the surrounded objects to the present selection.
- ❑ If you Shift-click an object that is already selected, Illustrator declares it.

Direct Selection Tool

The direct selection tool is the hollow (white) arrow in the upper right corner of the toolbox. Click with the direct selection tool to select an individual point or segment in a path. If you click a point, you select the point; if you click a segment, you select the segment. This works even if the path that contains the point or segment is part of a group.

The following list summarizes these and other ways to select elements with the direct selection tool:

- ❑ If the Use Area Select check box in the General Preferences dialog box is turned on (as it is by default), you can click inside a filled shape to select the entire path. This assumes that the shape has a fill.

- ❑ Shift-click a point or segment to add it to the current selection. You can also Shift-marquee around elements. If you Shift-click a point or segment that's already selected, it becomes deselected. The same goes for Shift-marqueeing.
- ❑ Alt-click a point or segment to select an entire path. This is a great way to select paths inside groups.
- ❑ Alt-marquee or Alt-Shift-click paths to select multiple paths at a time.

Selecting using Lassos

You may have noticed that the marquees created by the arrow tools are always rectangular. Illustrator 10 now gives you two lasso tools that let you round up selections in any shape you desire. And just like the selection tools, the lassos are divided into two different selection modes.

The Black Lasso

The black lasso (officially known as the lasso tool) selects entire objects – even if you only snare parts of them within the lasso marquee. Simply drag the lasso around the objects you want to select. A line indicates the area that is being selected. When you release the mouse, all the objects that were within the lasso marquee will be selected as shown below.

The White Lasso

The White lasso (officially known as the direct selection lasso tool) selects parts of objects. Drag around the points or segments you want to select. When you release the mouse, only those points or segments that were within the lasso marquee will be selected, as shown in the figure on the next page, the direct selection lasso allows you to select points that would require many different passes dragging with the arrow tools.

Adding More Lasso Selections

The lasso tools work slightly differently than the other selection tools. if you hold the shift key, you will see a small plus sign next to the lasso cursor. This indicates that the next loop of the lasso will add to the selection. But the lasso do not deselect selected items when you use the Shift key. They only add to the selection. To deselect as you lasso you have to press and hold down the Alt key.

Selecting Everything

If you want to select all paths in your drawing, choose Edit >> Select All or press Ctrl-A. Illustrator selects every last point segment and other element throughout the illustration, even if it's on the pasteboard.

Other Selection techniques

There are actually several other techniques for selecting things. For instance, you can select all the objects on layers, by using the Layers palette. You can also select objects by attributes using the Selection commands.

These commands are all found under the submenu after Edit>>Select. Various other methods of selections are:

Same Fill and Stroke

Selects all objects that have the same fill and stroke attributes.

Same Fill Color

Selects all objects that have the same fill color. The stroke colors may vary.

Same Stroke Color

Selects all objects that have the same stroke color. The stroke weight may vary as well as the fill colors.

Same Stroke Weight

Selects all objects that have the same stroke weight. The stroke color may vary as well as the fill attributes.

Same Blending Mode

Selects all objects that the same type of blending mode as found in the Transparency palette. All other attributes may vary.

Same Opacity

Selects all objects that have the same percentage of opacity applied. All other attributes may vary

Same Masks

Selects all objects that are acting as masks to hide areas of other objects.

Same Stray Points

Selects all single points. Single points can get left over when you delete portions of objects or forget and click once with the pen and then don't click again.

Same Brush Strokes

Selects all objects that have brush strokes applied.

Deselecting

To deselect all objects – regardless of form or gender – press Ctrl-Shift-A (Edit >>Deselect All) or just click with one of the selection tools on an empty portion of the drawing area.

You can make more discrete deselection using the Shift key:

- To deselect an entire path or group, shift-click the object with the arrow tool.
- To deselect a single point or segment, Shift-click it with the direct selection tool.
- To select a single path inside a group, alt-shift click it with the direct selection tool.
- You can also deselect elements and objects by Shift-marqueeing around them. Selected elements become deselected and deselected elements become selected.

Dragging

Once you're selected a point or segment, you can move it around, changing its location and stretching its path. In fact, dragging with the direct selection tool is the single most common method for reshaping a path inside Illustrator. You can move selected points independently of deselected points. And you can stretch segments or move Bezier control handles to alter the curvature of a path. The next few pages explain all aspects of dragging.

Dragging Points

To move one or more points in a path:

1. Select the points you want to move with the direct selection tool.
2. Drag any one of them.
3. Squeal with delight.

When you drag a selected point, all over selected points move the same distance and direction. When you move a point while a neighboring point remains stationary; the segment between the two points shrinks or stretches in length to accommodate the change in distance, as shown in the figure here.

Pen Tool

The pen tool is capable of creating anything from schematic newspaper charts to detailed scenes of heightened reality. For nearly a decade, Illustrator's pen tool was the reigning champ and no other program offered anything that came close. Now Adobe has taken Illustrator's pen tool and with a few microscopic exceptions, added it to InDesign. You can also find a more primitive version of the pen tool in Adobe Photoshop. It's a testament to the elegance of the original.

Pen Tool Basics

When drawing with the pen tool, you build a path by creating individual points. Illustrator automatically connects the points with segments. The following list summarizes how you can use the pen tool to build paths in Illustrator.

Path building

To build a path, create one pointer after another inside the drawing area until the path is the desired length and shape. You create and position a point by either clicking or dragging with the pen tool. Clicking creates a corner, dragging creates a smooth point. Illustrator draws a segment between each new point and its predecessor.

Adjusting a point

Midway into creating a path, you can reposition points or change the curvature of segments that you've already drawn. To move a point while you are still creating it, press and hold the spacebar. You can then reposition the point on the fly. Release the spacebar and continue creating points. If you've already created a point but wish to modify it before moving on to the next point, just press the Ctrl key to access the direct-selection tool, press Ctrl+Tab if the arrow tool comes up instead, and drag the points, segments and control handles as desired. When you've finished, release Ctrl and continue adding points.

Closing the path

To create a closed shape, click or drag on the first point in the path. Every point will then have one segment coming into it and another segment exiting it.

Leaving the path open

To leave a path open, so it has a specific beginning and ending, deactivate the path by pressing Ctrl+Shift+A (Edit>> Deselect All). Or you can press Ctrl to get the arrow or direct selection tool and click an empty portion of the drawing area. Either way, you deactivate the path so you can move on and create a new one.

Extending an open path

To reactivate an open path, click of drag one of its endpoints. Illustrator is then ready to draw a segment between the endpoint and the next point you create.

Joining two open paths

To join one open with another open path, click or drag an endpoint in the first path, then click or drag an endpoint in the second. Illustrator draws a segment between the two, bringing them together in everlasting peace and brotherhood.

Defining Points and Segments

Points in a path act a little road signs. Each points steers the path by specifying how a segment enters it and how another segment exists it. You specify the identify of each little road sign by clicking or dragging, sometimes with the Alt key gently but firmly pressed. The following items explain the specific kinds of points and segments you can create in Illustrator.

Corner point

Click with the pen tool to create a corner point, which represents the corner between two segments in a path.

Straight segment

Click at two different locations to create a straight segment between two corner points.

Smooth point

Drag with the pen tool to create a smooth point with two symmetrical Bezier control handles. A smooth point ensures that one segment fuses into another to form a continuous arc.

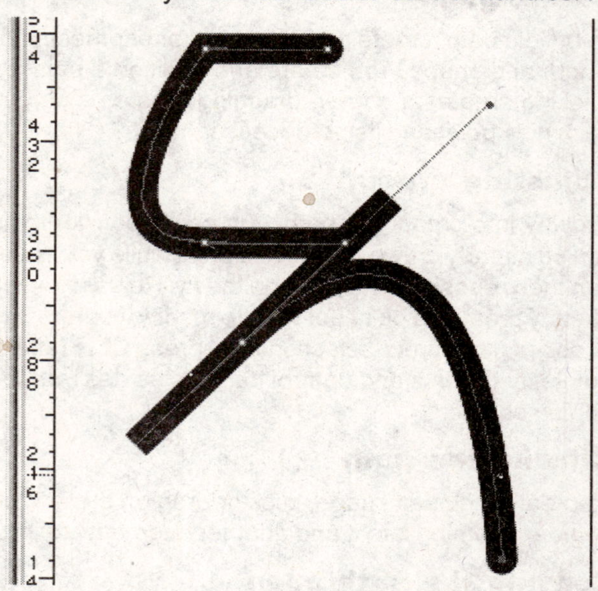

Curved segment

Drag at two different locations to create a curved segment between two smooth points.

Straight segment followed by curved

After drawing a straight segment drag from the corner point you just created to add a control handle. Then drag again at a different location to append a curved segment to the end of the straight segment.

Curved segment followed by straight

After drawing a curved segment click the smooth point you just created to delete the forward control handle. This converts the smooth point to a corner point with one handle. Then click again at a different location to append a straight segment to the end of the curved segment.

Cusp point

To convert a smooth point to a corner point with two independent handles (sometimes known as a cusp point), you have a couple of different options depending on the situation. First, after drawing a curved segment, don't release the mouse button. Add the Alt key and pivot to change the direction of the forward control handle. Then drag again at a new location to append a curved segment that sprouts off in a different direction. This creates a cusp.

Modifying the Closing Point

When you close a shape, you click, drag and alt-drag, just as you do when creating other points. But because you modify and close in one gesture, it seems a good idea to revisit these techniques within this slightly different context:

- ❑ Click the first point in a path to clip off any control handle that may have been threatening to effect the closing segment and you'll close the path with a corner point.
- ❑ If the first point in the path is a smooth point, drag it to make sure it remains smooth, thus closing the path with an arc.
- ❑ If the first point is a corner point, drag to add a control handle that curves the closing segment.
- ❑ To convert a smooth point to a cusp on closing. Alt-drag the first point in the path. In this case, you must press the Alt key before you start the drag. Pressing the alt key after you're into the drag has no effect.

Working with the Pen

In the next three sections, I will explain to you the way Pen tool works. First I will show you how to use corner points, then smooth points and finally cusps. Clicking with the pen tool is a wonderful way to create straight-sided polygon. Unlike the shapes you draw with the regular polygon tool, pen tool polygons may be any shape or size.

1. **Click to create a corner point** Select the pen tool and click in the drawing area to create a corner point. The little x next to the pen cursor disappears to show you that a path is now in progress. The new corner point appears as a filled square to show that it's selected. It is also open-ended, meaning that it doesn't have both a segment coming into it and a segment going out from it. In fact, this new corner point – point A – is not associated with any segment whatsoever.

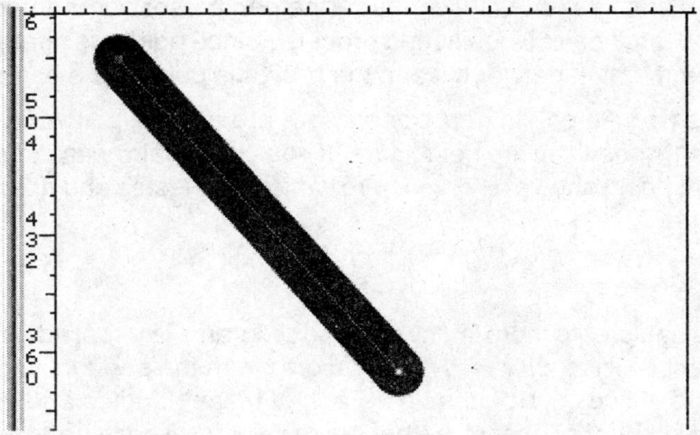

2. **Click to add another corner point** Click at a new location in the illustration to create a new corner point- we'll call it point B. Illustrator automatically draws a straight segment from Point A to point B, as shown here. Notice that point a now appears hollow

rather than filled, showing that point A is the member of a selected path, but is itself deselected. Point B is selected and open-ended. Illustrator automatically selects a point immediately after you create it and deselects all other points.

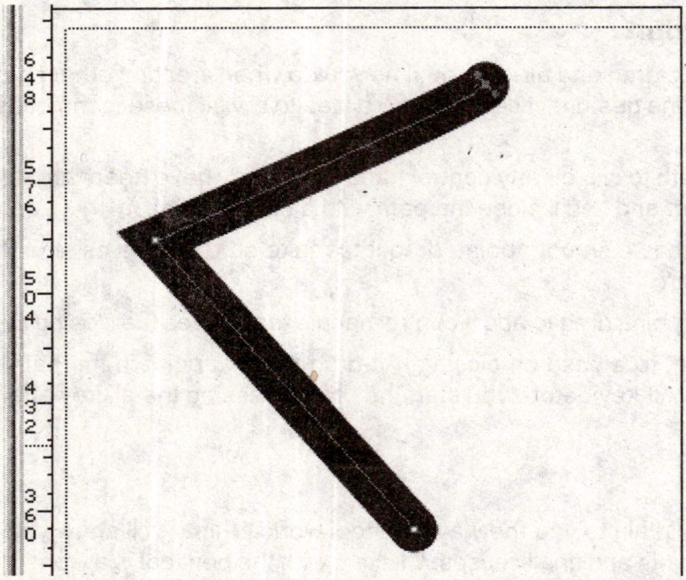

3. **Click to add yet another corner point** Click a third time with the pen tool to create a third corner point – point C. Since a point may be associated with no more than two segments, point B is no longer open-ended, as shown in the figure below. Such a point is called an interior point.
4. **Click the first point in the path** You can keep adding points to a path one at a time for as long as you like. When you're finished, you can close the path by again clicking on point A, as shown here. Illustrator displays the close cursor to show you that it's ready to draw the last segment. If you don't see the close cursor (the pen cursor augmented with a little 0 in the bottom right), you don't have it positioned properly. Since point A is open-ended, it willingly accepts the segment drawn between it and the previous point in the path.
5. **Click to start a new path** All points in a closed path are interior points. Illustrator displays the new path cursor, as shown in the next figure. If you click again, with the pen tool you create a new independent point, shown as origin here, which is selected and open ended in two directions, just like point A.

Drawing Curves

Free-form polygons are great, but you can create them in any drawing program. The real advantage to the pen tool is that it lets you draw very precise curves. When you drag with the pen tool to create a smooth point, you specify the location of two control handles. Each of these handles appears as a tiny circle perched at the end of a thin line that connects the handle to its point. These handles act as levers, bending segments relative to the smooth point itself.

The point at which you begin dragging with the pen tool determines the location of the smooth point; the at which you release becomes a control handle that affects the next segment you create. A second handle appears symmetrically from the first handle, on the opposite side of the smooth point. This handle determines the curvature of the most recent segment. You might think of a smooth point a if it were the center of a small seesaw, with the control handles acting as opposite ends. If you push down on one handle, the opposite handle goes up and vice versa.

Creating Corners

A smooth point must always have two Bezier control handles, each positioned in an imaginary straight line with the point itself. A corner point, however much more versatile. It can have zero, one or two handles. To create a corner point that has one or two control handles (sometimes called a cusp), you must manipulate an existing corner or smooth point while in the process of creating a path.

1. **Draw some smooth points** Begin by the drawing the path as shown in the figure here. You do this by dragging three times with the pen tool: First drag downward from first point, then drag leftward from second point and finally drag up from third point. The result is an active path composed of three smooth points.
2. **Click the last point created** Illustrator lets you alter the most recent point while in the process of creating a path. Suppose that you want to flatten off the top of the path to create a sort of tilted bowl. Because you can associate smooth points only with curved segments, you must convert the top two smooth points to corner points. To convert the most recent point – the one on the left – position the pen tool over last point so the pen changes to the cusp (the normal pen cursor with an additional little carat in the lower right corner). Then click to amputate the forward handle, which does not yet control a segment.

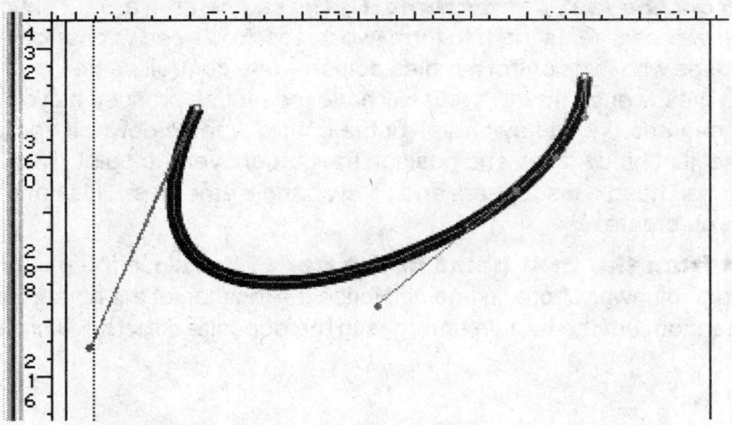

3. **Click the first point in the path** You now have an open path composed of two smooth points and a cusp. You still need to close the path and amputate a handle belonging to first point. A single operation–clicking on the first smooth point–accomplishes both maneuvers. It's that simple. With one click, you close the path and amputate the control handle that would otherwise have curved the closing segment. Hence, the new segment is straight, bordered on both sides by corner points with one handle each. If you don't release the mouse button, you can delete the forward handle from third point by another method. You construct the path as explained in step 1, except that you don't release the mouse button after dragging with the pen to form the forward control handle belonging to last point. Continue to hold down the mouse button and press the alt key. You can now drag the forward handle independently of the backward handle. Drag the forward handle back into last point until it disappears. The advantage is you modify the path as you drag. Just make sure the forward handle is completely gone.

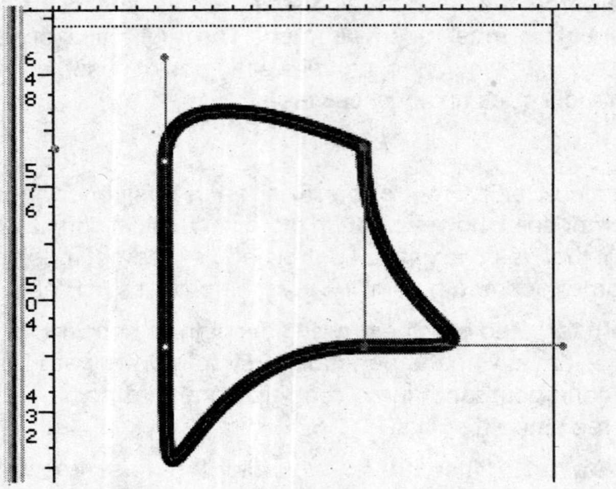

Converting Smooth Points to Cusps

These steps show you how to close the path from with a concave top, resulting in a crescent shape:

1. **Draw some smooth points** Begin again by drawing the path described in the first step of the previous section.
2. **Alt-drag down from the last point created** The segments in a crescent are curved, but the upper and lower segments meet to form two cusps. You need to change the two top smooth points to cusps with two control handles apiece – one controlling the upper segment and one controlling the lower segment. If you still have the mouse pressed as you create the smooth point, you can add the alt key and pivot the control handle down. If you've already released the mouse, just hold Alt key and position the cursor over the point. Then drag from third point. The existing handle disappears and a new handle emerges. This handle controls the next segment you create.
3. **Opt/alt-drag up from the first point in the path** You close the path in a similar manner, by Alt-dragging upward from first point. Notice the location of the cursor as you drag. You drag in one direction, but the handle emerges in the opposite direction. This is because

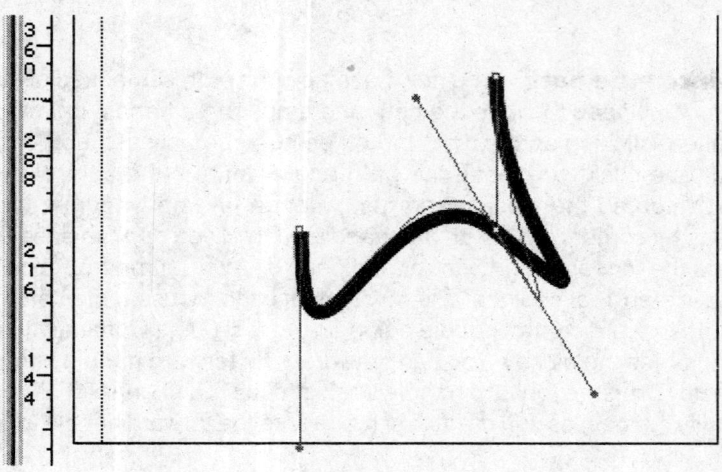

when dragging with the pen tool, you always drag in the direction of the forward segment – that is, the one that exists the current point. Illustrator positions the handle controlling the closing segment symmetrically to your drag, even if it is the only handle you're manipulating. It's kind of weird, but it's Illustrator's way.

Handling Corner Points

Now I tell you how to add a curved segment to a path composed of straight ones:

1. **Draw some corner points** Begin by creating the straight-sided path. It doesn't matter how many points are in the path, so long as they're all corner points.
2. **Drag from the last corner point created** Drag from the corner point you've created most recently to extract a single control handle. You may think you need to hold Alt key here, but you don't. Illustrator knows that if you drag you want to create curves. It won't convert the corner point to a smooth one, though. It simply adds a Bezier handle to create a curve for the segment you're about to create.
3. **Drag from the first point in the path** To close the path, drag from the first corner point in the path. Once again, you drag in the direction opposite the emerging Bezier control handle. Illustrator won't curve the first segment, only the one you're currently working on.

Adding Points to a Path

It is not that you are restricted to the number of points which are already there on the path, you can always add more points as per your needs.

1. **Appending a point to the end of an open path** If an existing path is open, you can add points to either end of it. First activate one of its end points by clicking or dragging it with the pen tool. When you position the pen tool over an inactive endpoint, you get the activate cursor, which looks like a pen with a little slash next to it.

   Drag from the point if you want to retain or add a control handle; click if you want to trim off a control handle or avoid adding one and Alt-drag if you want to change the direction of a handle. Then click and drag to add more points to the path. You can also lengthen an open path by dragging from one of its end points with the pencil tool. In the unlikely event the path touches a portion of a tracing template, you can even use the autotrace tool.
2. **Closing an open path** Once the path is active, you can close it. Just click, drag or Alt-drag the opposite endpoint with the pen tool. You can also close a path with the pencil tool by dragging from one endpoint to the other.
3. **Insert a point into a segment** To insert a new interior point into a path, select the add point tool and click anywhere along a segment (except on an existing point). Illustrator inserts the point and divides the segment in two. Illustrator automatically inserts a corner or smooth point depending on its reading of your path. You don't have to actually switch to the add point tool. If you've got the pen chose, simply position the cursor over an empty spot on any segment. The regular pen cursor gains a little plus sign (so it looks just like the add point cursor).

Removing Points from a Path

To delete an entire path, you just select it with the arrow tool and press the Backspace/Delete key. You can do it from menus too, just choose Edit>>Clear. To delete a point or segment, try out one of the following techniques.

1. **Delete a point and break the path** To delete a point, select it with the direct selection tool and press the Delete key. When you delete an interior point, you delete both segments associated with that point, resulting in a break in the path. If you delete an endpoint from an open path, you delete the single segment associated with the point.
2. **Delete a segment** You can delete a single interior segment from a path without removing a point. To do so, click the segment you want to delete with the direct selection tool and press Delete. Deleting a segment always creates a break in a path.
3. **Delete the rest of the path** After you delete a point or segment, Illustrator selects the remainder of the path. If the path is broken into two parts, both parts will be selected. To delete the whole path, just press Delete a second time. This can be a handy technique if you don't want to switch to the arrow tool. Just click some portion of the path and press Delete twice in a row to delete he whole path.
4. **Remove a point without breaking the path** If you want to get rid of a point but dan't want to create a break in the path, select the delete point tool and click the point you want to disappear. Illustrator draws a new segment between the two points neighboring the deleted point.

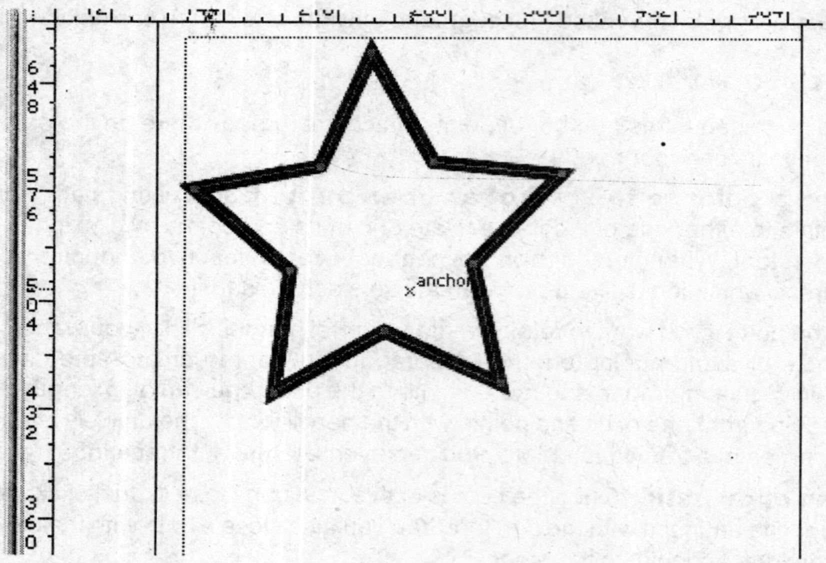

Converting Points between Corner and Smooth

The convert point tool lets you change a point in the middle of a path from corner to smooth or smooth to corner. When a path is shaped wrong, this tool is absolutely essential. You can change the identity of an interior point in any of the following ways:

- **Smooth to corner** Using the convert point tool, click a smooth point. This converts it to a corner point with no control handles.
- **Smooth to cusp** Drag a control handle belonging to a smooth point to move it independently of the other control handle, thus converting the smooth point to a cusp.
- **Corner or cusp to smooth** Drag from a corner point or cusp to convert it to a smooth point with two symmetrical control handles. Once you have the smooth point, you can use

the convert point tool on either handle to change the point into a cusp.

The figure on the next page shows a path created with the star tool. Like any star, it's made up entirely of corner points and straight segments. But with the help of the convert point tool, you can put some curve, as the following steps show.

1. **Drag from one of the points along the inner radius** Select the convert point tool and drag from one of the inner radius points as shown on the next page. The corner point changes to a smooth point with symmetrical control handles, bending both neighboring segments.
2. **Drag the inside control handle outside the star** Drag the control handle that moved inside the star to a position outside the star, so that the two spikes form mirror images of each other, as shown in the figure here. This converts the smooth point to a cusp, permitting the control handles to move independently.

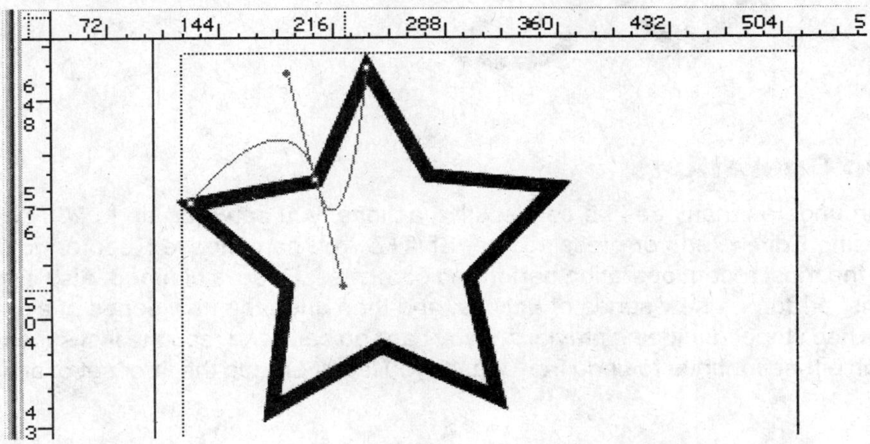

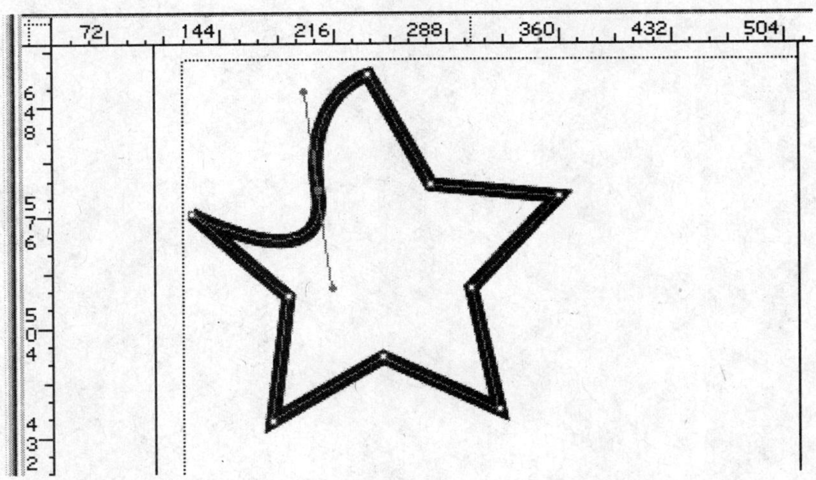

3. **Repeat Steps 1 and 2 on all the inner radius points** By dragging control handles from all the points and converting them to cusp points, you can create the flower shape shown in the figure here.

4. **Continue to adjust the handles until they're just right** With the convert poin tool, click and drag on any handle that does not suit your fancy.

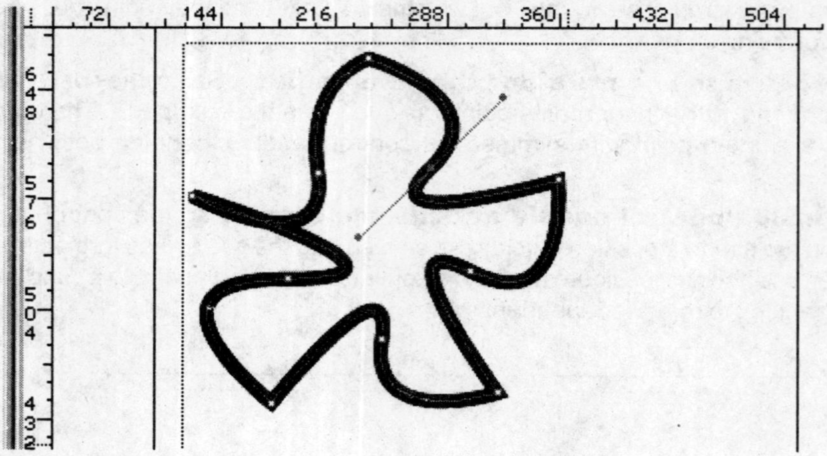

Redo Undo Operations

Just as you can undo as many as 200 consecutive actions, you can redo up to 200 consecutive undos by choosing Edit>>Redo or pressing Ctrl+Shift+Z. You can choose Redo only if the Undo command was the most recent operation performed otherwise, Redo is dimmed. Also if you undo a series of actions, perform a new series of actions, and then undo the new series of actions to the point where you had stopped undoing previously, you can't go back and redo the first series of undos. Instead, you can either continue to undo from where you let off or redo the later set of actions.

3 Handling Text in Illustrator CS 4

Introduction

Illustrator's text capabilities are very vast as would see in the course of this chapter. First we will understand how to create text and apply attributes like fonts, paragraph settings, spacings, etc. Later we look at more effective ways of handling text, like, converting text to a curve, setting text inside free-form text blocks, applying effects to Adobe's specialized Multiple Master fonts, converting letter outlines to fully editable paths and even present text in the Japanese vertical style.

First, we create text objects.

Creating Text Objects

Illustrator provides 6 tools for creating text, as was told to you in the first chapter. But, first let us concentrate on the type tool (the one that looks like a T). With the type tool, you can create a text object – which is any object that contains type – in one of two ways:

- ❑ Click with the type tool within the drawing area and a few words of type for a logo or headline. This kind of text block is called point text, because Illustrator aligns the text to the point at which you click.
- ❑ Drag with the type tool to draw a rectangular text block. Then enter your text from the keyboard. Illustrator fits the text to the rectangular text block, automatically shifting text that doesn't fit on one line down to the next. Create a text block when you want to enter a full sentence or more.

1. Select the type tool and click in some empty portion of the drawing area with the new block cursor. The new block cursor shows that you are about to create a new text object. After you click with the type tool, Illustrator creates an alignment point, which appears as an x in the outline mode. Illustrator aligns the text to this point.
2. Enter the desired text from your keyboard. By default, the text appears to the right of the alignment point. As you type, a blinking insertion marker flashes to the right of the last character. The insertion marker shows you where the next letter you enter will appear. With point text, Illustrator keeps all characters on a single line unless you tell it to do otherwise. This is why point text is better suited to a few words or less. If you want to move the insertion marker down to create a new line of type, press the Enter key.
3. When you have finished entering your text, hold the Ctrl key and click the text. Then release the Ctrl key. The text block appears selected as shown in the figure on the next page. The alignment point now looks like a filled square, just like a selected anchor point.

You can drag the alignment point with any of the three selection tools to reposition the text in the drawing area. You can also drag point text by its baseline which is the line that runs under each line of type. The baseline is the imaginary line on which letter sit. Some lowercase characters – g, j, p, q

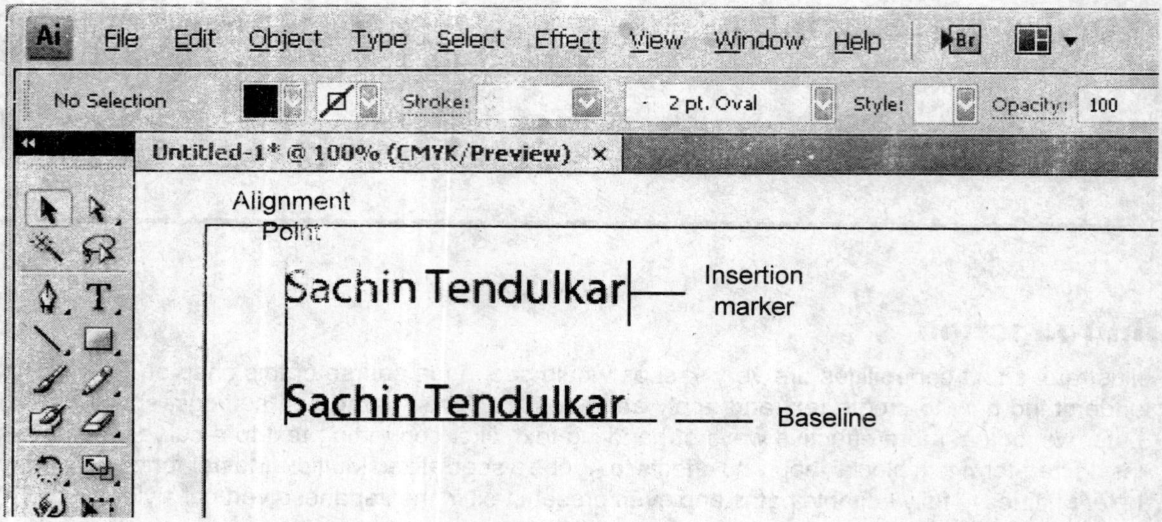

and y – descend below the baseline. Lastly, you can move point text by dragging on the text itself. The exception to this last technique is when the Type Area Select option of the Type and Auto Tracing Preference dialog box is turned off.

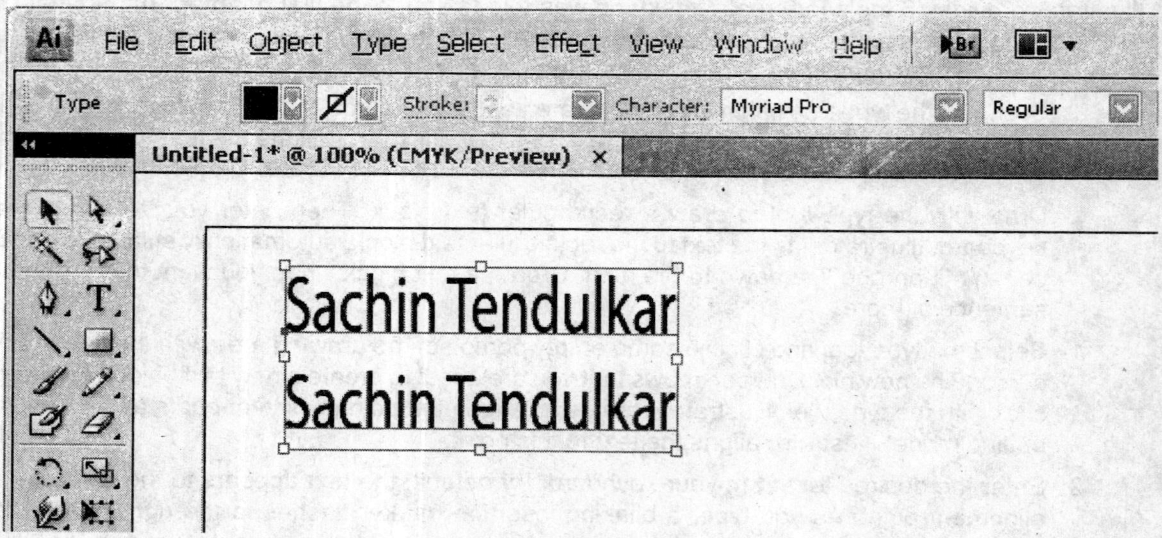

Text in Blocks

Point text is easy to create, but because Illustrator forces all text onto a single line unless told to do otherwise, point text is not well suited to whole paragraph and longer text. To accommodate lengthy text, you need to create a text block:

1. Drag with the type tool. This creates a rectangle, as shown in the example on the next page, just at if you were dragging with the rectangle tool. This rectangle represents the height and width of the new text block. When you release the mouse, Illustrator shows you a box with a blinking insertion marker. You will also see a center point, just as in a standard rectangle.

2. Enter type from the keyboard. If a letter would extend beyond the right edge of the text block, Illustrator sends the word down to start a new line of type. Known as automatic wrapping, this is precisely the capability that point text lacks.
3. After you stop entering text, hold the Ctrl key and click the text. Then release the Ctrl key. The text block appears selected, showing off four corner points connected by straight segments and a center point hovering in the middle. Baseline underscore the type to indicate that the letters themselves are selected.

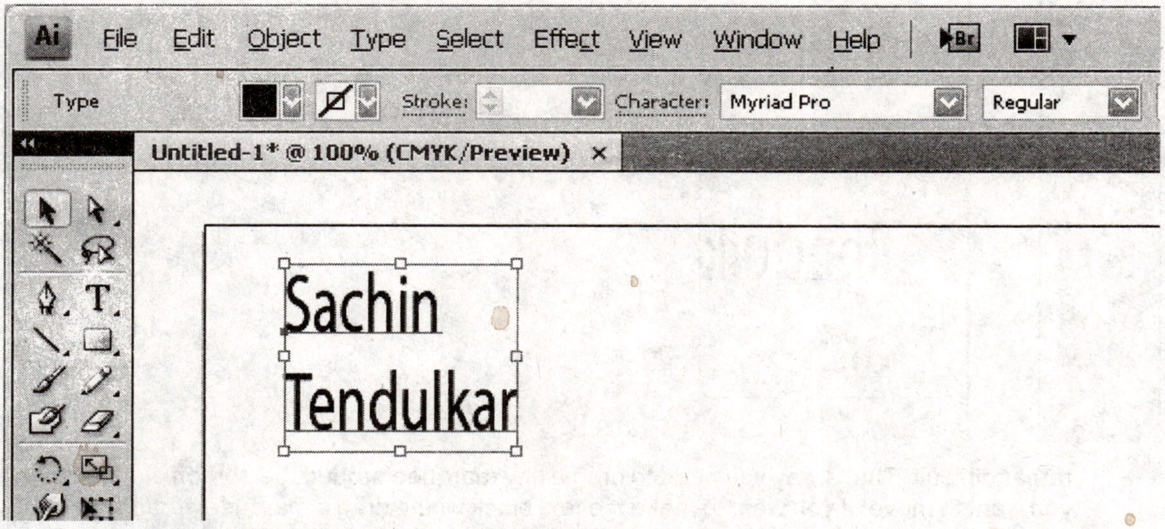

Resizing and Reshaping Text Blocks

You can reposition a text block by dragging either the rectangular boundary or one of the baseline with the arrow tool. Or you can drag directly on the text itself. You can also change the size and shape of a text block with the direct selection tool. For example, let's say that the next you entered from the keyboard doesn't entirely fit inside the text block. Or the text block isn't wide enough to accommodate a particularly long word.

The little square with a minus sign in it shows that Illustrator had to break the word everybody onto two lines. The square with a plus sign shows that there is more text than can fit inside the text block and is temporarily hidden. This text is called overflow text. By resizing a text block, you can fit long words on a single line, reveal overflow text or simply change how words wrap from one line to the next. To resize a text block, you have to use the direct selection tool to select and modify the rectangular boundary independently of the text inside it.

1. **Create your text block** After creating the text block, select the direct selection tool.
2. **Deselect the text block** If your first impulse is to resize the block by dragging a corner point, resist the feeling. You'll turn the block into a kite-shaped object. To reshape the block and keep it a rectangle, you have to select one of the segments and drag it, just as if you were resizing a standard rectangle. And – just to make things as painful as possible – you can't select a segment until you deselect path. So choose Select>>Deselect All or press Ctrl+Shift+A to deselect the text block.
3. **Select the right or bottom edge of the text block** If you're working in the preview mode, the text block outline disappears. This makes selecting an edge of the text block

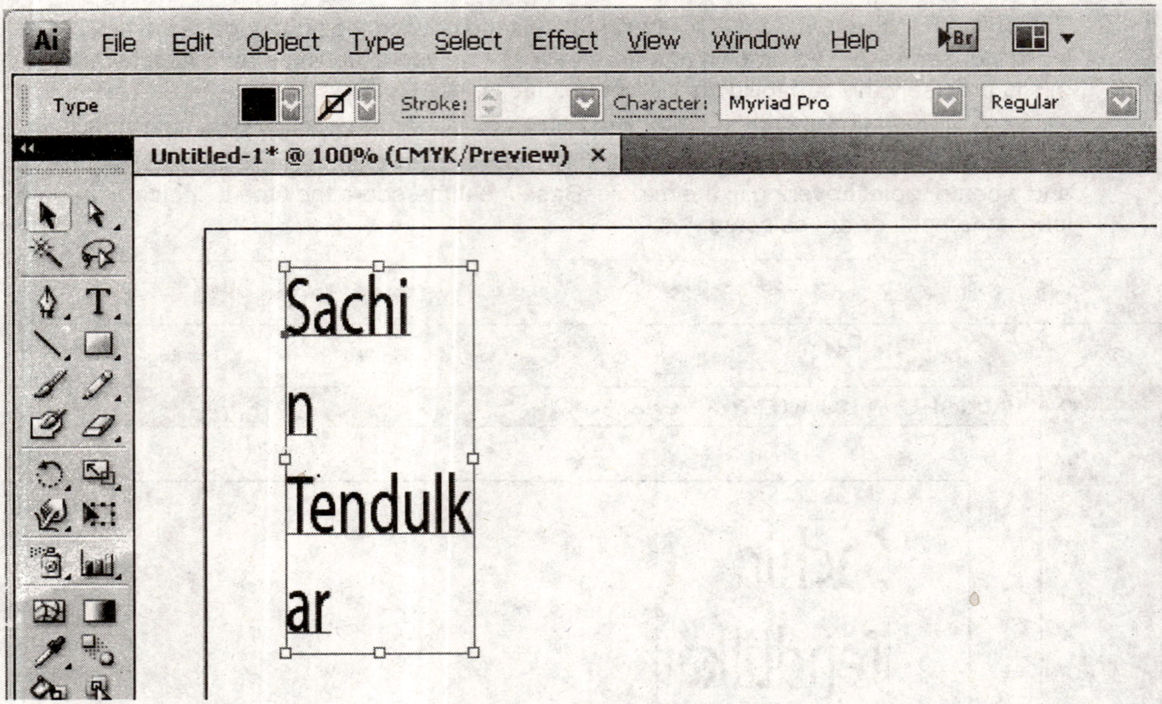

rather difficult. That's why you need to drag a tiny marquee around the portion of the outline you want to move. If you want to make the text block wider, drag a marquee around the right side. If you want to make the text block taller, marquee the bottom side. In either case, you select the desired edge.

4. **Shift-drag the edge** To maintain the rectangular shape of the text block, shift-drag the right segment to the right or Shift-drag the bottom segment downward.

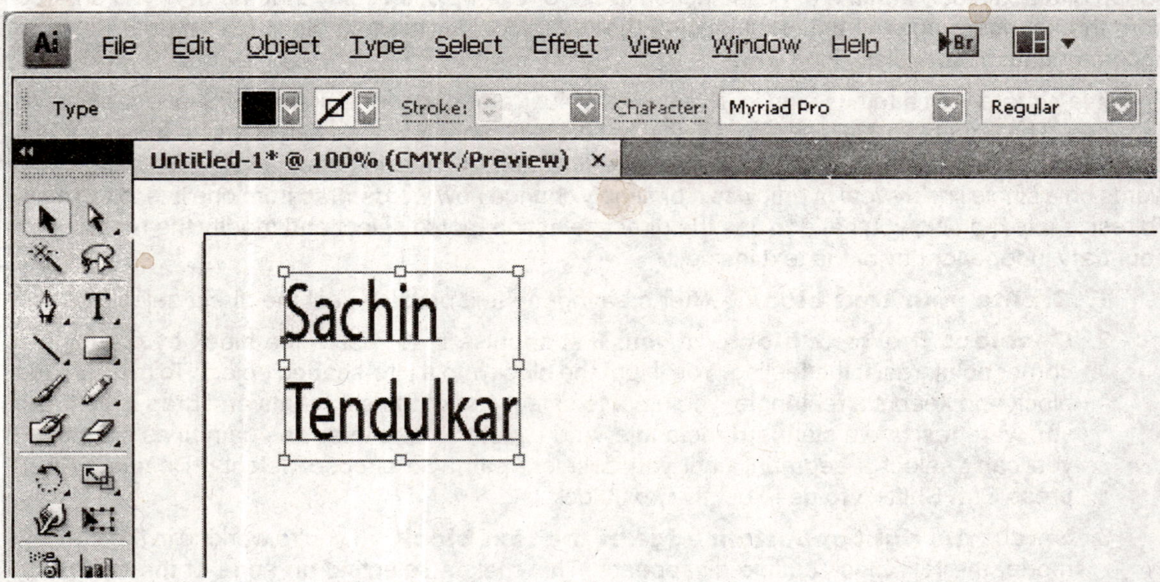

When you release the mouse button, Illustrator rewraps the text and displays as much overflow text as will fit. If there is still more overflow text, the little plus icon remains in the lower right corner of the text block. In addition to dragging points and segments, you can:

- Change the corner points to smooth points with the convert point tool.
- Drag the control handles to bend the segments.
- Insert or remove points with the add point and delete point tools.
- Select a segment and press Delete to open the path.
- Extend the open path using the pen or pencil tools.

Selecting and Editing Text

Before you can change a single character of type or change how text looks on the page, you have to select the type using the arrow or the type tool.

- Clicking along the baseline of a line of type with any selection tool selects all type in the object. If you change the font, type size, style or some other formatting attribute, you change all characters in the selected text object.
- You can shift-click to select multiple text objects. Any changes you make to the text formatting will apply to all the selected text objects. Illustrator doesn't format an entire text block if you select just a portion of the outline with the direct selection tool.
- If you select text with a type tool, you can edit that text by entering new text from the keyboard or format the selected text independently of other text in the object.

Selecting with the Type Tool

The type tool is the most common instrument for editing type in Illustrator because it affords the most control. The following items explain how to select type with the type tool:

- Drag over the characters that you want to select. Drag to the left or to the right to select characters on a single line; drag upward or downward to select characters on multiple lines. The selected text becomes highlighted as shown on next page. Selected text has to be contigous. You cannot select alternate words for example or for that matter select the first line, skip the second line and then select the third line.
- Double-click a word to select it. Hold down the mouse button on the second click and drag. Your selection will be whole worlds.
- Triple-click to select an entire paragraph, from one return character to the next. Hold down the mouse button on the third click and drag to select additional paragraphs.
- Click to set the insertion marker at one end of the text that you want to select and then Shift+click at the opposite end of the desired selection. Illustrator highlights all characters between the first click and the Shift+click.
- Click anywhere in a text block and press Ctrl-A or choose Edit >>Select All, to select all text in the object. After you click with the type tool to set the insertion marker inside a text object, you can use the arrow keys to move the insertion marker around or select text.
- Press the left or right arrow key to move the insertion marker to the left or right one character.
- Press the up or down arrow key to move the insertion marker up or down one line.

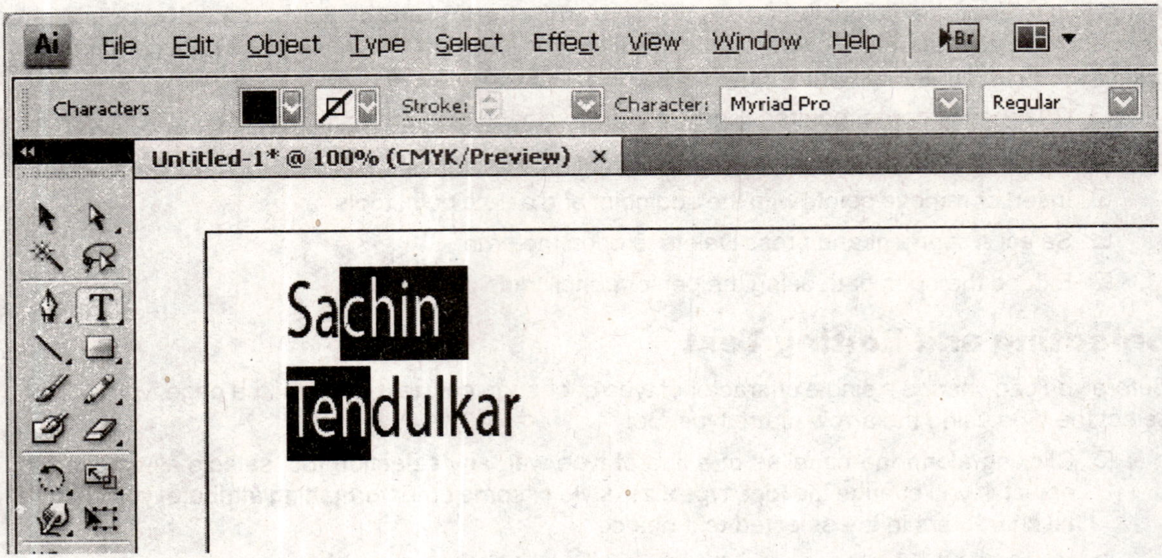

- Press Ctrl+right arrow move the insertion marker one whole word to the right. Press Ctrl+left arrow to move back a word.
- Press Ctrl+up arrow to move the insertion marker to the beginning of the paragraph. Press Ctl+down arrow to move it to the end of the paragraph.
- Press Shift along with any of these keystrokes to select text as you move the insertion marker. For example, press Shift+right arrow to select the character after the insertion marker. Press Ctrl+Shift+up arrow to select everything from the insertion marker to the beginning of the paragraph.

Adding Text

After you highlight some text, you can format it or replace it by entering new text from the keyboard.

- To delete selected text, press the Backspace/Delete key.
- You can remove the selected text and send it to the Clipboard by choosing Edit>>Cut or Ctrl-X).
- To leave the selected text intact and send a copy to the Clipboard choose Edit>>Copy or Ctrl-C.
- You can even replace the selected text with text that you cut or copied earlier by choosing Edit>>Paste or Ctrl-V. The pasted text retains its original formatting.

Formatting Text

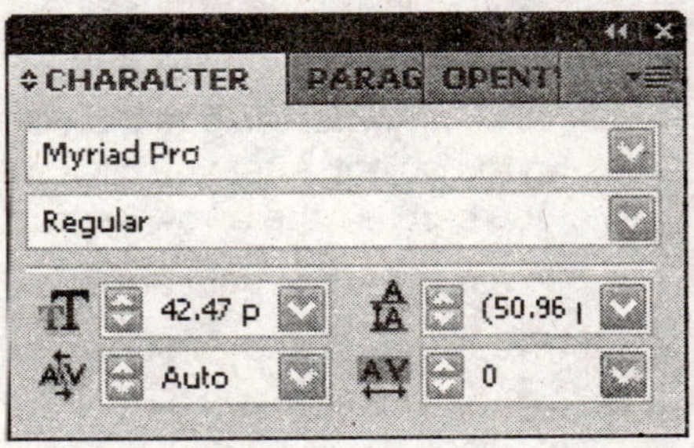

Formatting means nothing more than changing the way characters and lines of text look. Illustrator provides an exhaustive supply of formatting functions that let you modify far more than you'll ever want to. You can divide formatting attributes into two categories – those that apply to individual characters of type and those that apply to entire paragraphs.

- **Character-level formatting** includes option

such as typeface, size, leading, kerning and tracking, baseline shift and horizontal scaling. To change the formatting of one or more characters, you select the characters with the type tool and apply the desired options. Illustrator changes the highlighted characters and leaves surrounding characters unaltered.

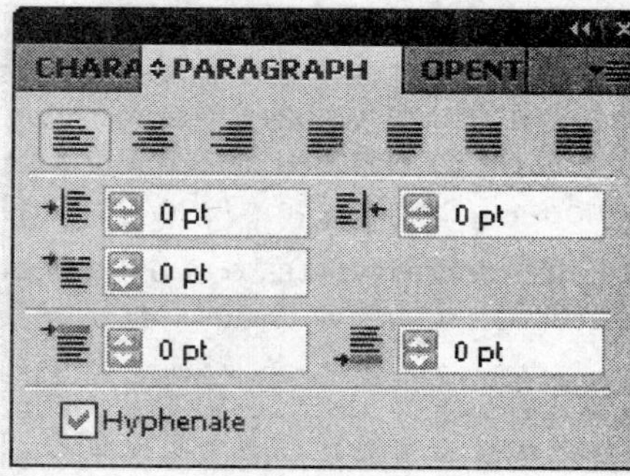

- **Paragraph-level formatting** includes indents, alignment, paragraph spacing, letter spacing and word spacing. To change the formatting of a single paragraph, you need only position the blinking insertion marker inside that paragraph. Illustrator changes the entire paragraph to matter how little of it you select. To change the formatting of multiple paragraphs, select at least one character in each of the paragraphs you want to modify.

Character-Level Formatting

To format characters, you can either choose commands from Type menu or use the options in the Character palette. The letter is the more convenient. To display the Character palette, choose Type>> Character or press Ctrl-T. By default, the Character palette shows only six options, as shown below. But if you choose the Show Options command from the pop-up menu, you expand the palette to display several more options, as shown next. Let us discuss the various options which you can change from this dialog box.

Selecting a Typeface

You can select a font from the Type>>Font submenu or from the Font pop-up menu in the Character palette. For example, to assign Arial Bold, you would choose Type>>Font>>Arial>>Bold. If you know the name of the font you want to apply, just enter the first few letters of its name into the Font option box in the Character palette. Each time you enter a character, Illustrator tries to guess which font you want.

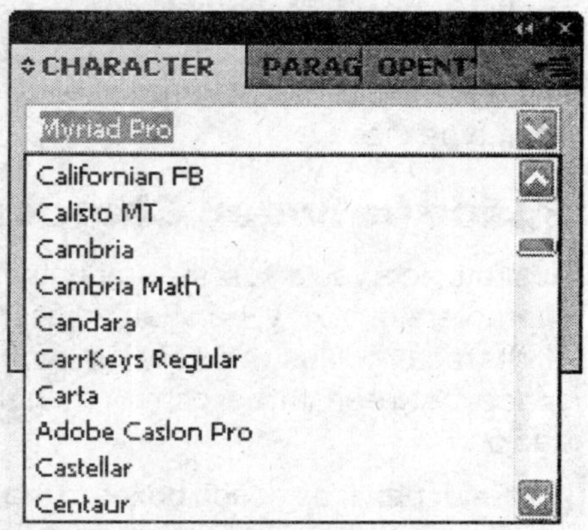

To change the style, press the Tab key and enter the first few letters of the style, such as B for Bold or I for italic. You can also right-click and choose a font from the Fonts submenu in the context-menu. You may notice that Illustrator doesn't let you apply electronic styles such as underline. Illustrators inability to assign electronic styles inhibits its compatibility with TrueType fonts.

If a TrueType font doesn't have a submenu of stylized fonts next to its name in the Type>>Font submenu, it means that the fonts on your machine don't include the stylized versions of that font.

Reducing/Enlarging Type

To change the size of any selected type, choose a size from the Type>>Size submenu. If you choose Others, you'll be sent to the size option in the Character palette.

Type size, as it is called, is measured in points from the top of an ascender (such as a d or an f) to the bottom of a descender (such as g or p). You can enter any value between 0.1 (1/10 the size of the smallest character) and 1296 (four times the size of the largest character) in 0.01–points increments.

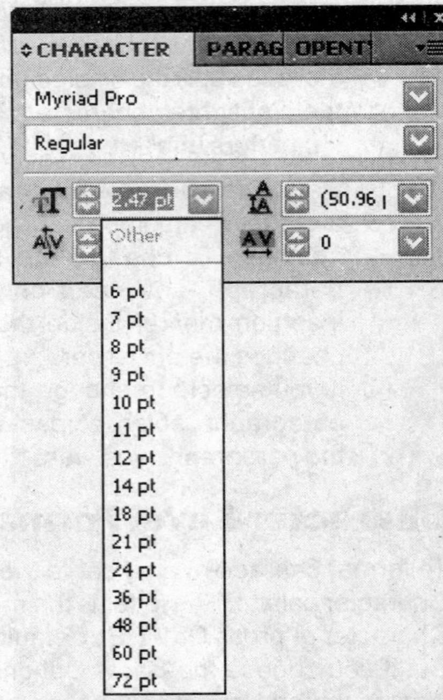

If you dramatically reduce the size of a line of type, it appears as a gray bar. Illustrator figures it's too small to be readable on screen, so why waste the time trying to draw it accurately? If you want to see text at smaller sizes, change the greeking amount in the Type and Auto Tracing Preferences.

To change the type size of the selected text by five times the Size/Loading value, do the following:

Press Ctrl-Alt-Shift-> or Ctrl-Alt-Shift-<

Distance between Lines

Leading specifies the distance between a selected line of type an the line below it, as measured in points form one baseline to the next. Therefore, 14-point leading leaves a couple of points of extra room between two lines of 12-point type. You can change the leading by entering a value into the Leading option box in the Character palette.

To speed things up, select some text and press Alt-down arrow to increase the leading or Alt-up arrow to decrease it.

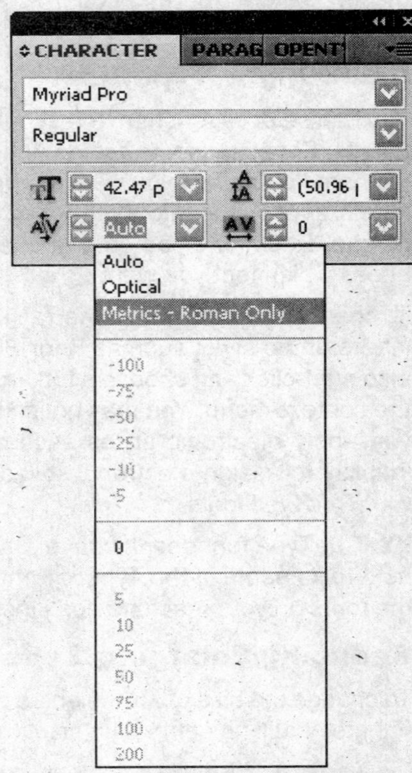

Select Auto from the Leading pop-up menu in the Character palette to make the leading equal to 120 percent of the current type size (rounded off to the nearest half-point). If a line of text contains characters with two different leading specifications, the larger leading prevails. If you begin a paragraph with a large capital letter, for example, you might combine a 24-point character and the 12-point character use auto leading, then the entire line will be set at 29-point leading (120 percent of the 24-point type size).

Space between Characters

Illustrator lets you adjust the amount of horizontal space between characters of text. When you adjust the space between a pair of characters, Illustrator calls it kerning. When you adjust the space between three or more characters, Illustrtor calls it tracking.

Illustrator provides option boxes in the Character palette for both kerning and tracking – commands for these don't exist in the Type menu and appear only in the Character palette. When you click with the type tool to position the insertion marker between two characters, you will want to use the Kerning option box. When you select so much as a single character, the Tracking option box is the one for you. Don't worry if you get them confused – enter a value in the Kerning option box when you're trying to change the tracking or vice versa – because Illustrator will promptly respond by either doing nothing or flashing some annoying warning that you're mistreating it.

Changing Height and Width of Characters

The next options in the Character palette, Vertical Scale and Horizontal Scale modify the height and width of selected characters, respectively. You can expand or condense type anywhere from 1 to 10,000 percent (1/100 to 100 times its normal width) by entering a new value into either the Vertical Scale or Horizontal Scale option box and pressing Return/Enter.

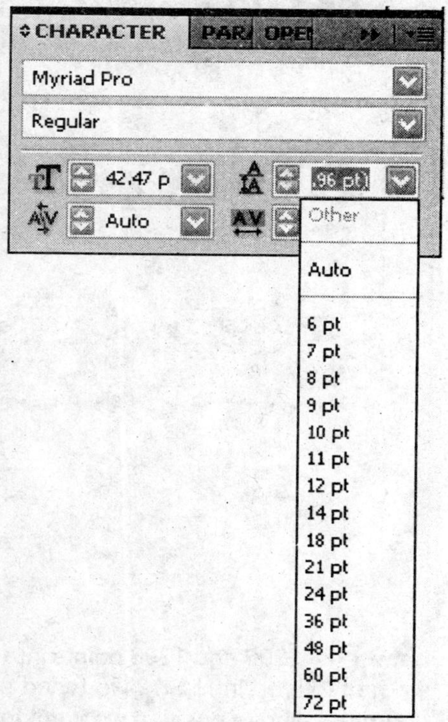

Changing the height or width of a character distorts. The Vertical Scale and Horizontal Scale options do not create the same effect as designer-condensed or expanded fonts. For example, the figure on the next page shows two variations on Arial for the alphabet XYZ. In the first example, I took 200-point Arial Bold and scaled it 50 percent horizontally. You would get almost the same result if you were to scale 115-point type vertically to 175 percent – go ahead and try it.

Notice how the horizontal bars of the X and Y are much thicker than the vertical stems. This is because Horizontal Scale affects vertical proportions and leaves horizontal proportions untouched. With this in mind, you should remember a few things when using the Vertical Scale or Horizontal Scale option:

- If you want the type to appear distorted, go for broke. There are no hard and fast rules in page design; type that specifically calls attention to itself can be just as effective as type that doesn't, if you have a bold design and an open-minded audience.
- If slightly widening or narrowing a few lines of type will make them fit better on the page, you can get away with Horizontal Scale values between 95 and 105 percent; no one will notice.
- Changing both the vertical and horizontal factors by the same amount is the same as changing the size. So if you enter 50 percent into both the Vertical Scale and Horizontal Scale option boxes, the result is the same as if you had change the value in the Size option box to half of its original value.

Superscript and Subscript

The Baseline Shift option in the lower half of the Character palette determines the distance between the selected type and its baseline. A positive value, or called Superscript, raises the characters above the normal text; a negative value, also called Subscript, lowers characters below the normal text. The default value of 0 leaves them sitting on the baseline, where they typically belong.

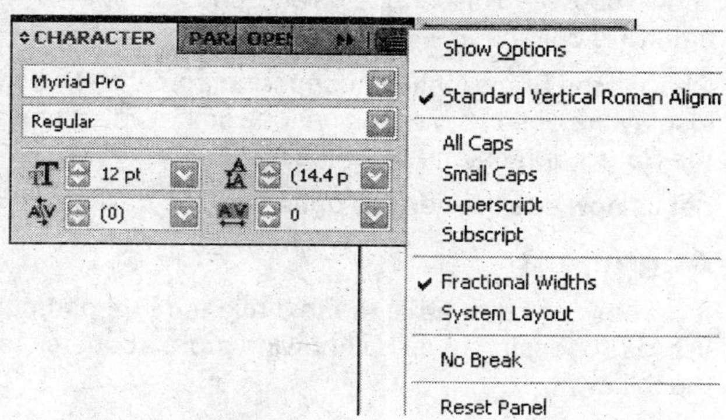

You can modify the baseline shift to create superscripts and subscripts or to adjust type along a path. To change the baseline shift, select some type and then enter any value

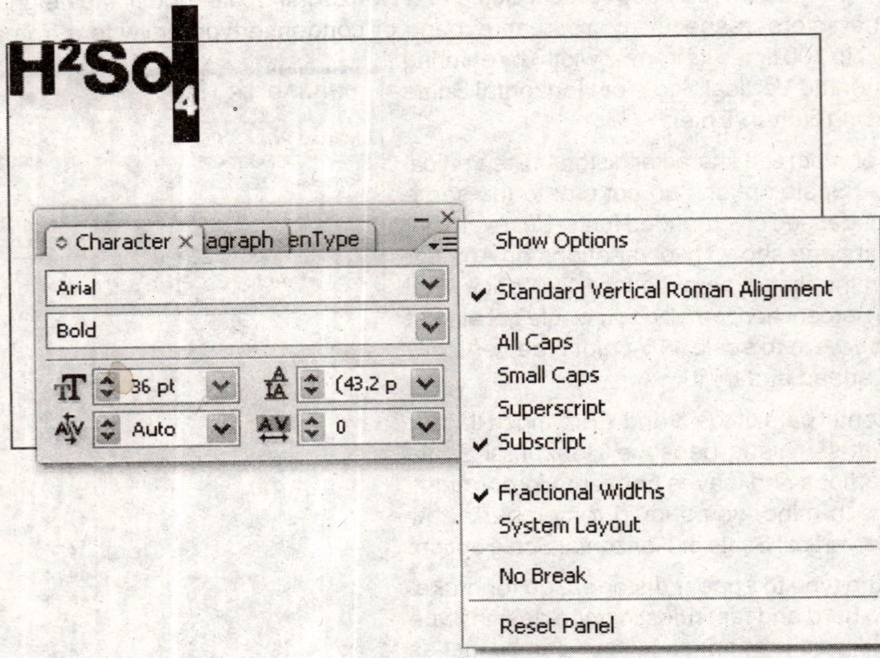

between – 1296 and 1296 points into the Baseline Shift option box. In the the above example, where we had to type in H_2So_4, we typed all the characters of the text in one go first. Then selected the character whose position we want to change, in this case 4. The text was changed to half the size, i.e., 18 instead of 36 and then gave it a –12 point shift, to make 4 as $_4$. Similar thing was done in the case of 2. Similarly, if you have to create mathematical expression $x^3 + 2x^2 + 4$, then you can do the same. The only difference here is that instead of –12 pt as done in the earlier cases, you do 12 pt for both 3 and 2 to make them ^{3} and ^{2}, as shown in the following figure.

Paragraph-Level Formatting

So far we have done some character level formatting, now we will try to concentrate on paragraph level formatting. Illustrator's paragraph formatting controls can be found on the Paragraph palette, as shown above. To display the palette, choose Type>>Paragraph or press Ctrl-M. By default the Paragraph palette is collapsed.

Choose the Show Options command from the Paragraph palette submenu to expand the palette and display the options. Various options of the dialog box are shown on the next page. You can show/hide the Paragraph palette by pressing Ctrl+M again.

Let us now see the various options of the paragraph dialog box.

Alignment

It is your choice to have the text aligned in a particular manner. Those of you who are familiar with Word Processing must be knowing more about text alignment than others. By alignment you can do the following:

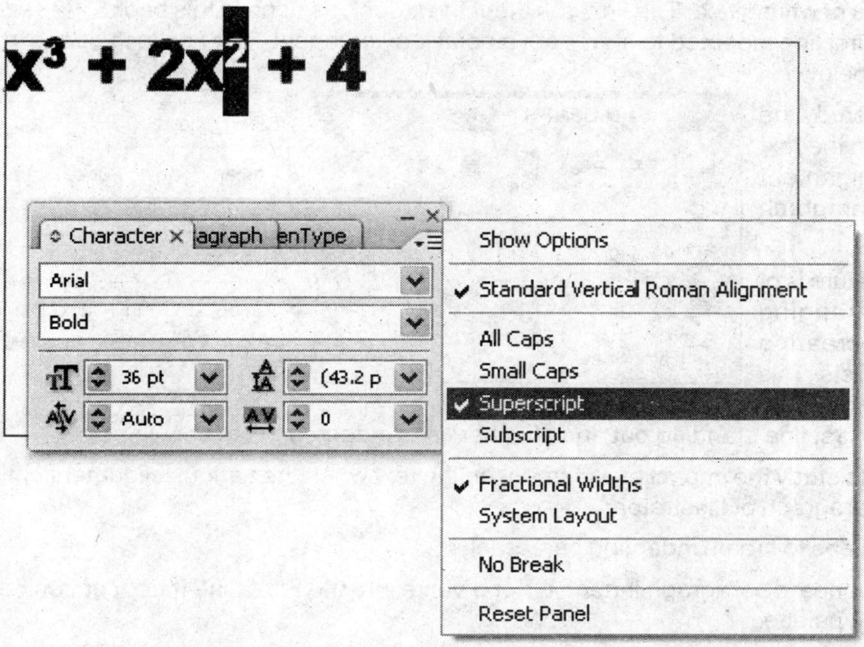

- To align a paragraph so that all the left edges line up (flush left, ragged right), press Ctrl-Shift-L or select the first alignment icon in the Paragraph palette. For example,

  We are here to study the impact of alignment on the text when the various alignment options are used in paragraph of Illustrator.

- To center all lines in a paragraph, press Ctrl-Shift-C or select the second Alignment icon in the Paragraph palette. For example,

  We are here to study the impact of alignment on the text when the various alignment options are used in paragraph of Illustrator.

- To make the right edges of a paragraph line up (flush right, ragged left), press Ctrl-Shift-R or select the third Alignment icon. For example,

  We are here to study the impact of alignment on the text when the various alignment options are used in paragraph of Illustrator.

- You can also justify a paragraph, which stretches all lines except the last line of a paragraph so they entirely fill the width of the next block. To justify a paragraph, press Ctrl-shift-J or select the fourth Alignment icon. For example,

  We are here to study the impact of alignment on the text when the various alignment options are used in paragraph of Illustrator.

- If you want to force justify the last line in a paragraph, press Ctrl-Shift-F or click the last Alignment icon in the Paragraph palette. This forces the last line to finish at the end of the line.

  We are here to study the impact of alignment on the text when the various alignment options are used in paragraph of Illustrator.

Indentation of Paragraphs

There are 2 main ways of writing text. The first is without the indent, as done in this book. The second option is to have the first line indented to start from a point leaving about 1/2 of an inch space in the beginning, as shown below.

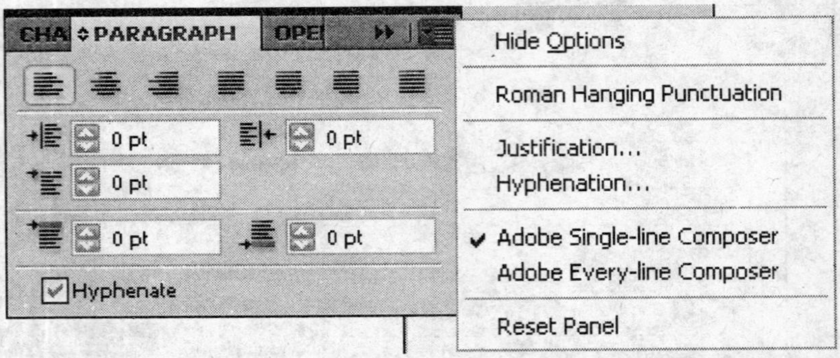

We are here to study the impact of alignment on the text when the various alignment options are used in paragraph of Illustrator.

Another interesting feature is of hanging indent. A hanging indent is great for creating bulleted or numbered lists. This is used when you have to highlight the text with first line standing out and all other lines indented in, as shown below.

- We are here to study the impact of alignment on the text when the various alignment options are used in paragraph of Illustrator.

Follow the following steps to create indenting paragraphs.

- ❑ To create a standard paragraph indent, enter a value into the First Line Indent option box in the Paragraph palette.
- ❑ If you assign a first-line indent to a paragraph, remember that you can break a word onto the next line of type without indenting it by pressing Shift-Enter to create a new line character. The words divided by the new line character appear on different lines, but are part of the same paragraph.
- ❑ To create a hanging indent, enter a positive value into the Left Indent option box and the inverse of that value in the First Line Indent option box.
- ❑ You can have to set the tab so the first lines up with the others. You can press the Tab key to get the bullet to insert a tab character. Then choose the Type>>Tab Rulers command to display the Tabs palette and created a left tab.

Paragraph Spacing

You can have some space after and before the paragraph. For this you have to use Spacing Before Paragraph option box to insert some extra space before a selected paragraph. This so-called paragraph leading helps separate one paragraph from another, much like a first-line indent. Most designers use first-line indents or paragraph leading to distinguish paragraphs, but not both. The two together are generally considered design overkill. In this particular book, a paragraph spacing of 4 points have been used.

Letters and Words Spacing

The middle options in the Paragraph palette let you control the amount of space that Illustrator places between words and characters in a text block. As you might imagine, word spacing controls the amount of space between words; letter spacing controls the amount of space between the letters.

There are two primary reasons for manipulating spacing:

- ❑ To give a paragraph a generally tighter or looser appearance. You control this general spacing using the Desired options.
- ❑ To determine the range of spacing manipulations Illustrators can use when justifying a paragraph. Illustrator tightens up some lines and loosens others to make them fit the exact width of your text block. You specify limits using the Min. and Max. options.

When spacing flush left, right or centered paragraphs, Illustrator relies entirely on the two Desired values. In fact, the other options are dimmed. All values are measured as a percentage of a standard space, as the information contained in the current font determines. For example, a Desire Word Spacing value of 100 percent inserts the width of one space character between each pair of words in a paragraph. Reducing of enlarging this percentage makes the space between words bigger or smaller. A Desired Letter Spacing of 10 percent inserts 10 inserts of the width of a space character between each pair of letters. Negative percentages squeeze letters together and a value of 0 percent spaces letters normally.

If you select one or more justified paragraphs, the Min and Max. options become available. These values give Illustrator some wiggle room when tightened and spreading lines of type. Word Spacing and Letter Spacing values must be within these ranges:

- ❑ The Min. Word Spacing value must be at least 0 percent; the Min. Letter Spacing must be at least -50 percent. Both must be less than their respective Desired values.
- ❑ The Max. Word spacing value can be no higher than 1,000 percent; Max. Letter Spacing can be no more than 500 percent. Neither can be less than its respective Desired value.
- ❑ Each desired value can be no less than its corresponding Min. value and no higher than the corresponding Max. value.

The examples on the next page show the various options.

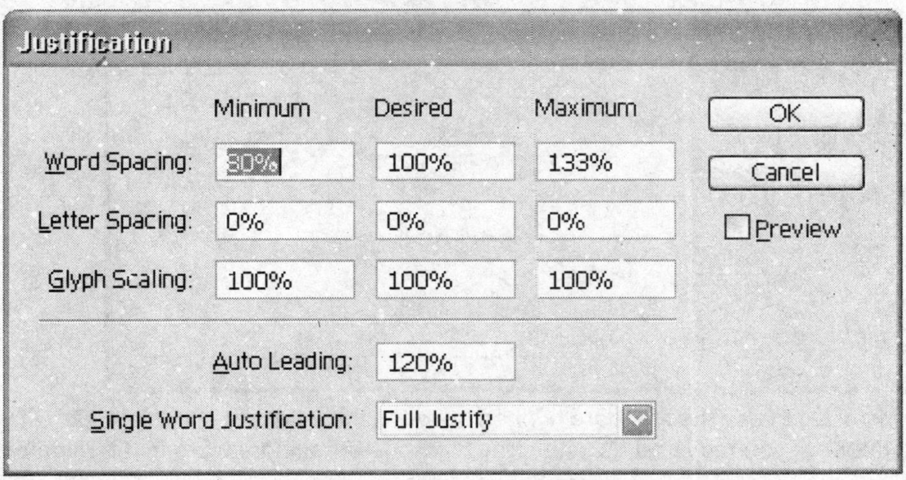

Activating Automatic Hyphenation

There are three ways to hyphenate text in Illustrator:

- ❑ Enter a standard hyphen character (-) between two words you want to hyphenate. This is usually found in hyphenated words like 3-inch mark or hyphenated names such as Biddle-

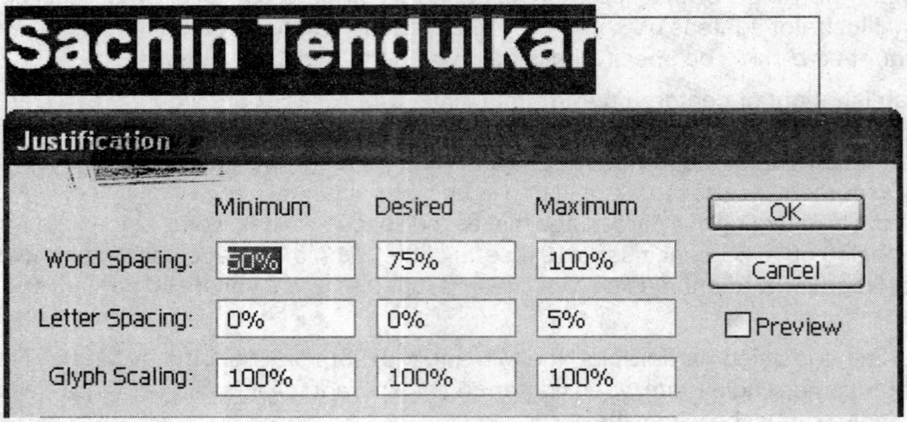

Barrows. Don't use the standard hyphen between the letters of a word, though. If you edit the text later on, you may end up with stray hyphens breaking a word in the middle of a line.

- A much better idea is to insert a discretionary hyphen, which disappears any time it is not needed. You can enter a discretionary hyphen by pressing Ctrl-Shift-hyphen(-). If no hyphen appears when you enter this character, it simply means that the addition of the hyphen does not help Illustrator break the word. You can try inserting the character at a different location or expanding the width of the text block to permit the word to break.
- The third option is to let Illustrator do the hyphenating for you by selecting the Auto Hyphenate check box in the Paragraph palette.

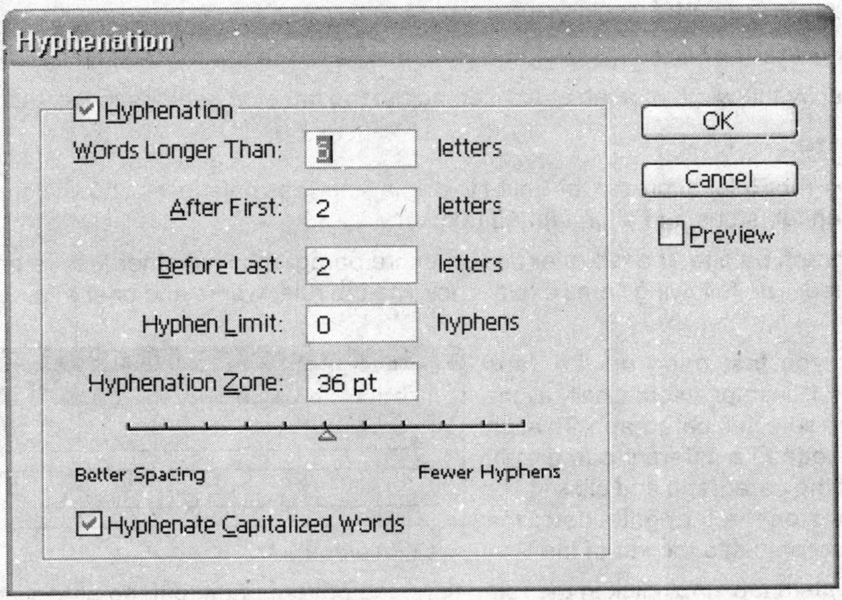

If you do decide to us automatic hyphenation then this is how you will proceed.

1. **Turn on Auto Hyphenate** With the arrow tool, select the text block you want to hyphenate turn on the Auto Hyphenate check box in the Paragraph palette. Illustrator adds hyphens where it deems necessary.
2. **Choose the Hyphenation Options** If you want to limit where and how hyphenation occurs, choose the Hyphenation command from the Paragraph palette pop-up menu. The Hyphenation Options dialog box, as shown above will appear.
3. **Specify how many letters must appear before and after a hyphen** In the Hyphenation Options dialog box, enter a value into the first Hyphenate option box to specify the minimum number of letters that can come between a hyphen and the beginning of a word. Enter a value into the next option box to determine the minimum number or letters between a hyphen and the end of a word. For example, with both values set to 2, Illustrator could split the word apple as ap-ple, because both the first and last syllables are at elast two letters long.
4. **Specify the possible number of consecutive hyphens** If you want to limit the number of consecutive lines of Illustrator can hyphenate, select the Limit check box and enter the maximum limit in the option box. By default, the value is set to 3, so Illustrator can hyphenate no more than three consecutive lines before it has to permit one line to go without hyphenation. But as far as we're concerned, any more than two hyphenated lines in a row looks amateurish and interferes with legibility.
5. **Prepare to groove as Illustrator implements all your secret hyphen-related desired** Click the OK button or press Enter.

Working with Tabs

Tabs have been there since the days of typewriter. But, unfortunately, there the tabs were restricted to only one, i.e., left one. Here we have the option of having 4 different type of tabs, i.e., Left, Right, Centre and Decimal. You use tabs to align character precisely.

There are really only two rules to using tabs:

1. Never press Tab twice in a row (thus creating two tab characters).
2. To specify the width of a tab character, adjust the tab stop settings in the Tabs palette.

Tabs Palette

Choose Type>>Tab Ruler or press Ctrl-Shift-t to display the Tabs palette, as shown here. This palette lets you position tab stops and align tabbed text.

Like the Paragraph palette, the tab ruler affects entire paragraphs, whether they're entirely or only partially selected. The following items explain how the tab ruler works and offer a few guidelines for using it.

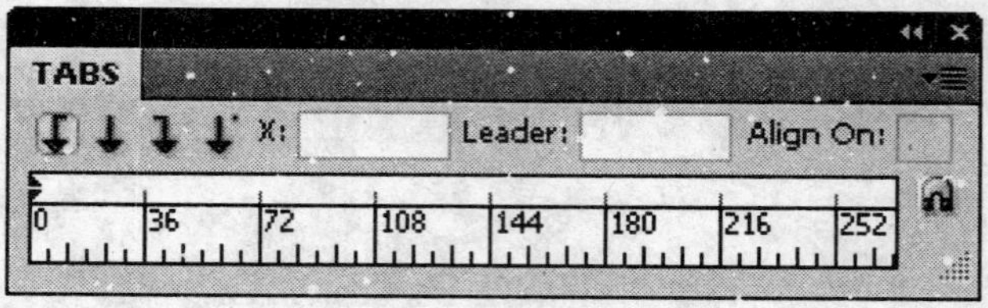

- ❑ When you first bring up the Tabs palette, Illustrator automatically aligns it to the selected paragraph. To align the palette to a different paragraph, select the paragraph and click in the size box on the far right side of the title bar (or just to the left of the Windows close box).
- ❑ To create a tab stop, click in the ruler along the bottom of the palette or click inside the tab strip just above the ruler. If you drag the tab stop, Illustrator projects a vertical alignment guide from the Tab palette. The line moves with the tab stop, permitting you to predict more accurately the results of your adjustment. The Tabs palette also tracks the numerical position of the tab stop – with respect to the left edge of the text block – just below title bar.
- ❑ When you create a new tab stop, all default tab stops (those little Ts) to the left of the new stop disappear. The default stops merely tell illustrator to space tabbed text every half inch.
- ❑ A question mark in the tab ruler means that at least one line of selected text does not align to that tab stop. Just click the tab stop to make all selected lines align.
- ❑ Select the Snap check box to align new and moved tab stops to the nearest increment on the ruler.
- ❑ To change the identity of a tab stop, select the tab stop by clicking on it, then select a different identity from the four buttons on the left side of the palette. From left to right, these buttons make tabbed text align with the left side, center, right side or decimal point.
- ❑ To delete a tab stop, drag it upward, off the tab strip and out of the palette. The X: item reads *delete*. To delete ail tab stops, Shift-drag upward on the leftmost tab stop in the ruler.
- ❑ You can also cycle through the units of measurement by pressing Ctrl-Shift-U.

The Text Eyedropper and Paint Bucket

Illustrator gives you a easy way to sample the text attributes from one set of text and then apply it to another. You do it by using the eyedropper and paint bucket tools. There are three parts to using these tools.

— The first part is to sample the text attributes using the eyedropper.

— The second is to apply the attributes using the paint bucket.

— The final part is to set which text attributes the tools should copy and apply.

Sucking up Attributes with the Eyedropper

To sample text attributes with the eyedropper tool, choose the eyedropper tool. Position the tool over the text that you want to sample. When a small T appears next to the eyedropper cursor, you know that the eyedropper is in the text mode.

Click or drag the eyedropper over the text that you want to sample. A click sucks up the text attributes exactly under the cursor. A drag samples the attributes from the text where the mouse button is released at the end of the drag. If you drag with the eyedropper, the tip of the eyedropper cursor turns black to show that the attributes are being sampled.

Next figure shows the text after and before using the eyedropper key.

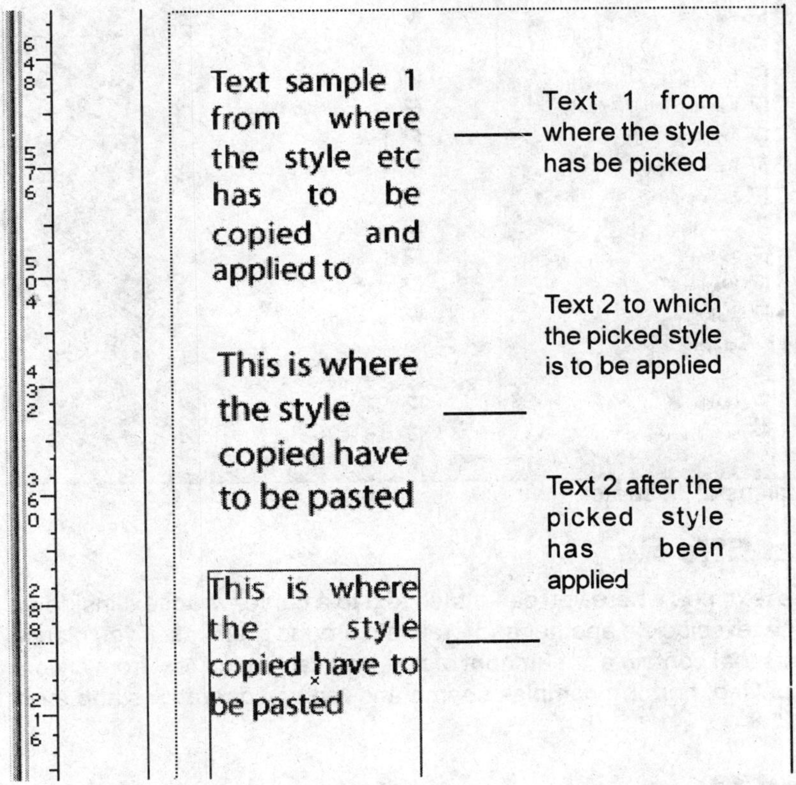

Pouring out Attributes with Paint Bucket

To apply text attributes, you can choose the paint bucket tool from the alternate eyedropper slot in toolbox. However, because, you most likely already have the eyedropper tool selected, simply hold the Alt key. This toggles between the eyedropper and paint bucket. Position the paint bucket over the text that you want to change. Look for the small T next to the cursor; this tells you that the paint bucket is in the text mode. Unlike the eyedropper, there is a real difference between clicking and dragging with the paint bucket. If you simply click with the paint bucket, you apply the text attributes to all the text in the text object.

However, you may want to apply text attributes to specific areas of a text object. To do that, you need to drag with the paint bucket tool across the text. As you drag, a box appears around the characters that are chosen. When you release the mouse button, those characters will be changed. If you don't see the T next to the paint bucket cursor, then the paint bucket will apply only the fill and stroke attributes of the text that has been sampled.

Configuring Eyedropper and Paint Bucket

By default, the eyedropper and paint bucket will sample and apply all the character and paragraph attributes of the text. However, you can configure the tools so that they sample and only certain attributes. For instance, you can set the tools so they sample and apply only character attributes, but not the paragraph ones.

To configure the tools, double-click either the eyedropper or the paint bucket in the toolbox. The Eyedropper/Paint Bucket Options dialog box appears as shown below. Use the check boxes to choose which attributes you want each tool to recognize. The settings for the eyedropper and point bucket remain in effect for new documents and new sessions of Illustrator.

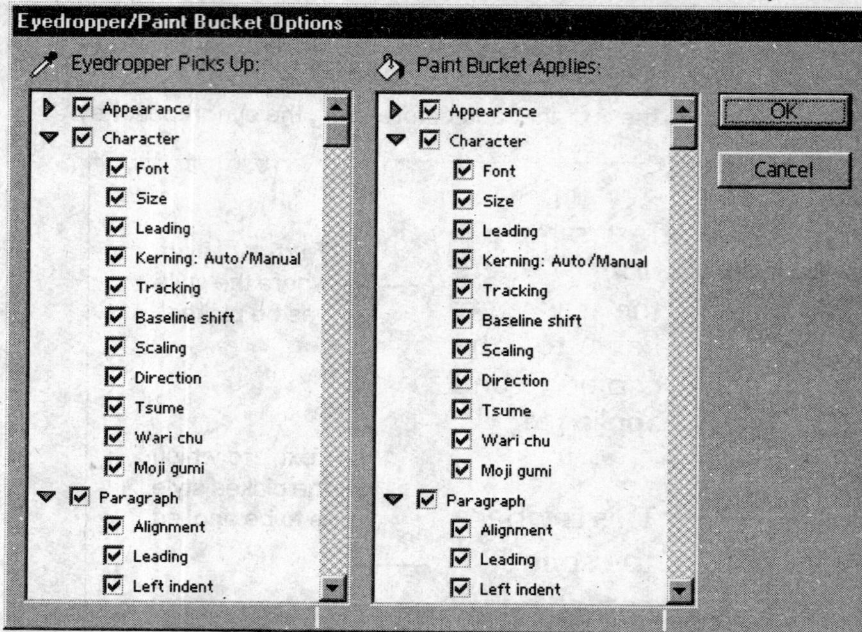

Creating Various Text Effects

Now we come to other part of the text, i.e., where you can attach text to a curve, wrap text inside an irregular outline, flow text from one text block to another and wrap text around graphics. If you plan to use Illustrator to create documents that contain a fair amount of text, you can import text from a word processor and then check the spelling, perform complex search and replace operations and even export the text back out to disk.

Merging Text with Curve

Illustrator lets you bind a line of text to a free-form path. To create type along the outline of a path, follow these simple steps:

1. **Draw a path** Curved paths work better than those with sharp corners, so you'll probably want to avoid corner points and cusps and stick with smooth points. Ellipses, spirals, and softly sloping paths work best. Grab the smooth tool if you need to smooth out a path.
2. **Select the path type tool** To get the path type tool, drag from the type tool in he toolbox to display a pop-up menu. The path type tool looks like a T on a slanted line.
3. **Click the path and start typing** The point at which you click determines the position of the blinking insertion marker. As you enter text from the keyboard, the characters follow the contours of the path. If your text appears on the underside of the path or if no text appears

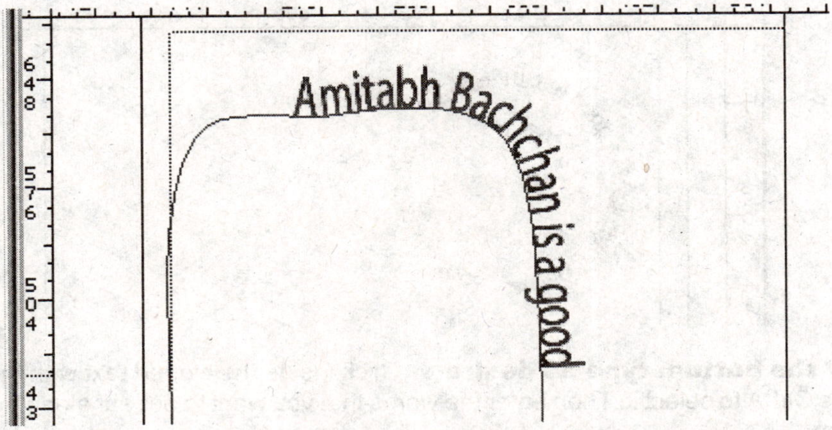

and all you see is a plus sing inside a little box, your need to flip the text to the other side of the path. Select the arrow tool and double-click the alignment handle, which looks like and I-beam attached to the path. Then select the type tool and click the path to continue adding text.

4. **Complete the path text** When you finish entering text, select another tool in the toolbox to finish the text object. The path text appears selected.

Shifting Type in Relation to Its Path

Illustrator lets you raise and lower type with respect to its path using baseline shift. The baseline of path text is the path itself so moving type away from the baseline likewise moves it away from the path. The following steps demonstrate why baseline shift is useful. They show you how to create text along the top and bottom halves of a circle – a job for baseline shift if there ever was one.

1. **Draw a circle** You know how to do it, shift-drag with the ellipse tool.
2. **Alt-click with the type tool at the top of the circle** Illustrator snaps the alignment handle to the top center of the shape.
3. **Enter the text you want to appear along the top of the path** Just enter the text which you want to, it can be just any text.
4. **Center the text** Press Ctrl-Shift-C or click the second icon in the Paragraph palette. As long as the alignment handle is positioned at the top of the shape, you can use Illustrator's alignment formatting functions to position text around the handle. It comes in handy when you want to get things exactly right.
5. **Format the text as desired** Press Ctrl-A to highlight the text. Then format at will. You may use any font or size, but on circle text looks good as Caps.
6. **Clone your text** This is the most important step and one of the trickiest to pull off. First select the path text with the arrow tool. Then drag the alignment handle around the path to the bottom of the circle. Without releasing – don't release till we say so – drag upward so the type flips to the other side of the path. Then drag down ever so carefully until your cursor snaps onto the bottom point in the circle. Finally, press the Alt key and release the mouse button. You can now release the alt key. A clone of the type moves and flips to the interior of a cloned circle.

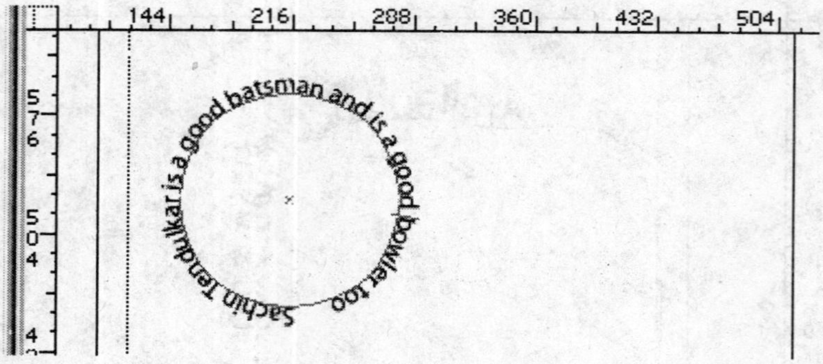

7. **Edit the bottom type as desired** Click inside the cloned text with the type tool and press Ctrl-A to select it. Then enter the words that you want to appear along the bottom of the circle.

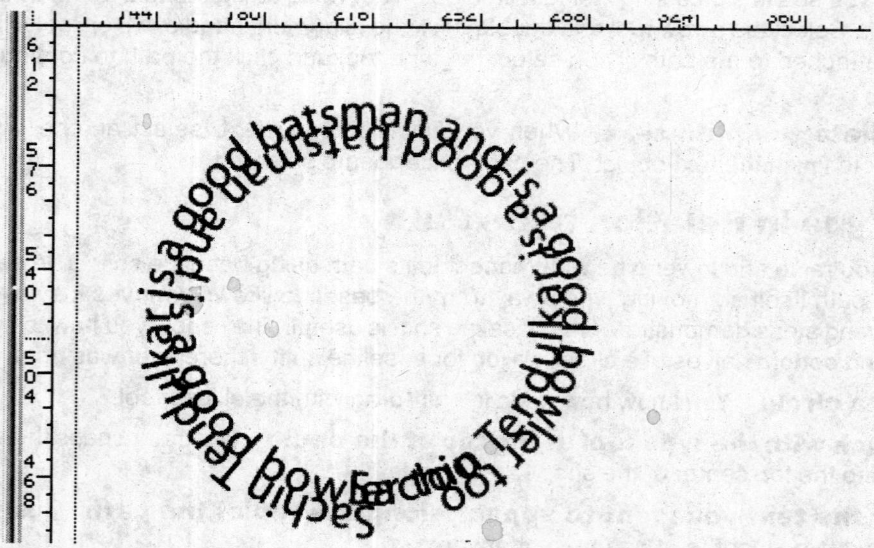

8. **Shift the bottom text downward** You've noticed that the upper and lower text blocks don't align properly. You need to move the lower text outward without flipping it. While the text is still active, press Ctrl-A to highlight the lower text block. Because you want to lower the type with respect to its path, press Alt-Shift-down arrow to move the type downward 2 points.
9. **Similarly lower the text along the top of the circle** Press Ctrl-Shift-A to deselect the text. Then click in the upper text block with the type tool and press Ctrl-A to highlight the first words you created. Press Alt-shift down arrow several times to lower the top text so it aligns with the bottom text.

Using Vertical Type

One of the other tool in the type tool is the one with vertical direction. When text is typed using this tool, you get the text typed vertically, as can be seen in the figure on the next page. See the type of text tool used in the toolbox. This is very useful for typing text which is used in the Chinese and Japanese typing, where the text appears from top to bottom.

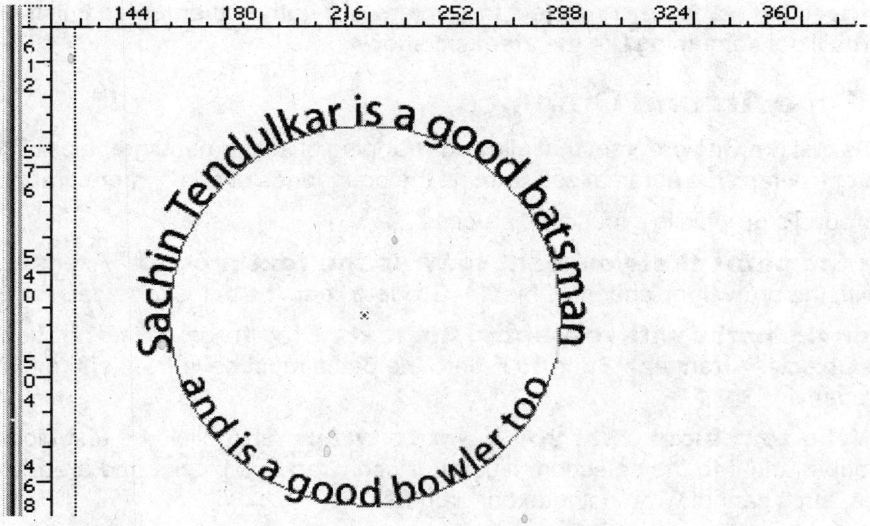

Taking out Alignment Handle

After you click a path with the type tool, Illustrator thinks you want to use the path to hold text for all time. Even if you delete all text from the path at some later date, the alignment handle will hang in there, showing you that this is still path text. Here's how to remove the alignment handie.

- ❑ Select the path by Alt-clicking it with the direct selection tool. Do not use the arrow tool.
- ❑ Press Ctrl-C or choose Edit>>Copy to copy the path to the Clipboard.
- ❑ Alt-click the path again. This selects the text and displays the alignment handle.
- ❑ Press the Delete key to destroy the path text for all time.
- ❑ Press Ctrl-F or choose Edit>>Paste In Front. The path is reborn on screen with no alignment handle. Stroke the path or fill it at will.

Wrapping Text to a Shape

You can create text inside polygons, stars or free-from shapes. You can even create text inside an open path if you want. To create type inside a path, do the following:

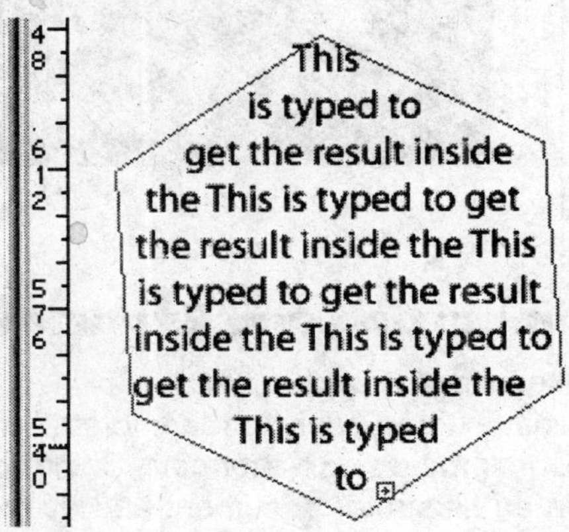

1. **Draw a path** Unlike path text, area text works just as well with corner points as with smooth points. But keep the corners abtuse – wide rather than sharp. It's very difficult and in many cases impossible, to fill sharp corners with text.
2. **Select the area type tool** Select the area type tool from the type tool pop-up menu in the tool box. The area type tool looks like a T trapped in Jell-O.
3. **Click along the outline of the path and enter some text** You must click the outline of the path; you can't click inside the path to add text. A blinking insertion marker appears at the top of the path. As you enter text, it fills the path. Words that would otherwise exceed the edge of the shape wrap to next line.

4. **Complete the path text** Select the type tool or some other tool to finish off the text block. You'll get something like the area text shown here.

Wrapping Type Around Graphics

Illustrator was the first drawing program that allowed wrapping of text around graphics. This feature instructs Illustrator to wrap type automatically around the boundaries of one or more graphic objects.

Wrapping text around a graphic is a four-step process.

1. **Select the paths that you want to wrap the text around** After selecting the paths with the arrow tool, choose Object>>Groupto keep the paths together.
2. **Position the paths with respect to the text** Drag the group into position and then choose Object>>Arrange>> Bring To Front. The paths must be in front of the text block to wrap properly.
3. **Select the text block that you want to wrap** Shift-click the text block with the arrow tool to add it to the selection. Illustrator can wrap text blocks and area text around graphics, but it cannot wrap point text or path text.
4. **Wrap the text** Choose Type>>Wrap>>Make and Illustrator wraps the text around the graphics and fuses text and paths into a single wrapped object.

Importing and Exporting Text

Despite Illustrator's text capabilities, you should find it easier to use a word processing program to edit text and apply formatting attributes. You can also export text from Illustrator into these same word processing file formats. Doing so allows you to recover and work with text that has been laid out in an Illustrator document and even lets you transfer text that has been laid out in an Illustrator document and even lets you transfer it to a mightier layout program such as QuarkXPress.

When importing a text file, Illustrator reads the file from disk and copies it to the illustration window. As this copy is being made, the text file passes through a filter that converts the file's formatting commands into formatting commands recognised by Illustrator. Illustrator lets you import text in the following formats.

- ❑ Microsoft Word 6, 95, 97, 98, 2000
- ❑ RTF (Rich Text Format), Microsoft's coded file format.
- ❑ Plain text with no formatting Whatsoever, also known as with no formatting whatsoever, also known as ASCII.

The following list describes how Illustrator handles a few prevailing formatting attributes an offers a few suggestions for preparing each:

- ❑ **Typeface** If Illustrator can't fine the typeface in your system – if the document was created on another machine, for example – it substitutes the default font, Myriad.
- ❑ **Type style** Illustrator does not apply electronic styles the way word processors do. As a result, bold and italics styles convert successfully, but most others do not. If Illustrator comes across a style for which a stylized font does not exist – underline, outline, strikethrough, small caps and so on – the program simply ignores the style. The exceptions are superscript and subscript styles, which transfer intact thanks to Illustrator's baseline shift function.
- ❑ **Type size and leading** All text retains the same size and leading specified in the word processor. If you assign automatic leading or single spacing inside the word processor, Illustrator substitutes its own automatic leading, which is 120 percent of the type size.
- ❑ **Alignment** Illustrator recognizes paragraphs that are aligned left, center and right, as well as justified text.
- ❑ **Paragraph returns** Illustrator successfully reads paragraph return character (which you create by pressing the Enter key).
- ❑ **Indents** All paragraph indents, including first-line, left and right indents remain intact. (Hanging indents won't look quite right, because Illustrator doesn't import tab stops.) Adjusting the margins in your word processor may also affect indentation in Illustrator. To clear the indents, just click the individual Indent option names in Illustration Paragraph palette.
- ❑ **Paragraph spacing** Some word processors divide paragraph spacing into two categories: "before spacing," which precedes the paragraph, and "after spacing," which follows the paragraph. Illustrator combines them into the Leading before —value in the Paragraph palette, essentially retaining the same effect.
- ❑ **Tabs, tab stops and tab leaders** Illustrator imports tab characters successfully. But it ignores the placement of tab stops and tab leaders (such as dots and dashes) are a complete mystery to the program. Use the Tabs palette to reset the tab stops as desired.
- ❑ **Special characters** Many word processors provide access to special characters that are not part of the standard character set. These include em spaces, nonbreaking hyphens, automatic page numbers, date and time stamps and so on. Of these, only the discretionary hyphen character transfers successfully.
- ❑ **Page markings** Illustrator ignores page breaks in imported text as well as headers, footers and footnotes.

If you can't find a formatting option in this list, chances are Illustrator simply ignores it.

Spell Checking

Spell checkers are a must for most of the programs, in fact, that even Illustrator offers one. So can check the spelling of your text in the following manner.

1. **Choose Edit>>Check Spelling** Because Illustrator automatically checks the spelling of all text, hidden or visible, in your drawing, you don't have to select any text. Illustrator sets about revealing your mistakes. If Illustrator doesn't locate any words missing from its dictionary, it displays an egostroking message about your excellent spelling. If the program finds mistakes, it lists all mistakes throughout the entire document in the Misspelled Words list at the top of the Check Spelling dialog box, as shown on the next page.
2. **Select all words that are spelling properly** Scroll through the Misspelled Words list to see which words are truly misspelled and which words Illustrator is simply too inexperienced in the ways of the world to know. If a word is spelled to your satisfaction, you can either add it to Illustrator's dictionary or simply skip the word for the time being.
3. **Click the Add to List button** This adds the selected words to Illustrator's auxiliary dictionary, so that the program will never again bug you about the spelling. If you'd rather ignore the words for the time being, click the Skip button. Click Skip all to tell Illustrator to ignore all occurrences of these particular words.
4. **Select a word that's misspelled** To correct a word that is indeed misspelled, select it from the Misspelled Words list. Illustrator highlights the first occurrence of the word in the story and displays a few alternative spellings in the Suggested Corrections list.
5. **Select the proper spelling** If one of the alternative spellings in the Suggested Corrections list is correct, click it. If none of the spellings is correct, enter the new spellings in the option box below the list.
6. **Click the Change button** Or you can press the Enter key or double-click the proper

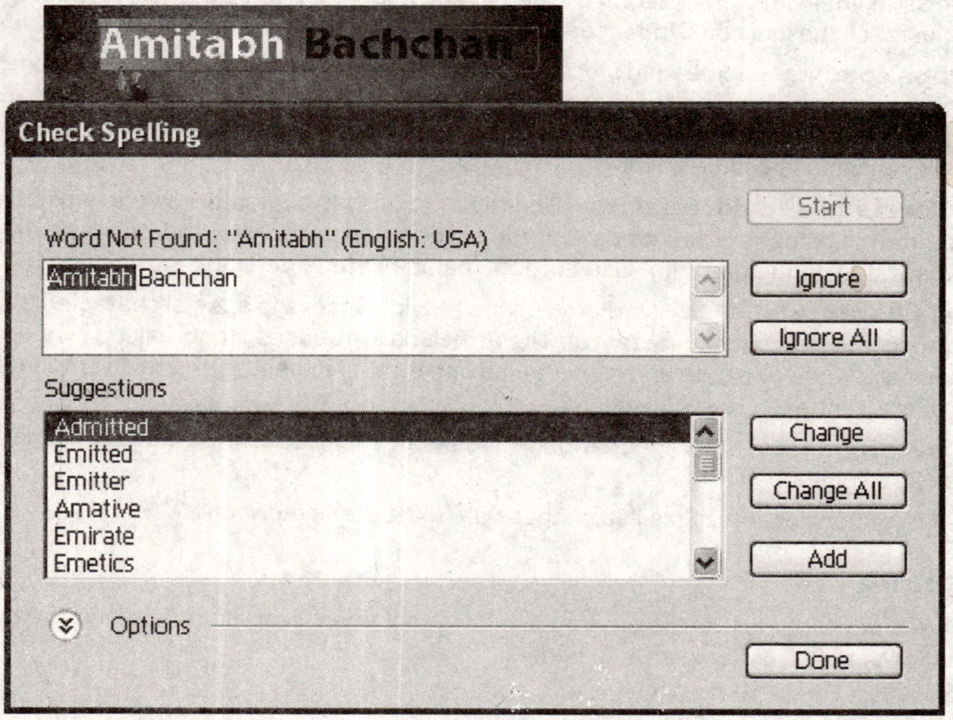

spelling in the Suggested Corrections list. If you know that many words are misspelled in the same say, click the Change All button to correct all misspellings at once. Illustrator corrects the spelling of the words in the illustration window and moves on to the next misspelled word.

7. **End the spell checking** After you tell Illustrator to either add, skip or change every word in the Misspelled Words list, an alert box tells you it's finished. If you want to cut things off early, click the Done button, press the Escape key, or press Ctrl-(Period).

Search and Replace

Another of word processing strong point is search and replace. It is available in Illustrator too. As you know it is used to find a particular word in the text and if required, replaced with another word. This is how it is done.

1. **Click with the type tool on the location where you want to begin the search** If you have selected the arrow tool, for example, Illustrator searches all stores throughout the entire drawing, from beginning to end. But if you want to limit your search to a specific area of a story, click in the story with the type tool. By default, Illustrator searches forward from the insertion marker' it does not search the text before the insertion marker. You can reserve the direction of the search by selecting the Search Backward check box.
2. **Choose Type>>Find/Change** Illustrator brings up the Find/change dialog box, as shown on the next page.
3. **Enter the text you want to find and the text you want to replace it with** Enter the search text in the Find What option box, press Tab and then enter the replacement text in the Change to option box. If you don't want to replace the text – you're just trying to find it – don't enter anything in the Change To option box.
4. **Click the Find Next button** Or press Enter. Illustrator highlights the first occurrence of the word in the illustration window.
5. **Replace the word and move on** Click the Change button to replace the selected text. Or click the Change/Find button to replace the text and then look for the next occurrence of the Find What text. Or click Change All to replace all Find What text with the contents of the Change To option box.

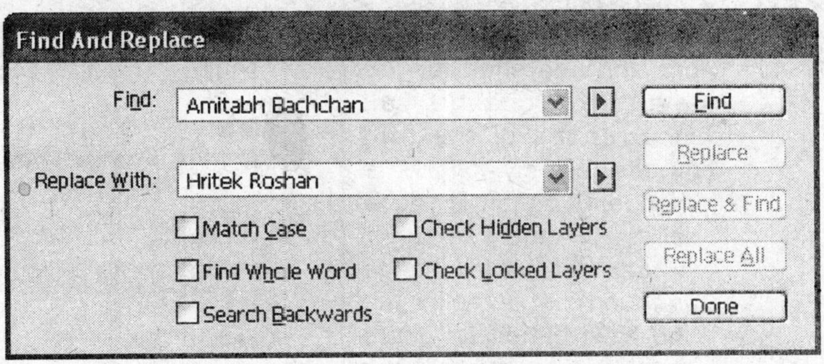

6. **When you're finished, click the Done button** Or press Ctrl-(period) or Esc.

You can modify your search by turning on and off the check boxes in the middle of the dialog box:

- ❑ **Whole Word** When you check this option, you limit the search to whole words that exactly match the Find What text. With this option unchecked, for example, searching for *and* would cause Illustrator to find the characters inside *grand* and *bland*. With Whole Word checked, the word *and* must appear by itself.
- ❑ **Case Sensitive** Select this check box to search for characters that exactly match the

uppercase and lowercase characters in the Find What text. Searching for And would find neither and nor AND when this option is selected.

- ❑ **Search Backward** This option begins the search at the insertion marker and proceeds backward toward the beginning of the story.
- ❑ **Wrap Around** To search the entire illustration, no matter where the insertion marker is currently located, select Wrap Around. This option begins the search at the insertion marker and proceeds to the end of the story, starts over at the next story, starts again at the beginning of the first story and winds up back at the insertion marker.

Replacing Fonts

You can press the Type>>Find Font key combination to launch another of Illustrator's amazing search functions. This time, instead of replacing words, Illustrator lets you search for one font and replace it with another. For this do the following:

1. **Choose Type>>Find Font** In response, the Find Font dialog box comes on screen, as shown on the next page.
2. **Select the font that you want to remove from the Fonts in Document list** Illustrator highlights each occurrence of the font in the illustration window.
3. **Select the substitute font from the Replace Font From list** Initially, this list contains only the names of those fonts that are used in the current illustration. If you want to choose from a wider variety of fonts, select the System command from the Replace Font From pop-up menu, which instructs Illustrator to list every font loaded on your system. You can pause the font listing by clicking anywhere on an empty portion of the dialog box. To start the listing again, turn on and off one of the check boxes at the bottom of the dialog box.
4. **Click Change or one of the other buttons** The Change button replaces the first occurrence of the bad font and searches for the next. To change all occurrences of the font simultaneously, click the Change All button. If you're feeling a little more selective, you can opt not to change the found font and click the Find Next button to ignore that occurrence of a font and move on to the next. The Skip button performs the exact same function as the Find Next button.
5. **Click the Done button when you're finished** Or press Return, Escape or Ctrl-. (period).

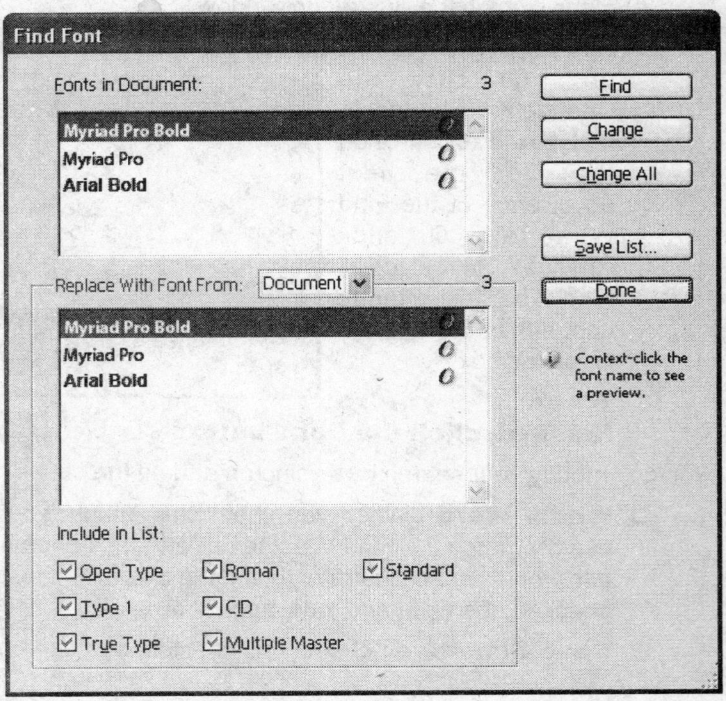

4 More Commands of Illustrator CS 4

Working with Lines and Brushes

Strokes are like lines but are different from lines. The main difference being that a line cannot be filled whereas the stroke can be. There are six basic attribute that can be applied to strokes in Illustrator. Five are controlled by the Stroke palette shown inhere. There are weight, bevels, caps, joins; and dashes. The sixth attribute – color – is applied from the Toolbox or the Color palette.

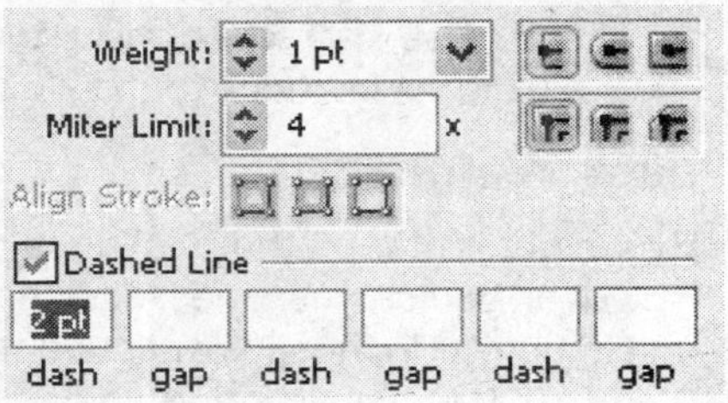

Stroking Type and Text Paths

Strokes are applied to objects differently depending on how the type is selected:

- If you select a text object with the arrow tool, applying a stroke affects all the type along the path.
- If you select the path with the direct selection tool, you can apply a stroke to the path only, leaving the text as is.
- Select text with the type tool to stroke single characters or words. In this case, the stroke is just another character-level attribute that affects the selected characters.

Applying Stroke from the Stroke Palette

The following steps explain how to use the options in the Toolbox an stroke palette to apply a stroke to a selected path or text object:

1. **Select the objects that you want to stroke.** If no object is selected, editing the stroke changes the setting for the next object that you create.
2. **Click the Stroke icon in the Color palette or the toolbox** This moves the Stroke icon to the front and makes the stroke the active feature. When the stroke is active, the Stroke icon overlaps the Fill icon.
3. **Choose a paint style** To color a stroke, choose a color from the Color palette. To remove the stroke, click the None icon or press the slash key (/) on the keyboard.
4. **If desired, apply a tint from the Color palette** Use either the Swatches palette or the Color palette. You can also drag a swatch from the swatch list in the Swatches palette and drop it into the Stroke icon in the toolbox. The Stroke icon doesn't have to be selected.
5. **Change the Weight value** The Weight value determines the thickness of the stroke (also known as stroke weight).
6. **Click the icons to set the Cap and Join options** These option buttons appear in the upper-right corner of the Stroke palette. You use the Cap icons to determine how the

stroke wraps around the ends of an open path. You use the Join icons to control the appearance of the stroke at corner points. The Miter Limit option box appears to the left of the options only when the first Join icon is selected. Otherwise, the option box is dimmed.

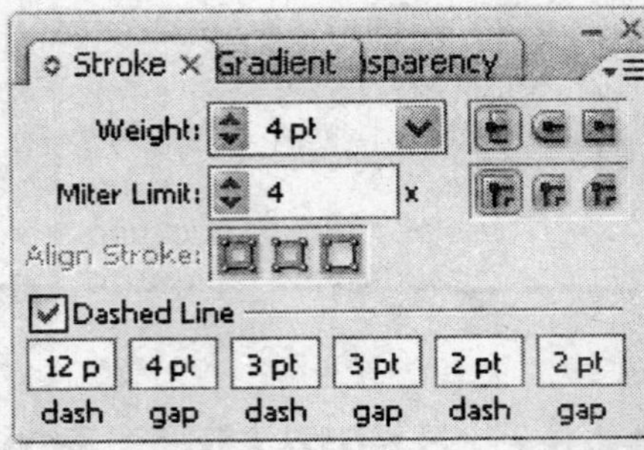

7. **Select the Dashed Line check box to create a dashed outline** The enter values into the Dash and Gap option boxes along the bottom of the dialog box to specify the length of each dash and each gap between dashes. (This option, too, will be explained just up ahead, good and trusting reader.) If you don't want dashed stroke, leave it unchecked.
8. **Press the Return/Enter key or click inside the illustration window** Illustrator returns its focus to the illustration window.

Line Weight

By weight it means the thickness of a stroke. Line weight is most commonly measured in points. However, you can use the Units and Undo section of the Preferences dialog box to set the line weight unit to points, inches, picas, centimetres, milimeters and pixels. You can enter nay number between 0 and 1000 (which is longer than a foot), accurate to 0.01 point. Lines of different weight are shown here.

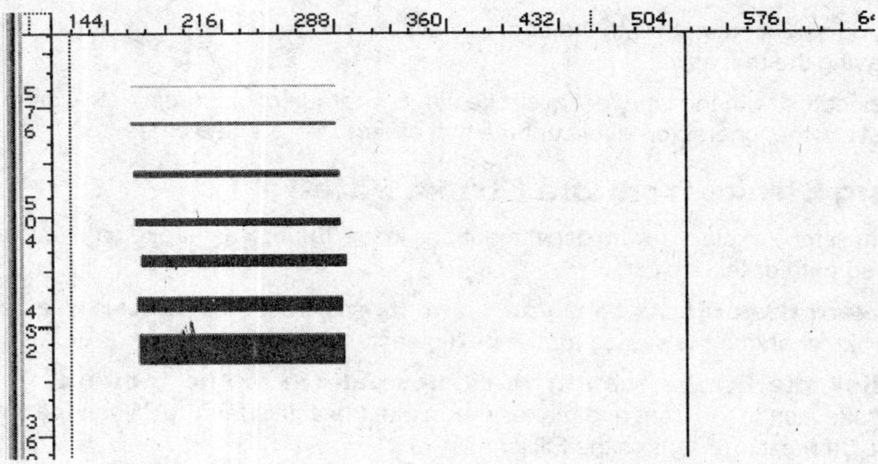

Line Caps

You can select from three types of line caps, which determine the appearance of a stroke at its endpoint. Line caps are generally useful only when you're stroking an open path. The only exception to this is when you use line caps in combination with dash patterns, in which case Illustrator applies the cap to each and every dash.

The three Cap icons in the Stroke palette works as follows:

Butt cap The first Cap icon is the butt cap option, the default setting and the most commonly used line cap. Notice the black line that runs through the center of each of the Cap icons. This indicates the position of the path reltive to the stroke. When the butt cap option is selected, the stroke ends immediately as an endpoint and is perpendicular to the final course of the path.

Round cap The second icon represents a round cap, which wraps the stroke around the path to circle the endpoint. The radius of the circle is half the line weight. If you have a 4-point line weight, for example, the round cap extends exactly 2 points out from the endpoint. Round caps are used to soften the appearance of a line. The line appears to taper, rather than abruptly end. We frequently apply round caps when using thick strokes.

Square cap Last and least is the square cap icon – Illustrator calls it the Projecting Cap. Here, a square is attached to the end of a line; the endpoint is the center of the square. Like the round cap, the square cap sticks out half the line weight from the endpoint. The only difference is that the square cap has very definite corners, making it appear to jut out more dramatically.

All 3 options are shown next.

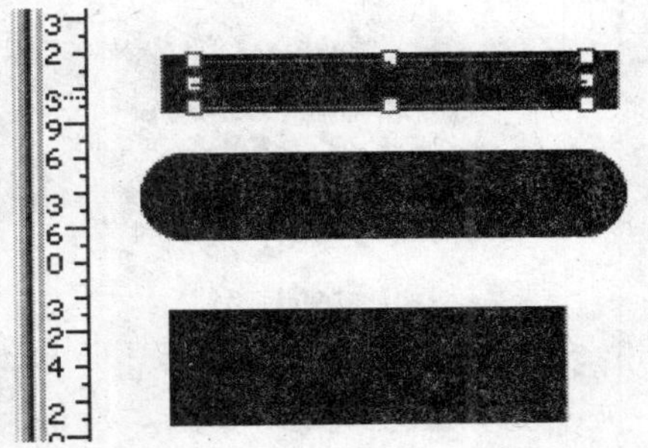

Use square caps when you want to close a gap. For example, if you want the stroke from an open path to meet with a point of another path, the square cap option gives a little overlap where the two point meet.

Line Joins

The Stroke palette offers three line joins, which determine the appearance of a stroke at the corner of a path. The stroke always form a continuous curve at each smooth point in a path, but you can use line joins. Compare its perfect spikes to the rounded and chopped off corners in the other stars.

Miter join The first Join icon represents a miter join, which is the defalut setting. If a corner has a miter join, the outside edges of the stroke extend all the way out until they meet to form a crisp corner. The first star is troked with miter joins.

Round join The second icon is the round join option, which is identical in principle to the round cap. Half of the line weight wraps around the corner point to form an arc. Round joins and round caps are so similar, in fact, that they are almost exclusively used together. The only time you should avoid using round joins is when a dash pattern is involved. Because round joins actually form complete circles around corner points, they can interrupt the flow of the dashes.

Bevel join: Use the third and last icon to apply a bevel join. Very similar to a butt cap, the bevel join shears the stroke off at the corner point. The bevel join creates a flat edge at each corner point. The length of this flat edge varies depending on the angle of the segments. A gradual angle results in a short bevel; a sharp angle results in a longer one.

Dash Patterns

To create a dash pattern, select the Dashed Line check box, which brings to life six previously dimmed option boxes. Each option box represents an interval, measured in points, during which the stroke is on or off over the course of the path. The Dash values determine the length of the gaps between the dashes. You don't have to fill all Dash and Gap options with values. In fact, most folks simply fill in the first pair of option boxes and leave the rest blank. Whatever you do, Illustrator repeats the values you enter and ignores the empty option boxes.

Next figure shows the line with various dashes.

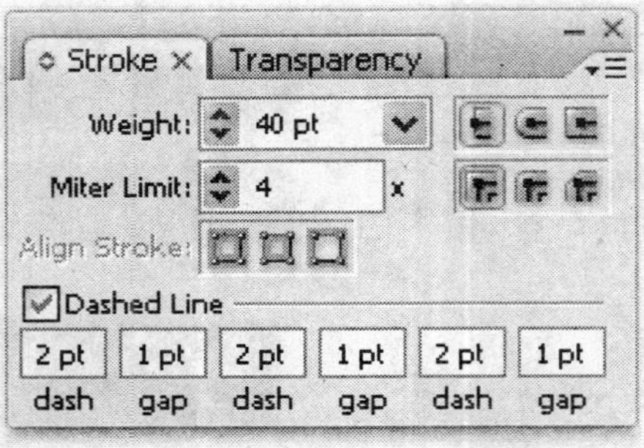

Using Brushes

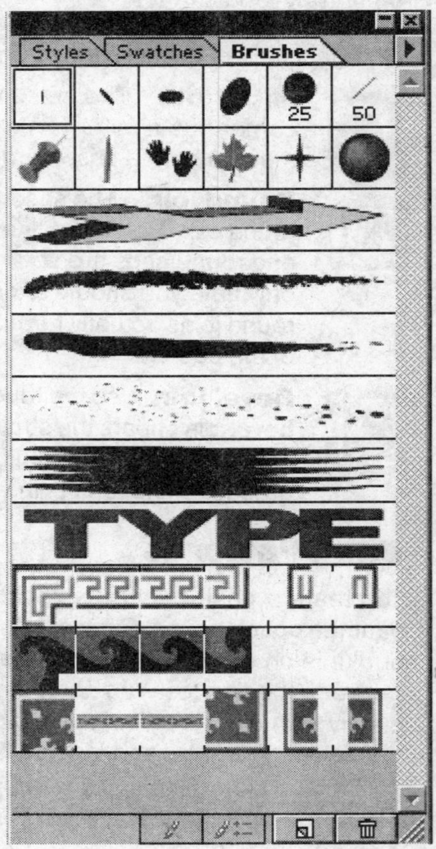

Brushes are special artwork that it applied to strokes that makes them look much more like traditional brush strokes. They are also used to apply artwork in repeating or scattered patterns along a path. There are four different types of brushes in Illustrator. By default, the Brushes palette contains a number of examples of each, as shown on a later page. You can use the paintbrush tool to draw with brushes.

Any path you create with the brush tool automatically adopts a brush stroke along its length. One of the great things about brushes is that they are not limited to the paths created with the brush tool. The fact is that you can apply a brush to any selected path. Simply select the path and click one of the Brushes palettes' entries. You can change the display of the Brushes palette using the palette menu. Choose View By Name to see the brushes listed with their names.

Choose each of the Show options to display or hide each of the types of brushes.

- **Calligraphic Brushes** A calligraphic brush simulates the lines created with a fountain pen. You have control over the roundness of the brush tip, the angle of the tip and its size. Although you can use a mouse when drawing with a calligraphic brush, they are ideal for pressure sensitive tablets. With such a tablet, you can vary all three of the brush's attributes as a function of how hard you press with the tablet's stylus.

- **Scatter Brushes** A scatter brush takes a single object or a group of objects and repeats them a number of times along the length of the path. You can control the size of the objects, the spacing (or the distance between the objects along the path), the scattering (or the distance the objects stray to the side of the paths) and the rotation of the objects. You can also vary the appearance of scatter brushes using a pressure sensitive tablet.
- **Art Brushes** An art brush takes a single drawing and stretches it the length of the path. You can decide in which direction the brush will flip across the path. Art brushes can be used to simulate the look of natural paintbrushes or to curve artwork such as arrows and type along a path.
- **Pattern Brushes** A pattern brush is a compilation of individual blocks that link together to form a continuous chain. They are ideal for borders because you can specify the design of both the beginning and the end of the path, the appearance of the inner and outer corners and all the parts that make up all the pieces in between.

Creating and Applying Brushes

To design a new brush, you need to assemble all its components and choose New Brush from the Brushes palette's pop-up menu (or you can click the New Brush icon at the bottom of the Brushes palette). Illustrator then gives you the option of creating any one of the four types of brushes. A candidate for a new art brush cannot contain gradients, live blends, rasterized objects, other brushes or unconverted type. You can, however, use regular old paths with flat fills and strokes or objects with transparency settings. These paths can't be masked.

The best rule of thumb when creating brushes is to keep it simple. Although most of the brushes features are not new, using transparency with brushes is new. It allows you to create a more natural look such as watercolors, where paint form one stroke builds up as it crosses another stroke builds up as it crosses another stroke.

- Brushes created in a document are stored only in that document.
- Illustrator installs other brushes that you can access via Window >>Brush Libraries and then choose the brushes from the sub-menu.
- There are hundreds of other brushes on the Illustrator CD under Illustrator Extras: Brush Libraries.
- You can import the brushes from one document to another via Window >> Brush Libraries >> Other Libraries. You can then choose the document that you want to import the brushes from. The brushes appear in a palette where you can select the brushes.

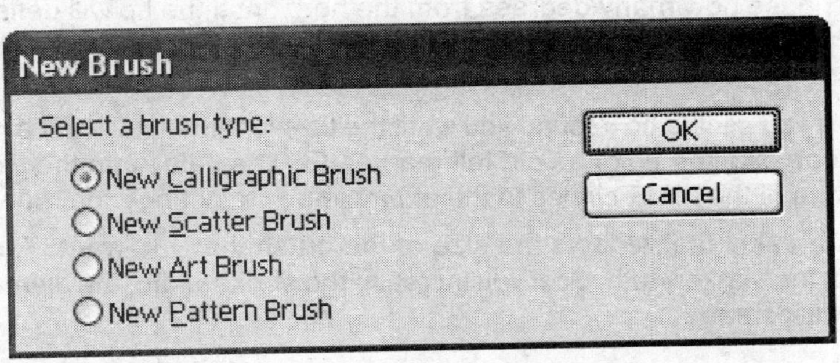

- ❑ Choose Persistent from the palette menu of an imported brush library to have it always open when Illustrator is launched.
- ❑ You can apply an brush to any selected object by clicking the brush in the Brushes palette.
- ❑ You can draw interactively with a brush by choosing the Paintbrush tool and then selecting a brush.
- ❑ Choose view by Name to list the brushes with their names in the Brushes palette.
- ❑ Like pattern swatches, you can drag the scatter, art and pattern brush objects out of the Brushes palette. The artwork used to create the brush, together with a bounding box, appears on your page.

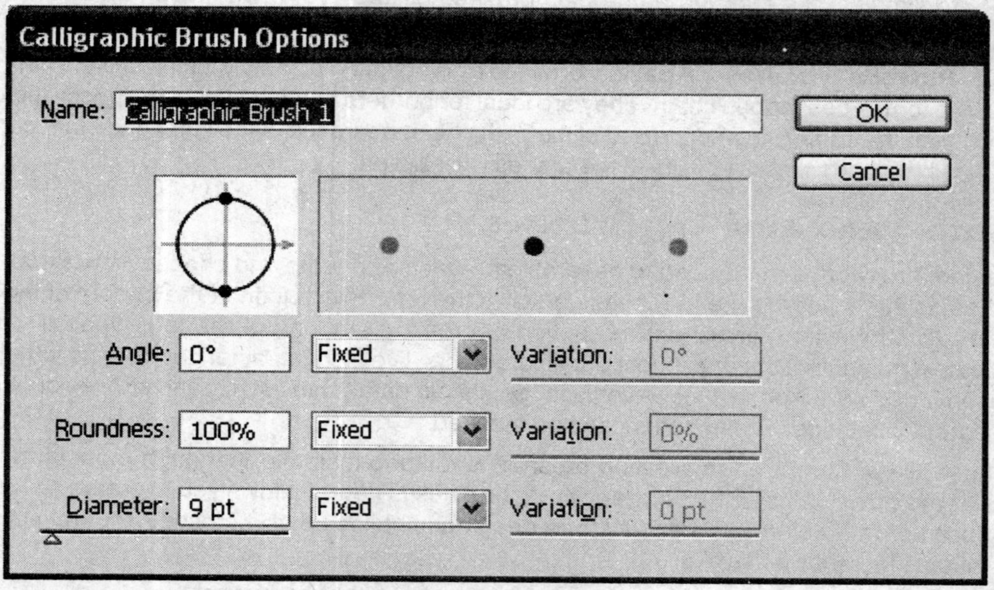

Defining Calligraphic Brushes

The calligraphic brush is the only brush that doesn't require you to create the artwork for the brush before you design the brush options. Choose New Brush from the Brush palette's pop-up menu and choose New Calligraphic Brush from the New Brush dialog box, as shown on the next page.

Various options of the dialog box are:

1. **Name** The name you apply to the brush is visible if you place your cursor over the brush or if you choose View by Name from the Brushes palette menu.
2. **Angle** You can choose how many degrees from the horizontal the tip will deflect. Either enter a value into the Angle option box or drag the arrow in the example box to change the angle.
3. **Roundness** Here you decide how round you want the tip—whether you want a nice round tip or more oblong one, like the tip of an old felt marker. Enter a value into the Roundness dialog box or drag one of the black circles in the example box to change the roundness.
4. **Diameter** Enter a value that reflects the size of the brush that you want. The value is relative to the size of the stroke width. So if you increase the stroke width, the diameter of the calligraphic brush will increase.

All the options except name, come with a pop-up list that gives you control over how Illustrator will apply the options.

1. **Fixed** This means that the attribute will always use the same value. If you use a pressure-sensitive drawing tablet, any changes in the pressure will be ignored.
2. **Random** The is means that Illustrator will vary the value as you apply the brush. A second slider bar to the right of the pop-up menu will appear. Here you decide the amount that the original value can vary.
3. **Pressure** If you use a pressure-sensitive drawing tablet, you can opt to have Illustrator take this into account. When selected, a second slider bar will activate to the right of the pop-up menu. With it you decide how much more or less the original value will vary to reflect the pressure you apply to the tablet.

Creating Scatter Brushes

For a new scatter brush, you first need to design the objects you want to have scattered on either side of the path. With your artwork selected, click the New Brush icon from the Brushes palette and select the New Scatter brush. The Scatter Brush Options dialog box appears as shown on the next page.

This dialog box has the following options.

1. **Name** The name you apply to the brush is visible if you place your cursor over the brush or if you choose View by Name from the Brushes palette menu.
2. **Size** Enter any value of 1 percent or greater. This controls the size of the brush in relation to the original object that was used to define the brush. 100 percent keeps the same size as the original. Anything less makes smaller objects. However, you can also control the size of the scatter brush by increasing or decreasing the stroke width applied to the scatter brush.
3. **Spacing** Here you choose how far apart you want the objects to space themselves along the path. Enter any value of 1 percent or greater. The smaller the value the more tightly the objects will be spaced.
4. **Scatter** This is the distance that the objects will appear above and below the path. A value of 0 percent positions the objects directly on the path. Enter any value between plus or minus 1000 percent. Positive values position the objects above the path. Negative values position the objects below the path. If you want the objects on both sides of the path, use the Random or Pressure setting and then enter both plus and minus values. This sets a range for the scatter on either side of the path. Keep these values small if you want to stress the shape of the path.
5. **Rotation** The scatter brush objects can rotate as they appear along the path. Also you decide whether the objects will rotate relative to the page or the path.
6. **Fixed, Random, Pressure** All of these options come with the same pop-up menus as occur in the options for the New Calligraphic Brush. You can choose to have the scatter objects appear uniformly along the path or vary them, either randomly or as dictated by the pressure you apply to your drawing table.
7. **Colorization** The Colorization settings allow you to set how the scatter brush responds to changes in the stroke color.

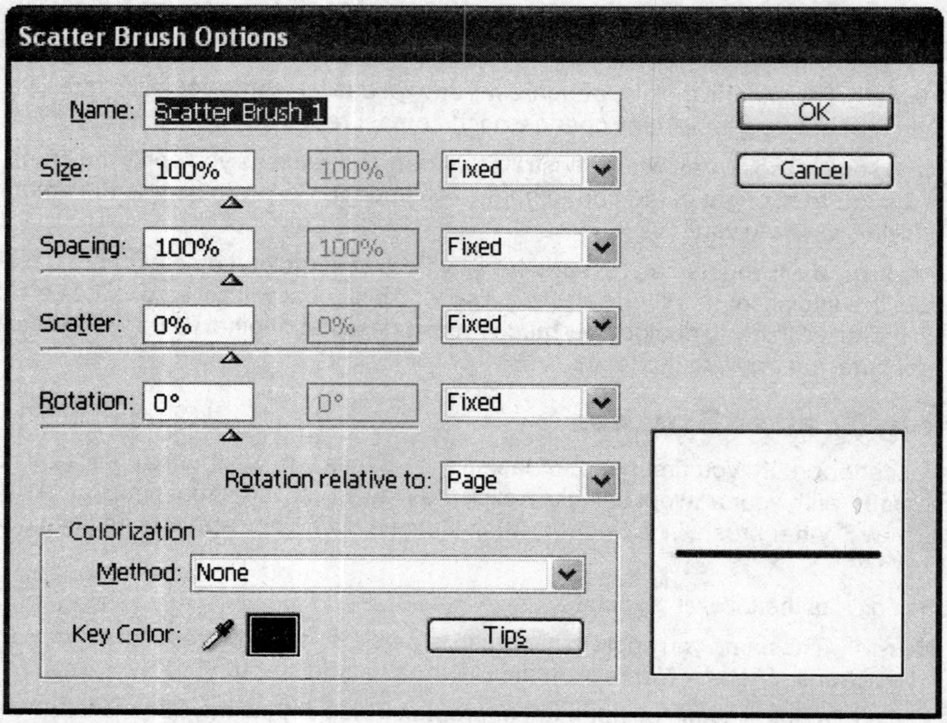

Defining Art Brushes

Once again, you need to design the brush first. Because the object will be stretched along the path, you can design the brush with a front and a back.

Select the design and then click the New Brush icon at the bottom of the Brushes palette. Then select the Art Brush option. The Art Brush Options dialog box appears, as shown on here.

Various options of the dialog box are:

1. **Name** The name you apply to the brush is visible if you place your cursor over the brush or if you choose View by Name from the Brushes palette menu.
2. **Direction** This determines the direction that the artwork will lie with respect to the path and the direction in which it was drawn. If you have long objects, you will most always want the direction to stretch from left to right or right to left. If you choose up to down or down to up, this will distort the object so that as that its width stretches along the path.
3. **Size** Enter a value to set the thickness of the brush. If you want to uniformly change the size, click the Proportional check box.
4. **Flip** You can choose to flip the object along the axis of the path or across its axis.

Creating Pattern Brushes

Pattern brushes are the most complex type or brush. The design elements for a pattern brush come from pattern swatches in the Swatches palette.

Once you have the patterns in the Swatches palette you can design the pattern brush by clicking the New Brush icon and then choosing the Pattern brush option.

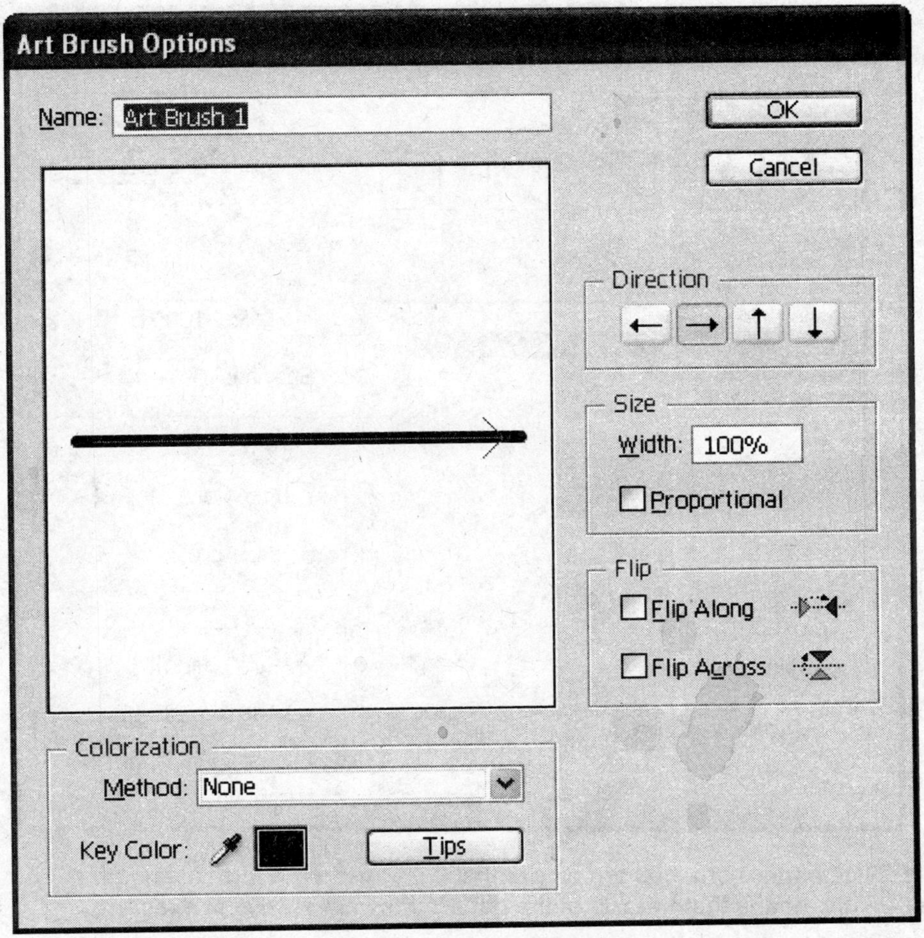

This opens the Pattern Brush Options dialog box as seen here.

Various options of the dialog box are:

1. **Tiles** There are given tile icons to a pattern brush. Click the tile icons to select which part of the path you want to apply the pattern to. The side tile runs along the path.

   The outer corner tile is applied to all left-hand turns for corner points along the path. The start tile is applied to the beginning of the path. The end tile is applied to the end of the path.

2. **Patterns** This patterns that are defined in the document are listed below the tiles. You can choose the name of the pattern, which is listed in the dialog box.

   The listing for Original uses the original swatches that were defined for the brush. This allows your pattern brush to contain tiles that may no longer be defined in the Swatches palette. None applies no tile for that part of the pattern brush.

3. **Size** Choose the thickness of the brush. If you want to uniformly change the size, click the Proportional check box.

4. **Flip** You can choose to flip the object along the axis of the path or across its axis.

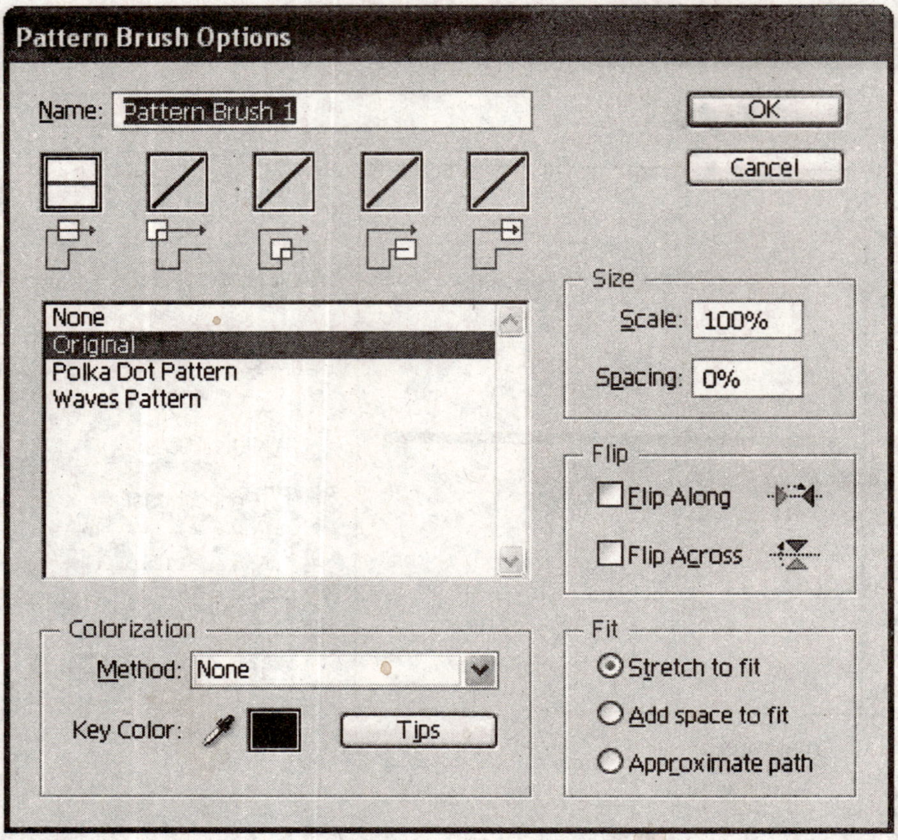

5. **Fit** The pattern brushes are blocks that link together to form a smooth pattern along the path. This means that the bits of the pattern may not always fit exactly.

You have three choice of how Illustrator will fit the brush to the path.

Stretch to Fit It will stretch the brush elements as needed to just fit the brush to the path. This means that Illustrator will need to distort the brush elements.

Use this option for most pattern brushes where you want to keep a seamless transition between tiles.

Add Space to Fit It means that Illustrator will add tiny spaces to the brush as necessary. If won't distort any brush elements, but it may give a disjointed appearance to your path.

Use this option for pattern brushes such as weather isobars that should not be distorted.

Approximate Path It is only appropriate for patterns applied as borders for rectangles. This option lets Illustrator move the pattern from the center of the path to the outside or inside so that it can better fit the tiles to shape of the path.

Drawing Line and Arc Segments

Use the line and arc segment tools to quickly and easily create individual lines and arcs by dragging. The Line and Arc Segment dialog boxes display the values of the last segment created. You can reset to the default values in the dialog box by pressing Alt and clicking Reset.

To draw a line segment:

Select the line segment tool, click where you want the line to begin, and drag to where you want the line to end.

As you drag, do any of the following:

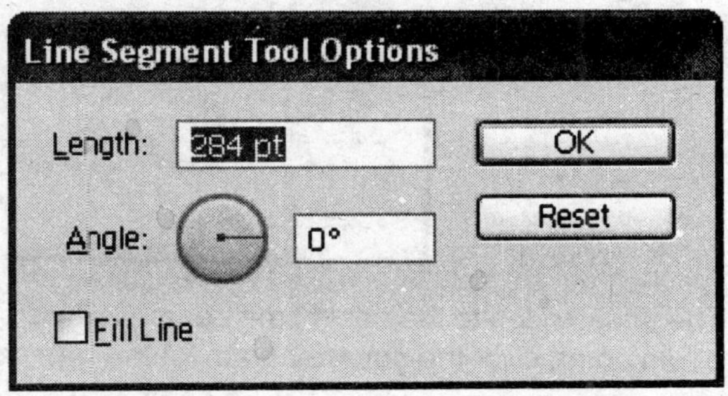

1. Press Alt to extend the line from both sides of the origin point.
2. Press the spacebar to move the line as you draw.
3. Press '(grave accent) to create multiple line segments as you move the mouse.
4. Press ~ (tilde) to constrain multiple lines to 45° angles.
5. Press Shift to constrain a single line to 45°.

To draw a line segment by specifying properties:

1. Select the line segment tool, and click where you want to place the segment.
2. In the Line Segment dialog box, enter the length and angle you want.
3. Select Fill Line if you want the line to use the current fill color (otherwise the fill is set to none).
4. Click OK.

To draw an arc segment:

Select the arc segment tool , click where you want the arc to begin, and drag to create an arc.

As you drag, do any of the following:

1. Press Alt to extend the arc from both sides of the origin point.
2. Press the spacebar to move the arc as you draw.
3. Press '(grave accent) to create multiple arc segments as you move the mouse.
4. Press C to switch between an open and closed arc.
5. Press F to flip the arc, keeping the origin point constant.
6. Press Up Arrow or Down Arrow to increase or decrease the arc's angle.

To draw an arc segment by specifying properties:

1. Select the arc segment tool, and click where you want to place the segment.
2. In the Arc Segment dialog box, enter the options you want.
3. Select Fill Line if you want the line to use the current fill color (otherwise the fill is set to none).
4. Click OK.

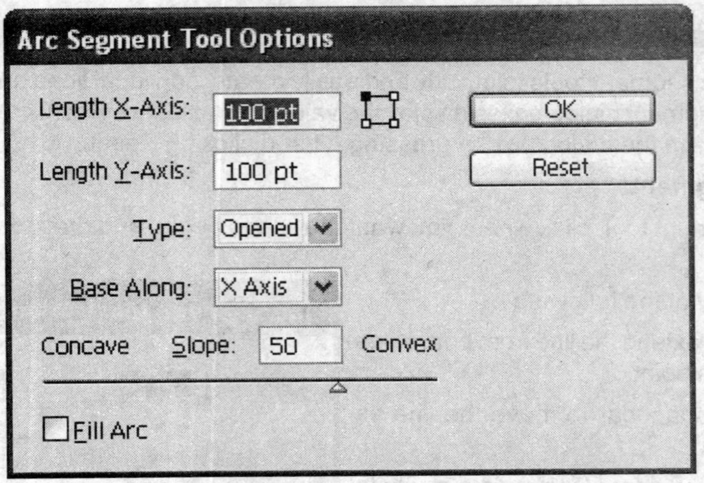

The square icon to the right of the Length X-Axis option sets the origin point for the arc. To change the origin point, click the square on any of the four corners.

Drawing Rectangular Grids

You can draw rectangular grids by dragging or by setting specific grid parameters in the Rectangular Grid Tool Options dialog box.

To Draw a Rectangular Grid:

Select the rectangular grid tool, and drag diagonally. As you drag, do any of the following:

1. Press Shift to constrain the grid to a square.
2. Press Alt to extend the grid from all sides of the origin point.
3. Press Shift + Alt to constrain the grid to a square as it extends from the origin point.
4. Press the spacebar to move the grid as you draw.
5. Hold down ~ (tilde) to create multiple grids.

To adjust the grid's dividers, do any of the following as you drag:

1. Press Up Arrow or Down Arrow to add or remove horizontal lines.
2. Press Right Arrow or Left Arrow to add or remove vertical lines.

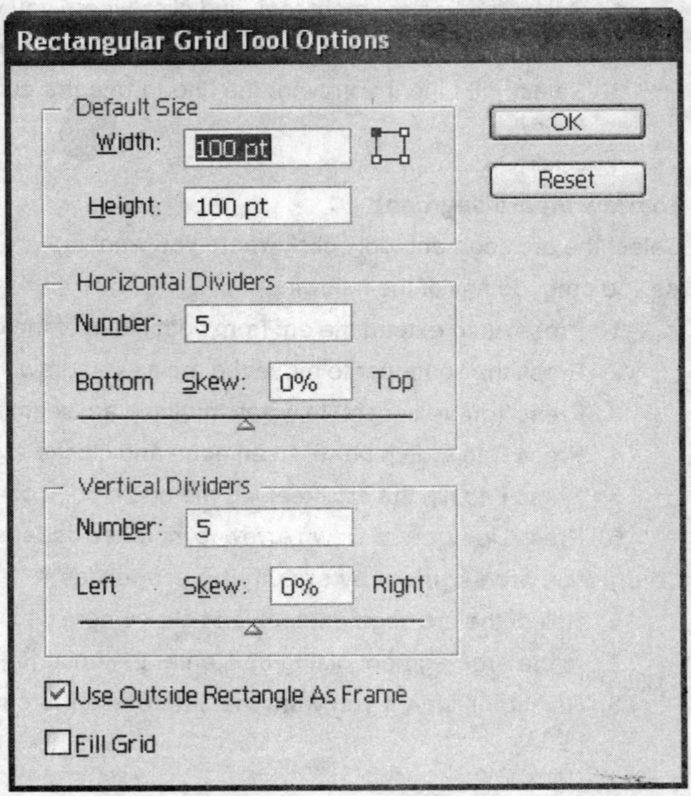

3. Press F to decrease the logarithmic skew value for the horizontal dividers by 10%.
4. Press V to increase the logarithmic skew value for the horizontal dividers by 10%.
5. Press X to decrease the logarithmic skew value for the vertical dividers by 10%.
6. Press C to increase the logarithmic skew value for the vertical dividers by 10%.

To create a rectangular grid by specifying properties:

Select the rectangular grid tool, and click in the artboard to set the grid's origin point and display the Rectangular Grid Tool Options dialog box. In the Rectangular Grid Tool Options dialog box, do any of the following and then click OK:

- For Default Size, enter Width and Height values for the entire grid. Then click a corner of the Origin Point icon to determine the point from where the grid is drawn.
- For Horizontal Dividers, enter the number of horizontal dividers you want to appear between the top and bottom of the grid. Then enter a Skew value to determine how the horizontal dividers are weighted to one side or the other.
- For Vertical Dividers, enter the number of dividers you want to appear between the left and right sides of the grid. Then enter a Skew value to determine how the vertical dividers are weighted toward the top or bottom of the grid.
- Select Use Outside Rectangle As A Frame to replace the top, bottom, left, and right segments with a separate rectangular object.
- Select Fill Grid to fill the grid with the current fill color (otherwise, the fill is set to none).

Drawing polar grids

You draw polar grids by dragging or by setting specific grid parameters in the Polar Grid Tool Options dialog box.

To Draw a Polar Grid:

Select the polar grid tool, and drag diagonally. As you drag, do any of the following:

1. Press Shift to constrain the grid to a circle.
2. Press Alt to extend the grid from all sides of the origin point.
3. Press Shift + Alt to constrain it to a circle as it extends from the origin point.
4. Press the spacebar to move the grid as you draw.
5. Hold down ~ (tilde) to create multiple polar grids.

To adjust the grid's dividers, do any of the following as you drag:

1. Press Up Arrow or Down Arrow to add or remove concentric circles.
2. Press Right Arrow or Left Arrow to add or remove radial lines.
3. Press X to change the logarithmic skew value for the concentric dividers inward by 10%.
4. Press C to change the logarithmic skew value for the concentric dividers outward by 10%.
5. Press F to change the logarithmic skew value for the radial dividers counterclockwise by 10%.
6. Press V to change the logarithmic skew value for the radial dividers clockwise by 10%.

To create a polar grid by specifying properties:

Select the polar grid tool, and click where you want to create the grid's origin point and open the Polar Grid Tool Options dialog box.

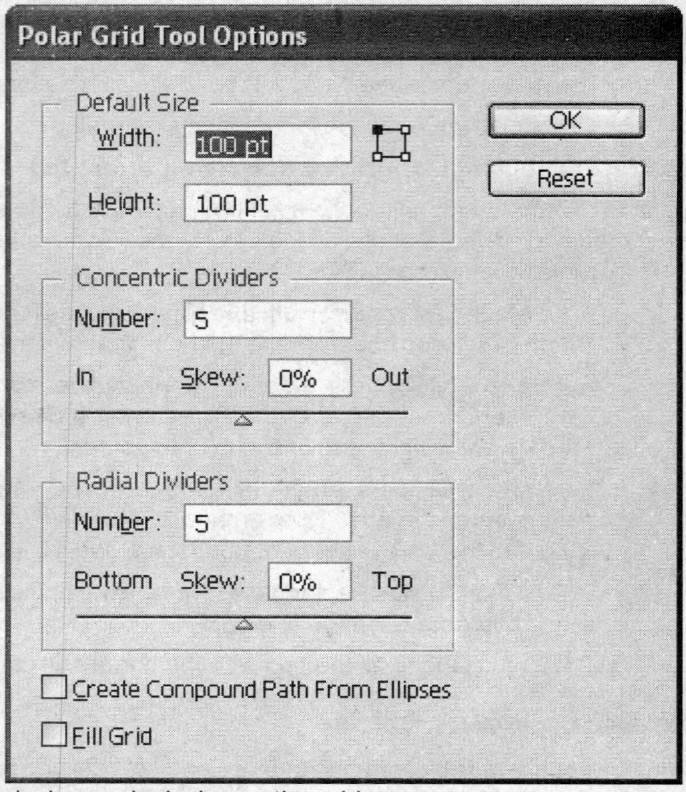

In the Polar Grid Tool Options dialog box, do any of the following and then click OK:

- For Default Size, enter Width and Height values for the entire grid. Then click a corner of the Origin Point icon to determine the point from where the grid is drawn.
- For Concentric Dividers, enter the number of circular concentric dividers you want to appear in the grid. Then enter a Skew value to determine how the concentric dividers are weighted toward the inside or outside of the grid.
- For Radial Dividers, enter the number of radial dividers you want to appear between the center and the circumference of the grid. Then enter a Skew value to determine how the radial dividers are weighted counterclockwise or clockwise on the grid.
- Select Create Compound Path From Ellipses to convert the concentric circles into a separate compound path and fill every other circle.
- Select Fill Grid to fill the grid with the current fill color (otherwise, the fill is set to none).

Transformations

Transactions allow you to change the shape of the objects. Illustrator has its own set of tools to do the same. Let us start with first one which is scale tool.

The Scale Tool

Select one or more objects in your drawing area and drag it with the scale tool. Illustrator enlarges or reduces the selection with respect to its center. If you drag away from the center of the selection, you enlarge the objects. If you drag toward the center, you reduce them. You can scale a selection with respect to any point in the illustration window. This origin point (also called a reference point or scale origin) represents the center of the transformation.

Scaling with the Shift Key

As you do when drawing and reshaping paths, you can use the Shift key to constrain a transformation. However, Illustrator actually has three different constrains for the Shift key:

- ❑ You can Shift-drag on a diagonal to scale a selection proportionally, so the height and width of a selected object are equally affected. Or you can scale the selection exclusively horizontally or vertically while pressing Shift.

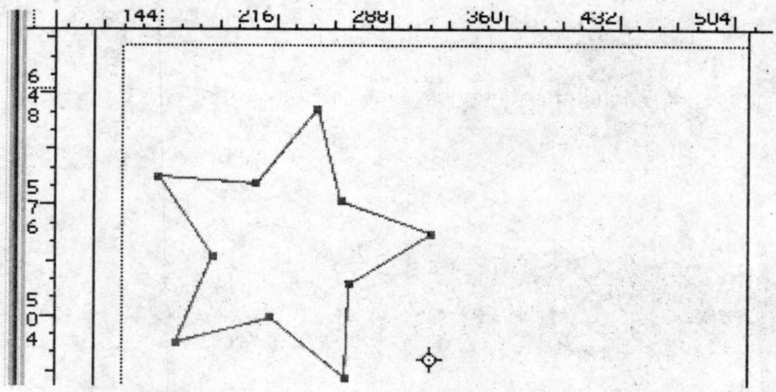

- Shift-drag to the left or right so that only the width of the object is affected. This is called a horizontal scale.

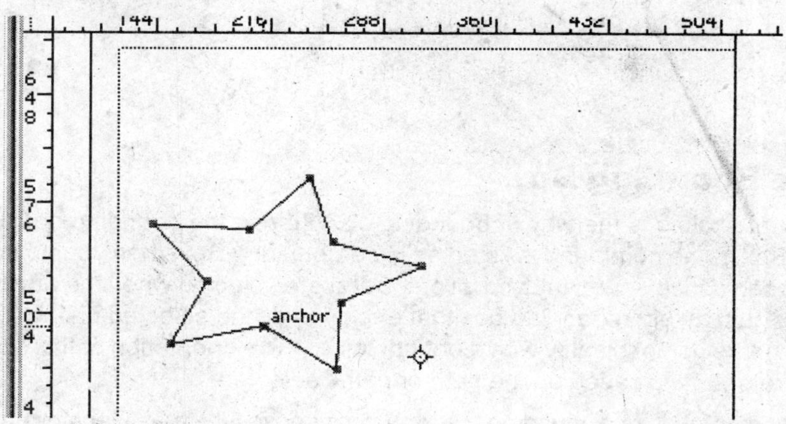

- Shift-drag up or down so that only the height of the object is affected. This is called a vertical scale.

If the shape seems to jump around a lot while you press the Shift key, it's because you began your drag in a bad place. Release and press Ctrl-Z to put things back where they were. Then start your drag in a diagonal direction from the origin.

Duplicating Objects as You Scale Them

The scale tool also lets you clone objects as you scale them. To scale a clone and leave the original unchanged, press the Alt key after you start the drag and keep the key pressed until after you release the mouse button. If you enlarge the selection, you may cover up the original with the clone, but the original will be there, lurking in the background. You can now create a series of scaled clones by choosing Transform Again. This is a particularly useful technique for creating perspective effects. By reducing a series of clones towards far-off origin, you create the effect of shapes slowly receding into the distance.

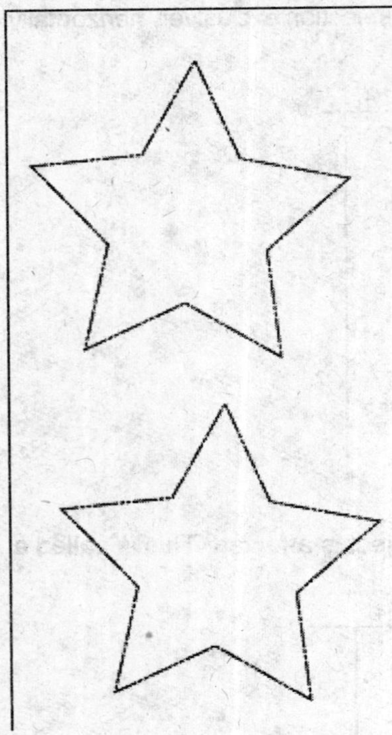

Scaling with the Bounding Box

Another very simple way of scaling is the way of bounding box. To use the bounding box, choose View>>Show Bounding Box. If the command is listed as Hide Bounding Box, then you do have the Bounding Box option chosen. Once done, any and all paths that are selected when the arrow tool is chosen will automatically gain an eight-handled box that enclosed all the selected paths – in other words, partially selected paths do not display with a bounding box. The orientation of this bounding box is initially up to Illustrator and is based on the path or paths selected.

If you don't like the default orientation of a bounding box, you can choose Object>>Transform>>Reset Bounding Box. When you select more than one path, the bounding box will usually align in such a way that it is square with the page. Anytime you want, you can reset the bounding box so that it is square with the page by choosing Object>>Transform>>Reset Bounding Box.

The real power of the bounding box is in its use:

- Drag on a corner handle to scale the selected objects. Shift-drag a corner handle to scale proportionally. In either case, the opposite corner serves as the scale origin.
- Alt-drag on a corner handle to scale the object around its center. Alt-Shift-drag a corner handle to scale proportionally around the object's center.
- Drag on one of the bounding box's side handles (including the top and bottom handles) to limit the scaling to either horizontal or vertical changes. The opposite side's handle serves as the scale origin.
- Shift-drag a side handle to once again scale proportionally, except that in this case the opposite side's handle serves as the scale origin.

- ❑ Alt-drag a side handle to horizontally or vertically scale the object from the center.
- ❑ Use Transform Again to repeat the transformation from the bounding box.

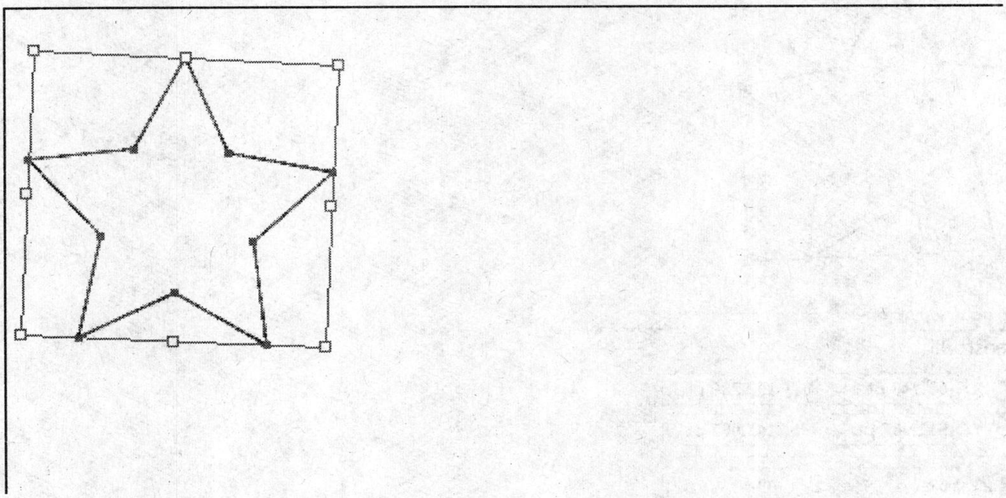

Resizing by the Numbers

The scale tool is one of our favourite tools, but it's not the only way to resize objects in Illustrator. You can also enlarge and reduce object sizes by entering precise numeric values into two different dialog boxes and one palette.

Scaling from the Transform Palette

Let's start with most convenient of the three scaling options, the Transform palette. Instead of a single Scale option box, you enter values in the W (for width) and H (for height) option boxes to scale objects. Although it may seem quite obvious how to use the palette, there are actually some hidden features:

- ❑ Enter an amount in either the width (W) or height (H) option boxes. Use the Tab key to jump from one box to another. Press Enter or click on the page to change the focus from the Transform palette.
- ❑ Use the reference point icon to change the point around which the transformation occurs. The reference points are measured with respect to the selection's rectangular bounding box.
- ❑ To scale by percentages enter a number followed by the % symbol into either the W or H option boxes. You can enter different percentages to scale the object non-proportionally. You can also enter a single number in either the width or the height option box. Then press Ctrl-Enter to apply the value to both the width and height.
- ❑ Press Ctrl-Alt-Enter to apply the values to a copy. This also changes your focus from the Transform palette.
- ❑ Press Ctrl-Alt-Tab to apply the values to a copy of the original – without leaving the Transform palette.
- ❑ Use Transform Again to reapply a percentage transformation change.

OK, so may be you knew the above features of the Transform palette. But we bet you didn't know these hidden features:

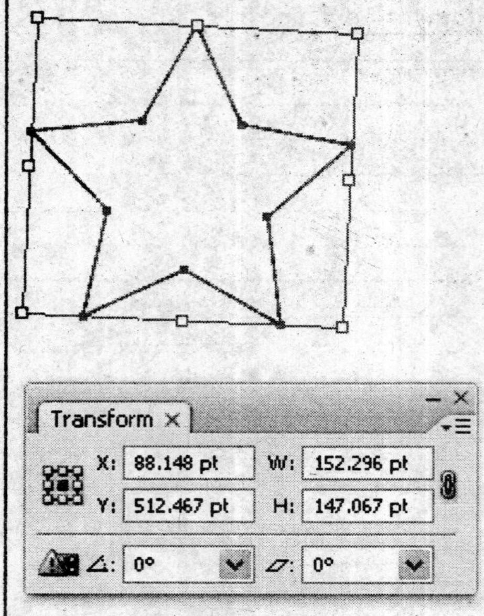

- Press Ctrl-Shift-Enter to scale uniformly and leave the focus on the last used option box.
- Press Alt-Enter to apply the scaling to a clone of the path. Press Alt-Shift-Enter to scale a clone and leave the focus on the last used option box.
- Press Ctrl-Alt-Enter to uniformly scale a clone.
- Press Ctrl-Alt-Shift-Enter to uniformly scale a clone and leave the focus on the last used option.

Using the Scale Dialog Box

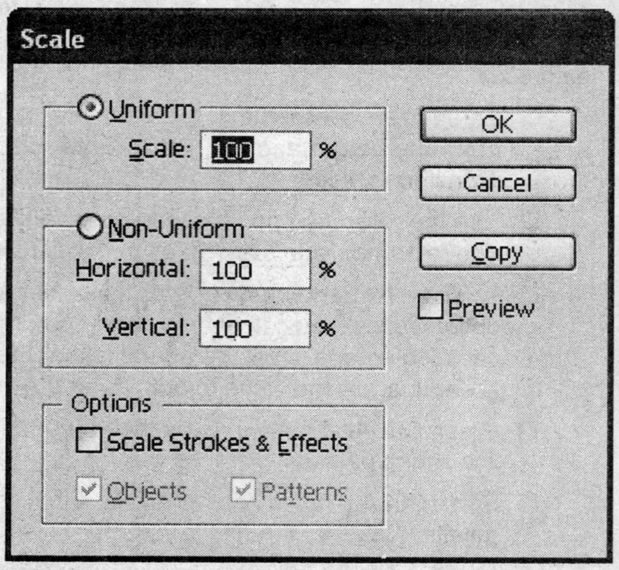

After selecting a few objects on your Things To Scale list, double-click the scale tool icon in the toolbox. This brings up the Scale dialog box on the screen. Illustrator automatically positions the origin point in the center of the selection. If you want to position the origin point yourself, Alt-click in the illustration window to the scale tool cursor. Alt-clicking with any transformation tool simultaneously positions the origin point and displays the appropriate dialog box. Here's how the Scale dialog box can be used:

- Choose Uniform and enter a value in the Scale option box to proportionally scale the width and height of the selection. This value is accurate to 0.001 percent – ten times more accurate than the scale value in the Transform palette.

- Choose Non-uniform and enter a value in either the Horizontal or Vertical option boxes to scale the object non-proportionally.
- Check Scale Strokes and Effects to scale any stroke weights or effects applied to objects. The stroke weights change only when objects are scaled uniformly. Effects are scaled whenever the box is checked. If the check box is off, strokes and effects are unaffected.
- Illustrator remembers this Scale Strokes and Effects setting the next time you Shift-drag with the scale tool. So if find that your line weight are getting thicker and thinner as you scale them, you know the culprit. Double-click the scale tool icon and turn off the Scale Line Weight check box. Or change the setting in the General Preferences.
- The objects and Patterns check boxes are used strictly when working with tiled fills.
- Use the Preview check box to see the possible yet currently unrealized future. Click it on and off to see your changes appear and disappear.
- To scale the selection, press Enter or click the OK button. Click the Copy button to clone the selection and scale it.

Scaling Partial Objects

You can use the scale tool or Scale dialog box to scale partially selected paths and text objects. For example, you can use the scale tool to enlarge a text blocks without changing the size of the text inside it. Alt-click the rectangular text container with the direct selection tool and then click with the scale tool to set the origin point and drag away. So long as you haven't selected any text, Illustrator enlarges or reduces the containers and rewraps the text inside. You can also scale selected points and segments in a path. The primary advantage of this technique is that you can move points symmetrically. Illustrator doesn't provide any specific mans for moving points away from or toward an origin point. Moving is the one transformation that has nothing to do with origins (which is why we don't discuss it in this chapter). The closest thing to an origin base moved function is the scale tool.

You can also use the scale tool to move objects in equal and opposite directions. Use the direct selection tool to select just the top and bottom points in the object on the left. Using the origin point in the center of the object, drag the top object up. This will send the bottom object down at the same distance. This ensured the finished object was the same on top and bottom. So in addition to its normal resizing functions, the scale tool does double duty as a symmetrical move tool.

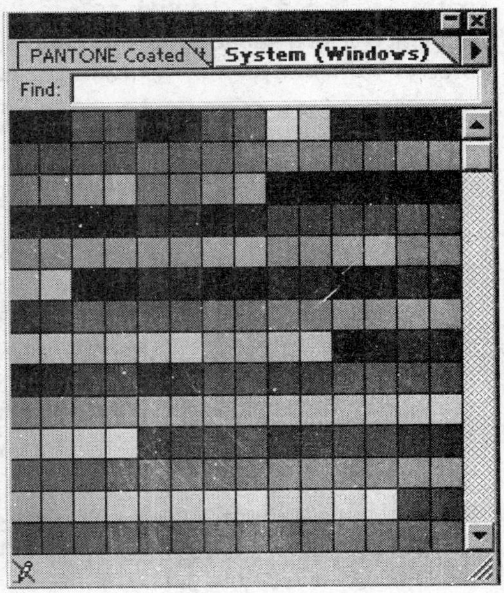

Working with Colours

You define all new process colors in the Color palette by adjusting the difrerent slider bars. Depending on which color model you are using (all of which are accessed through the Color palette's pop-up menu), the slider bars will vary the CMYK, RGB or HSB amounts.

You can define spot colors or import them from third-party swatch libraries. Once you've created colors in the Color palette, you can either use the color right away or you can sae it for later. If you want to save a color so that you can use it over and over again, choose the New Swatch command from the Swatches palette's pop-up menu or simply drag the color onto the Swatches palette.

You will then have the option of naming the color as well as deciding whether you wish to convert it to a spot color. You can also use one of the predefined colors in the Swatches palette. Or you can load entire libraries of spot colors from the Window >> Swatch Libraries submenu.

Onscreen Color controls

There are four onscreen elements that allow you to work with colors. In the Color palette, you can choose the color model that will best mix your favourite shade of "tickle-me" pink. The Swatches palette stores a number of predefined solid colors (as well as predefined gradients and patterns, both discussed in upcoming chapters.) And the Toolbox and Appearance palette, as well as the Color Palette, let you change the focus from fill to stroke.

Using the Color Palette

The Color Palette is the easiest way to pick the values for a color. First, use the Color palette menu to pick the color model (CMYK, RGB, HSB, Grayscale or Web-safe) you want to use. Click the spectrum bar along the bottom of the Color palette to approximate the color of your dreams. Modify the sliders by dragging on the little trangle that accompanies each bar or change the values in the option boxes to the right or each bar.

The Color palette's pop-up menu contains two commands that systematically change the values of the current color: Invert and Complement. The Invert command changes the color to its opposite along the RGB scale. For example, a color made up of 100 red, 150 blue and 200 green inverts to 155 red, 105 blue and 55 green. The original value and the inverted value for each component must add up to 255. Even if you work in the CMYK colorspace, the Invert command uses RGB values to calculate the inverse color.

The Complement compound alters color sin a similar manner (although the result is quite contrary to what you might except based on any color theory with which we are familiar). Whereas the Invert command bases its changes on 255, the Complement command uses the sum of the lowest and highest RGB values. Say we start with a battleship blue that breaks down into 55 red, 95 green and 120 blue.

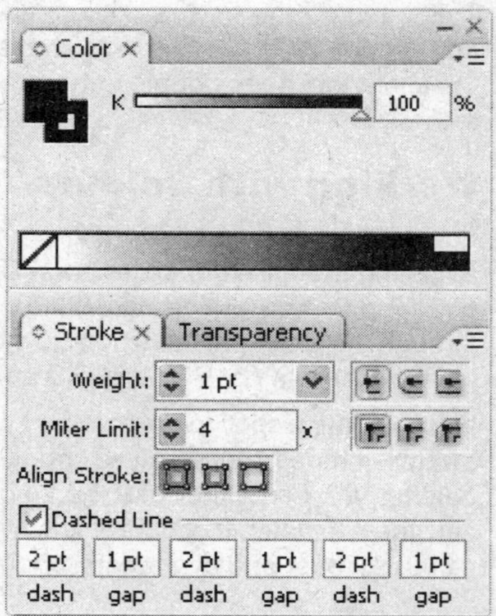

Complement would add the lowest and highest values (55 and 120, yielding 175) and then subtract each value from this total. The resulting components would be 120 red (175-55), 80 green (175-95) and 55 blue (175 – 55). Again, Illustrator doesn't change the colorspace of the original, it's just that the math only works in terms of RGB.

To create white, drag all the sliders to the left in the CMYK mode or just click the White box at the right end of the spectrum bar in the Color palette. If you're working in greyscale, you can also move the K slider triangle all the way to the left or enter 0 into the option box.

To color an object black, drag the black slider all the way to the right or click the Black box (just below the White box) on the spectrum bar. In greyscale, you have the option of either moving the K slider triangle to the far right or entering 100 into the option box.

If you're working in the CMYK colorspace, Illustrator will automatically change an out-of-gamut color to a closely-matching color that lies within the CMYK spectrum. If the color that Illustrator chooses is not to your liking, use the slider bars to tweak the color to meet your needs.

Applying Colors

Once you enter a value in the option box of the Color Palette, Illustrator automatically updates the colors of selected objects every time you drag a slider triangle or press Enter or Tab key. Click a colour in the Swatches palette to compel Illustrator to affect the fill or stroke of the selected objects.

- Changing a colour in the Color or Swatches palette changes the colour of the selected objects, but only the color of their fill or stroke, depending on which icon is active in the Color palette and the toolbox. The attribute icon (Fill or Stroke) that overlaps the other is the active icon. Illustrator offers a few ways for you to change the color of the attribute (fill or stroke) that is not active.

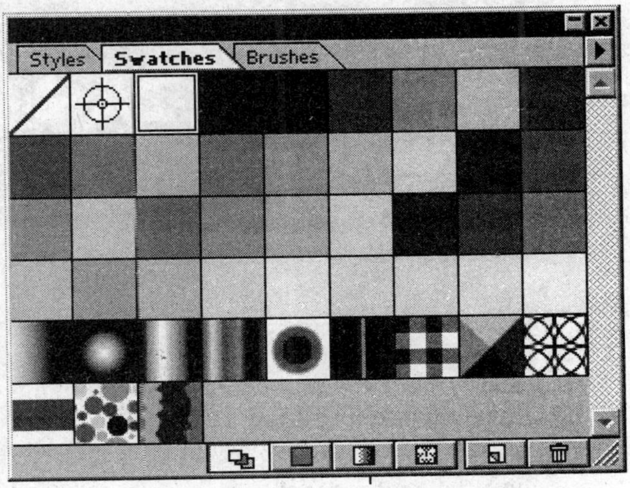

- Drag a color from either the Color or Swatch palette onto any object – even if it's not selected – to change the fill color of the object. Hold the Shift key to change the stroke color.
- You can drag a color swatch from the Swatches palette and drop it onto the Fill or Stroke icon. It doesn't matter which icon is active. You need to be careful to drop the swatch squarely on the icon of the attribute that you want to change.
- Another way to change the color of the icon that's not currently active is to Opt-click the spectrum bar at the bottom of the Color palette. The active icon will remain unchanged but the other icon will adopt the color on which you just clicked.
- Drag the color from the Fill or Stroke icon onto the other icon to match both colors.

The power of these techniques is that they allow you to edit the fill and stroke on an object without first activating the Fill and Stroke icons.

Using the Slider Bars

You wouldn't think something like slider bars would deserve their own section, but Adobe has built a bunch of little convenience features into the slider bars in the Color palette:

- Notice how the slider bars appear in different colors? This shows you what colors you'll get if you drag the slider triangle to that position. Each time you drag a slider triangle (or enter a value into an option box and press the Tab key), Illustrator updates the colors in the slider bars. This way, you're constantly aware of the effect that modifying a primary pigment will produce.
- If you like a color along the length of a slider bar, just click it. The slider triangle for that ink will immediately jump to the clicked position. To create a lighter or darker tint of a process color, Shift-drag the slider triangle. As you drag, all the slider bars change to demonstrate the

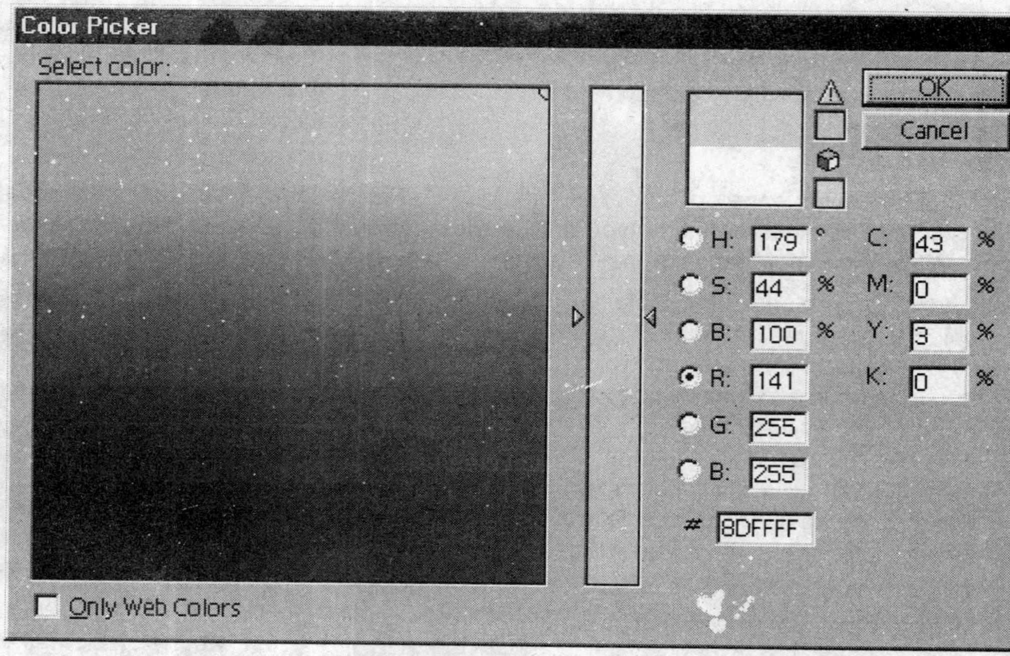

tint. To gain the most control, Shift-drag the triangle associated with the highest intensity color. (Any ink set to 0 percent does not move, because adding the ink would change the color rather than the tint.

- You can also shift-click a spot along a slider Bar to adjust the tint by leaps and bounds. All inks (not to 0 percent) change to maintain a constant hue. If the point at which you click is too high to maintain a constant tint, only that one ink will change. To make certain you change the tint and not the one ink, Shift-click and hold anywhere along the slider bar and then move your mouse until the sliders all move to some legal position.
- And, as you can in any palette, you can advance from one option box to the next by pressing the Tab key. Or you can move in reverse order by pressing Shift-Tab. If you wish to apply a new value and keep that option box active (allowing you to test a number of different settings quickly), press Shift-Return/enter.
- If you're an adept Photoshop user and you're wondering whether you can use the up and down arrow keys to modify option box values as you can in the fab image editor, the answer is no. Where slider bars are concerned, the two programs go their own ways.

Using Swatches Palette

The Swatches palette provides a handful of options for organizing swatches. For example, you can choose to display the swatches by name or by icon (large or small) as shown on the next page. If you let your cursor hover over a swatch in either icon view, the name of the swatch appears (provided you have the Show Tool Tips option selected in the General Preferences). You can control the organization of the Swatches palette by the following methods:

- To sort the swatches by either name or kind, choose the appropriate command from the pop-up menu in the Swatches palette. Sorting by kind groups similar swatches together. All the process colors appear first, followed by the spot colors, gradients and finally the pattern swatches.

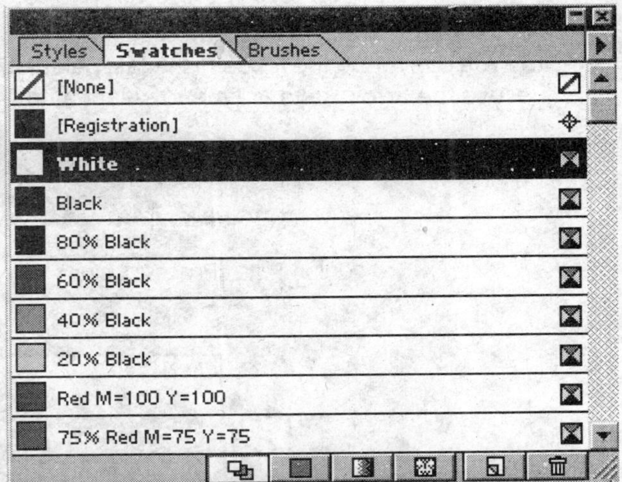

- ❑ Choose the appropriate command from the pop-up menu to view swatches by their name or simply by an icon that samples their color.
- ❑ Use the four icons along the bottom left of the Swatches palette to control which type of swatches display. Click the second, third, or fourth icon to restrict the display of swatches only to colors, gradients or palettes respectively. Click the first icon to show all swatches.

The Swatches palette offers another function that helps you organize your swatches. From the pop-up menu, choose the Select All Unused command to select all swatches that are not applied to paths or text blocks in any open illustration. Once the swatches are selected, you can drag them to a new location in the swatch list or delete them all by Opt/alt-clicking the Delete button. You can even duplicate them if you so choose.

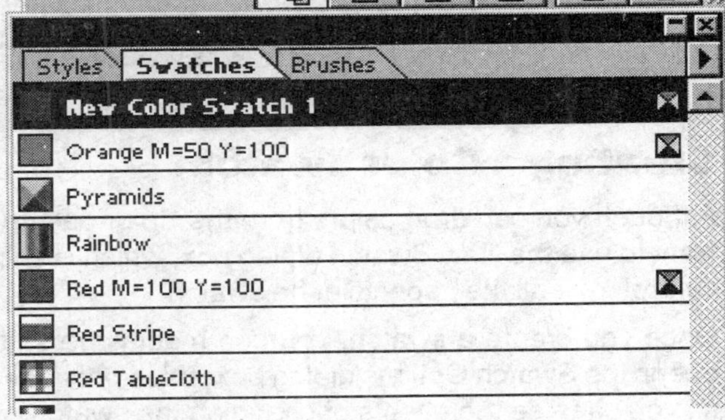

Setting the Swatches Palette Focus

This is one of the esoteric techniques that only ten people in the entire world actually use completely. However, the ten that do use the techniques swear they are very helpful and easy to remember. But we must be getting old because we can never remember all the features:

- ❑ You don't have to always use the mouse to select a swatch. You can set the focus to the Swatches palette by holding Ctrl-Alt and then clicking inside the palette. A black line appears inside the palette.

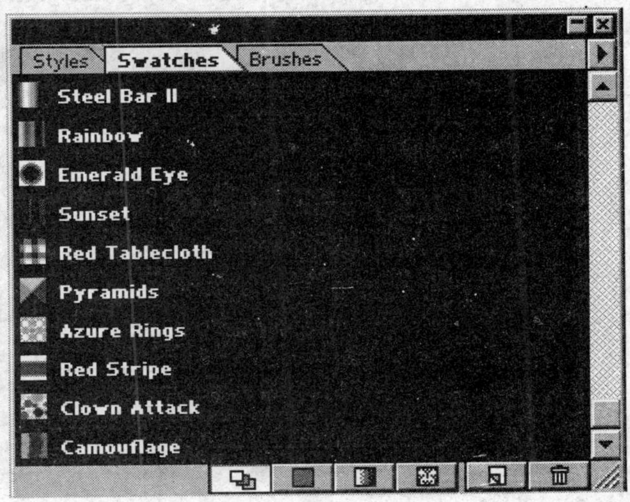

- ❑ Once you have set the focus inside the Swatches palette, you can scroll around the swatches by pressing the arrow keys.
- ❑ With the focus inside the Swatches palette, you can type the first few letters of the swatch's name to instantly go to that swatch. However, there is a much easier way to type to find specific colors, as we'll over in just a moment.

- Once you have selected a swatch, press Enter to switch the focus back to the document.
- You can return the focus to the last palette that was in focus by pressing Ctrl-~. You can then use the arrow keys or type to select a new swatch.

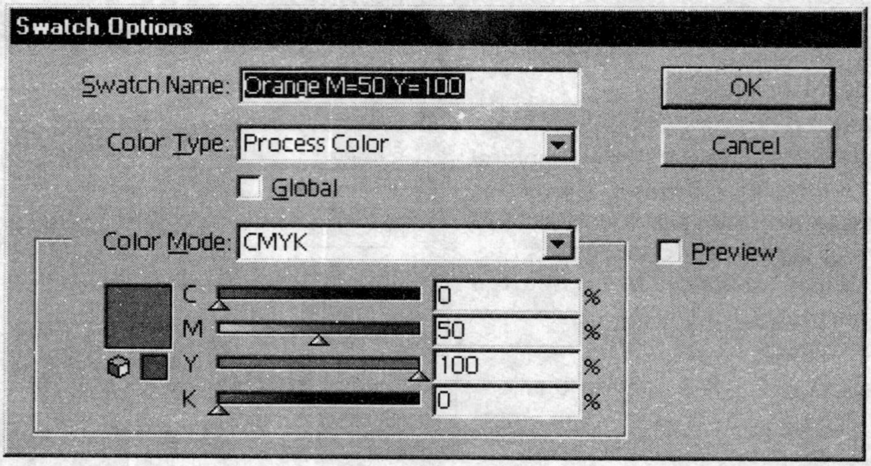

Creating a Color Swatch

Although you can drag colors from the Color palette into the Swatches palette, you will most likely want to use the New Swatch dialog box, which is shown on the next page. This gives you complete control over all the aspects of he swatch.

Once you create a swatch, you can modify the settings by double-clicking the swatch icon. This opens the Swatch Options dialog box which provides all the original options as well as a preview box so you can see the effects of changing the swatch color.

- First and foremost, give your color a name. It doesn't really matter what the name is. You can name the swatch with the percentage values of the colors or you can name it after your favorite Uncle Irving.
- From the Color Type menu, you can decide whether your newly-created color should be a process color or a spot color. If you designate a color as process in a CMYK colorspace, you

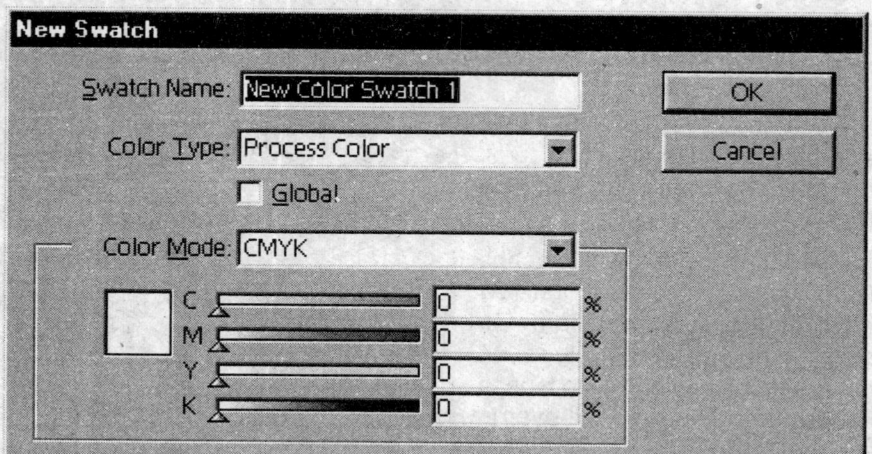

are instructing Illustrator to create the color by mixing the percentages of the CMYK colors. If you use RGB or HSB values to define your color, Illustrator will automatically convert the color into CMYK values.

- If you designate a color as spot, you are instructing Illustrator to separate the color onto its own plate when the artwork is separated into film for commercial printing. It really doesn't matter what percentages you assign to a spot color – however, the name of the color is important. See the section on working with spot colors for how to coordinate colors among documents.
- You can also check the Global option. This means that if you change the definition of a swatch all items that use the color will change. If you leave the Global option turned off, any changes to the swatch will apply only to new objects that use the color.
- Use the Color Mode list to choose what types of sliders you want to use to define your colors. If you are working in the CMYK colorspace, RGB, HSB or Web-Safe RGB colors are automatically converted into CMYK colors. If you are working in the RGB colorspace, HSB and CMYK colors are automatically converted into RGB colors.

Adjusting Colors

The Filter >> Colors >> Adjust Colors command is Illustrator's most capable color correction command. Choose the Adjust Colors filters to display the Adjust Colors dialog box, as shown here. There are four different types of colors that can be adjusted using this command.

- If you have any Global or Spot colors, the Global setting allows you to increase or decrease all those colors by using one tint slider. Any non-global process colors will not be affected in this mode:
- If you are working in the CMYK colorspace, the CMYK mode allows you to increase or decrease the cyan, magenta, yellow and black percentages of all non-global process colors. If you check Convert, any Global or Spot colors will also be adjusted at that time. Also, the Convert setting allows you to add color to objects colored with the grayscale color mode.

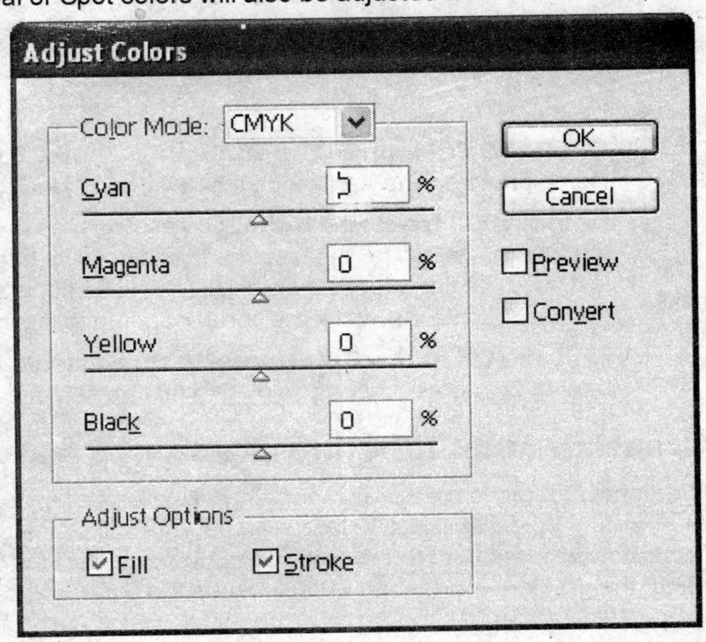

- If you are working in the RGB colorspace, the RGB mode allows you to increase or decrease the red, green and blue percentages of all non-global colors. If you check Convert, any Global or Spot colors will also be adjusted at that time.
- If you choose the Grayscale mode, all grayscale colors can be increased or decreased using a single black slider. If you check Convert, all other colors will be converted to grayscale values and then adjusted as you move the black slider.

The Grayscale mode is excellent for converting color jobs into grayscale and then varying the contrast of the Illustration.

The Adjust Colors dialog box also offers the following check boxes.

- **Fill** Select this option if you want to modify the fills of selected objects. Turn off the option if you want to change only strokes.
- **Stroke** Same thing as Fill, only opposite. Turn on the check box if you want to adjust strokes; turn it off if you want to affect only fills.
- **Convert** Select this check box to modify all colors of the selected objects according to the option box values. If you turn off this check box, you can adjust a color only in terms of its original color model.
- **Preview** Select this check box to keep apprised of the effects of your color modifications as you work inside the Adjust Color dialog box. Keep this option on to avoid surprise.

Applying a Single Fill

Whether you're filling path or text blocks, follow these steps to apply a ingle fill to an object:

- **Select the path or characters that you want to fill** You can use the arrow, direct selection or type tool. In fact, you can be in the middle of drawing a path with the pen tool and still fill a path. As long as you can see selection handles or highlighted text in the illustration window, you can apply a fill. If no object is selected, modifying the fill changes the default settings.

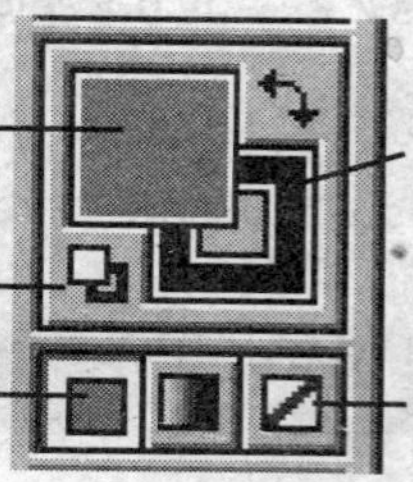

- **Click the Fill icon in the toolbox** Or, if the Stroke icon is active – overlapping the Fill icon – press X. The X key toggle between the two icons.
- **Select a fill from the Color, Swatches, or Gradient palettes** Or you can press the comma key (,) for the last used solid color or pattern or press the period key (.) For the last used gradient. Press the slash key (/) to be done with all this filling and have a transparent object. You can also click the corresponding icons in the lower portion of the toolbox.
- **Edit the fill in the Color palette as desired** For example, you can adjust the slider bars to change a process color. Or you can select a color from a gradient and change it.

Creating and Changing Gradient Swatches

Gradients are fragile creatures. After you create a gradient it exists in the Gradient palette and it will exist in any object that are selected while you make the gradient. But that's it. And if you quite Illustrator (or if, heaven forbid, your computer crashes) at that point, you will lose the information about the gradient. Fortunately, you can use the Swatches palette to store gradients.

- Drag the gradient from the Fill box in the Gradient palette into the Swatches palette. The gradient appears as a new swatch.
- With the gradient selected in the Gradient palette, click the New Swatch icon in the Swatches palette or choose New Swatch from the Swatches palette menu. This automatically adds the gradient to the bottom of the Swatches palette.
- Alt-click the New Swatch icon to open the New Swatch dialog box where you can name the gradient.
- Double-click the gradient icon in the Swatches palette to change the name of the gradient.
- Hold the Alt key as you drag a gradient onto an existing gradient swatch to change the definition of the gradient. This also changes the appearance of all objects that had the gradient applied.
- To create a new gradation based on a selected one, click the Duplicate Swatch command in the Swatches palette's pop-up menu. Illustrator creates a clone of the gradation. You can now edit it as usual.

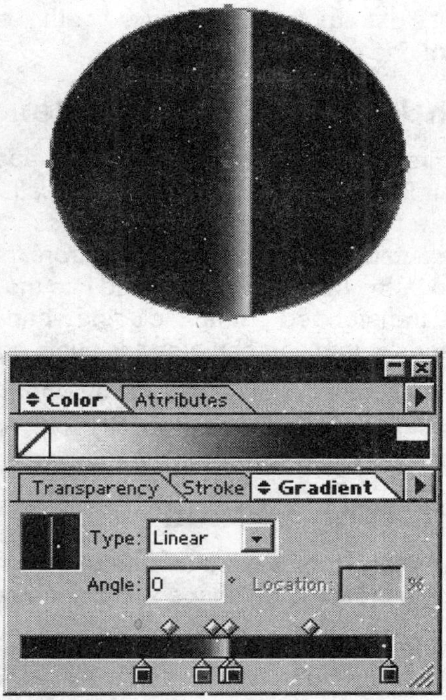

On this page, you see the various type of gradients that Illustrator offers, i.e., Radial and Linear. The difference is obvious from the figures. With this I conclude this book on Illustrator but there is more to Illustrator than this. Well, to learn completely about this software, you will have to go though the software and learn by experience, for the time being this is enough.

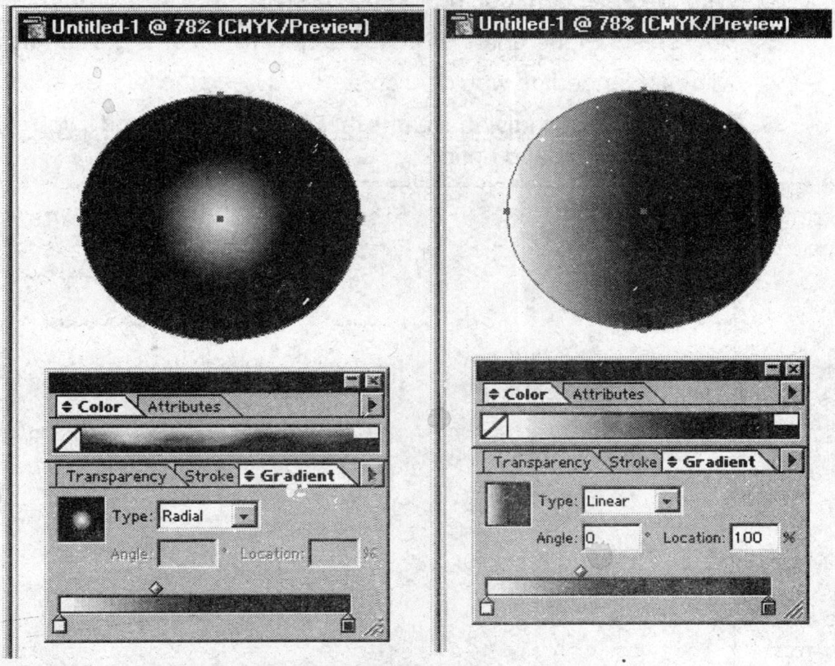

Working with Compound Paths and Masks

Two of the most difficult areas of Illustrator to master are masks and compound paths. Of course, these are also two of the program's most powerful functions. A "mask" is used to hide portions of an image (mask them out) and compound paths are paths that consist of two or more separate paths that Illustrator treats as a single path. This chapter also deals with blends, which allow you to morph from one path to another.

Understanding Path Blends

At first glance, gradients and blend appear to be the same except gradients are easy to use and blends seem to be much more difficult. Gradients are used only as Fills. Gradients can be either linear or radial, meaning htat color can change from side to side, top to bottom or from the center to the outside. Blends are series of transformed paths between two end paths. The paths between the end paths mutate from one end into the other. All the attributes of the end paths change throughout the transformed paths, including shape, size and all Paint Style attributes. The major benefit of blends is that you can blend multiple colors at one time.

Two blending choices exist: You can blend either by using the Blend tool or by choosing Object >>Blend>>Make[Ctrl + Alt + B]. You can create a blend with multiple shapes by pressing the right combination of keyboard commands.

Creating a blend

The Blend tool is used to create blends, which are group of paths (commonly referred to as blend steps) that change shape and color as each path is created closer to the opposite end path.

Follow these steps to create a blend:

1. Using the Circle tool, create a small (1-inch) circle. With the Star tool, create a star.
2. With the selection tool, now select both of them as shown below.
3. Now select Blend option from the Object menu and click at Make command.
4. A linear blendeding would be created between the two, as shown below.
5. You can edit the individual paths that make up the blend if you expand the blend object using the Object> Expand option.

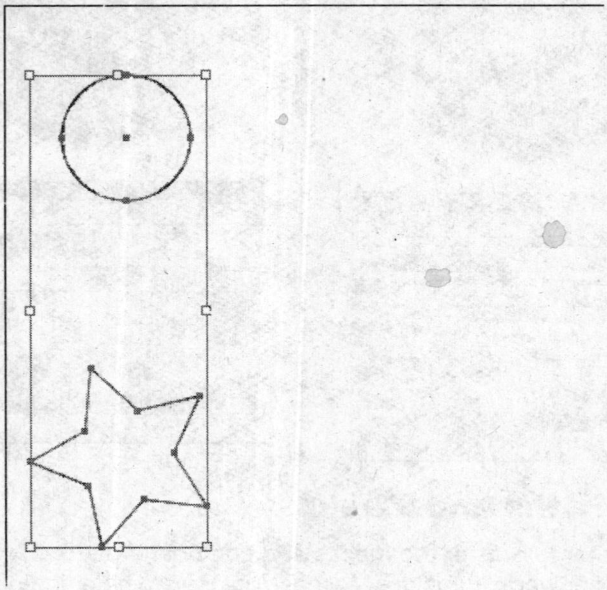

Creating Linear Blends

Color blends are made by creating two end paths, usually identical in shape and size, giving each path different Paint Style attributes and creating a series of steps between them with the Blend tool. The more end paths that are created, the more colors you can create.

The following steps describe how to create a basic linear blend.

1. Draw a vertical path with the Pen tool. Give it a Fill of None and Stroke of 2 points black.
2. Alt + copy the path to the right. Give the new path a Stroke of 2 points white.
3. With the Blend tool, click the path on the left and then the path on the right.
4. Deselect all [Ctr + Shift + a] to see the result.

Blend Options

Adobe has enhanced the Blending functions of Illustrator by improving the Blend tool and by adding a Blend submenu under the Object menu. The Blend submenu options are Make, Release, Blend Options, Expand, Replace Spine, Reverse Spine, and Reverse Front to Back. The Blend tool enables you to blend between specific points and with Illustrator's Live Blend capability, you do not need to release a blend to change it. Live Blending enables you to change the shape or color of a blend and update it automatically. You can use the Direct Selection tool to select the path and edit or change the color and the blend updates.

Using the Blend option

After choosing Object>>Blend>>Blend Options or by double clicking on the Blend tool, you can access the Blend Options box, shown next. This dialog box includes three Spacing options, which are Smooth Color, Specified Steps and Specified Distance.

The Orientation options are Align to Page and Align to Path.

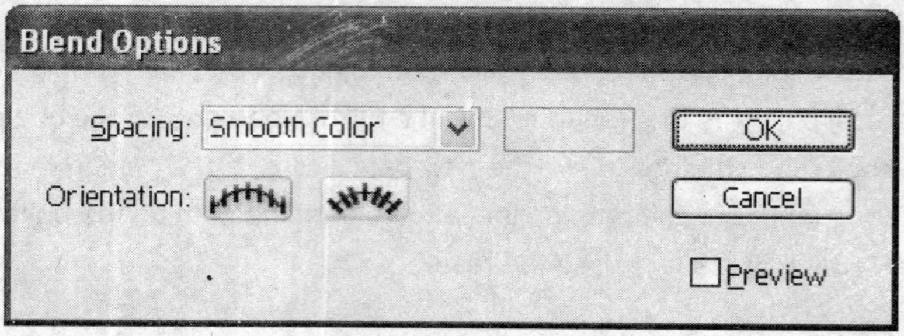

The Blend options work as follows:

- **Smooth Color** automatically determines the number of steps needed to make this blend look as smooth as possible.
- **Specified Steps** lets you choose how far apart each blend step is from another blend step.
- **Specified Distance** enables you to type in the distance between the steps.
- **Align to Page** runs the blend vertically or horizontally depending on your page orientation.
- **Align to path** runs the blend perpendicular to the path.

Blending Multiple Objects

To blend multiple objects in one step, select all the objects you want to blend and choose Object>>Blend>>Make. You can also use the Blend tool and click all the objects you want to blend.

Editing blends

The Blend tool enables you to edit blends without having to redo the entire blend. You have many different ways to edit a blend, such as moving the blend objects, replacing the blend spline with another rpath, or releasing or reversing the blend.

Changing Blend Colors on the Fly

The Live Blend option lets you change the colors of a blend without having to redo the whole blend. With the Direct Selection tool, select the path that you want to change the color of in the blended shape. Select a new Fill or Stroke color. The blend is updated instantly with the new color.

Moving a Blended Object

Another great aspect of Live Blends is its capability to edit the blend at any time and have it automatically update on the fly. A spine is created when a blend is made. With the Direct Selection tool you an select an anchor point on the spline and move it. This changes the location of that point and the blend updates accordingly.

Editing a Blended Object

Now you can edit lines by adding, deleting or moving any part of your blend and it updates automatically. You can delete add points or change the shape of a path with the Direct Selection tool.

Adjusting the Blend Options

The Blend Options dialog box lets you change the Spacing and Orientation aspects. Select the blend you want to adjust and either double-click the Blend tool or choose Object>>Blend>>Blend Options to open the dialog box to change the settings.

Expanding a Blend

If you want to edit the individual elements of a blend, you have to release it first. By choosing Object>>Blend>>Expand, the blend expands into a mess of shapes. The shapes will all still be grouped, but you can edit them individually after. Ungrouping them. You can tell when a group of objects is no longer a blend because the spline will no longer be visible.

Replacing the Spine

The Replace Spine option enables you to apply a blend to a selected path. To apply this effect, select the Stroked path and your blend and choose Replace Spine from the Blends submenu. Draw a path in the shape you want the spine of the blend to follow. Select the blend with the spine you want to change and the new path that is to become the new spine. Choose Object>>Blend>>Replace Spine. The blend update automatically.

Reversing the Spine

This option reverses the sequence of the objects you are blending. If you have a rectangle on the right blended to a circle on the left, choosing Reverse Spine puts the circle on the right and the rectangle on the left. Reversing the spine flips the position of the shapes on the spine.

Reversing Front to Back

The Reverse Front to Back option reverses the order in which your paths were drw when you created your blend. If you draw a circle first and a star second, choosing Reverse Front to Back displays the star on top and the circle underneath.

Changing into filled shapes

Choosing the Expand option enables you to change any blend or gradient into filled shapes.

Masking blends

Blends by themselves are great, but when masked by other paths, they can take on a life of their own. Use the following stepps to create a color wheel that illustrates this concept.

1. Using the Pen tool, draw a straight segment and give it a 2-point green (100% Cyan, 100% Yellow) Stroke and a Fill of None in the Color palette.
2. Choose the Rotate tool, press Alt and click one end point of the path to set the origin. Type 60 for the angle in the Rotate dialog box and press the Copy button (Alt+Enter). This procedure creates a copy of the Stroke at a 60-degree angle, with one end point directly on top of one of the existing ones.
3. Choose Object>>Transform>>Transform Again (Ctrl+D). Another Stroke is created at a 60-degree angle from the second. Continue to choose Transform Again until six Strokes exist. Each of these Strokes is used as an end path.
4. Color each Strokes as follows, moving closewise: 1. Green (100% Cyan, 100% Yellow); 2. Yellow (100% Yellow); 3. Red (100% Magents, 100% Yellow); 4. Magenta(100% Magenta); 5. Blue (100% Cyan, 100% Magenta); 6. Cyan (100% Cyan).

5. Blend each pair of end paths together either using the Blend tool on each end path or by choosing (Ctrl + Alt + B). The only catch in using the Blend function from the object menu is that you still have to manually blend the last end points. When all the end paths are blended together, the result is a beautifully-colored hexagon. Because of the shape, the end paths really stand out as points on the hexagon.
6. To complete the illusion of a perfect color wheel, the blend needs to be a circle. Using the Ellipse tool, draw a circle so that the edges are just inside the flat sides of the hexagon, with its center corresponding to the center of the hexagon. This process is easiest to do by Alt + clicking with the Ellipse tool at the center of the hexagon and pressing the Shift key as the oval is being drawn. Select the circle, the blend steps and the end paths, and choose Object>>Clipping Masks>>Make.
7. For a more realistic color wheel effect (one that resembles Apple's color wheel), create a Black Stroke on the mask and a small circle at the center that has a Fill of White and a Stroke of Black.

Creating Color Blends

Although there are many different ways to use blends, one aspect of blending directly relates to the Fill colors – Color Blends. These have some functionality that is uniquely different from gradients such as defining a different path along which the colors can change.

Multiple colors with linear blends

To create linear blends that have multiple colors, you must create intermediate end paths, one for each additional color within the blend, as follows:

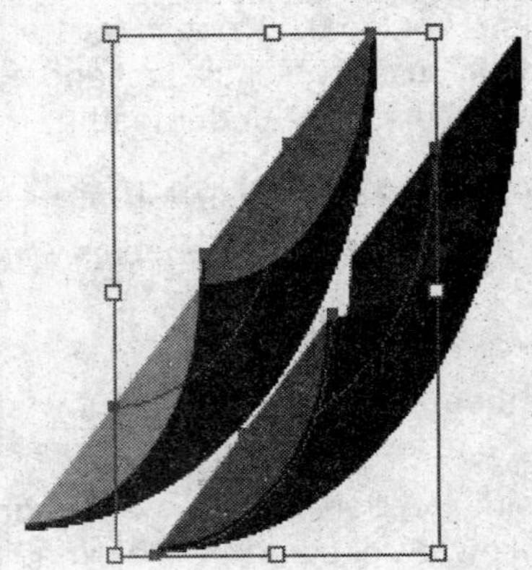

1. Create two end paths at the edges of where you want the entire blend to begin and end. Don't worry about colors at this time.
2. Select the two paths and choose Object>>Blends>>Make (Ctrl+Alt+B]). Then choose Object>>Blends>>Blend Options. Change the Smooth Options to Specified Steps. Choose your orientation and enter a number for the steps. (I have entered 3 to create three evenly spaced paths between the two end paths).
3. Expand the newly created Strokes by choosing Object>>Blends>>Expand, color each of the Strokes of the paths differently and give them a weight of 2 points. Select all of the paths and choose Object >>Blends>>Make (Ctrl + Alt + B).
4. The result should look like the blend of colors shown next in the figure.

Creating Shape Blends

The difference between colour blends and shape blends is their emphasis. Colour blends emphasize a color change; shape blends emphasize blending between different shapes. You should remember a number of things when creating the end paths that form a shape blend.

Both paths must be either open or closed. If open, only end points can be clicked to blend between the two paths. For the best results, both paths should have the same number of anchor points selected before blending and the selected points should be in a relatively similar location.

Illustrator pairs up points on end paths and the segments between them so that when it creates the blend steps, the lines are in about the same position.

Computer Vents

Look on the side of your monitor or on the side of a computer or hard drive case. You undoubtedly see vents or simulated vents running back along these items for design purposes. This type of blend (changing the angle of straight lines) is the most basic of shape blends and is easy to create.

The following steps describes the process for creating computer vents and figure illustrates this process.

1. Draw a rectangular shape that has been distorted to appear like the side of your monitor (use the Pen tool). Choose a Fill of 25% Black and a Stroke of 0.5 point 50% Black

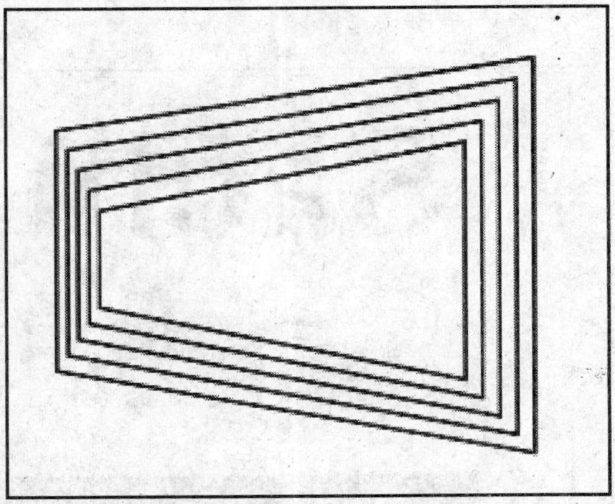

2. Select the shape and double-click the Scale tool. Enter 90 percent in the Uniform field of the Scale dialog box and click Copy (Alt + Return).
3. With the Direct Selection tool, select and delete the two vertical segments of the shape. Select both of the horizontal segments and change the Fill to None.
4. Blend the two paths together. Then choose Object>>Blend>> Blend Options and change the Spacing to Specified Steps and the number to 15. One side of a monitor is now complete.
5. Select all the paths and copy them up 0.5 point by using the copy button in the Move dialog box. Change the Stroke to 75% Gray.
6. Draw a circle over the center of the group and select the group and the circle. Choose Object>>Masks>>Make and you have a "real" vent in the simulated one. Maybe you can make a better one than the one I have made.

Creating Realism with Shape Blends

To create a realistic effect with shape blends, the paths used to create the blends need to resemble object you see in life. Look around and try to find a solid colored object – doesn't the color appear to change from one part of the object to another? Shadows and reflections are everywhere. Colors change gradually from light to dark, not in straight lines but in smooth, rounded curves. Blends can be used to simulate reflections and shadows. Reflection are usually created with shape blends; shadows are usually created with Stroke blends.

In the following example, we show you how to simulate reflections with shape blends. This process is a little tricky for any artist because the environment determines the reflection. The artwork you create will be viewed in any number of environments, so the reflections have to compensate for these differences. The chrome-like in the word SACHIN in figure was created by masking shape blends designed to look like a reflective surface.

The following procedure shows you how to achieve this:

1. Type the word or words you want to use for masking the reflecting surface. The typeface and the word itself have an impact on how the finished artwork is perceived. I have chosen the word SACHIN and the typeface Arial.
2. Choose Type>>Create Outline(Ctrl + Shift + O). Choose a Fill of White for the text and a Stroke of Black. At this point, most of the serifs on the letters overlap.
3. Select all the letters and choose Unite from the Pathfinder palette. This command gets rid of any unsightly seams between the letters. Create a rectangle and place it behind the letters.
4. Set the Auto Trace Tolerance option to 2 in the General Preference dialog box (Edit>>Preferences>>General). Using the Pencil tool, draw a horizontal line from left to right across the rectangle. With a low Auto Trace Tolerance setting, this step should result in a path with many points.

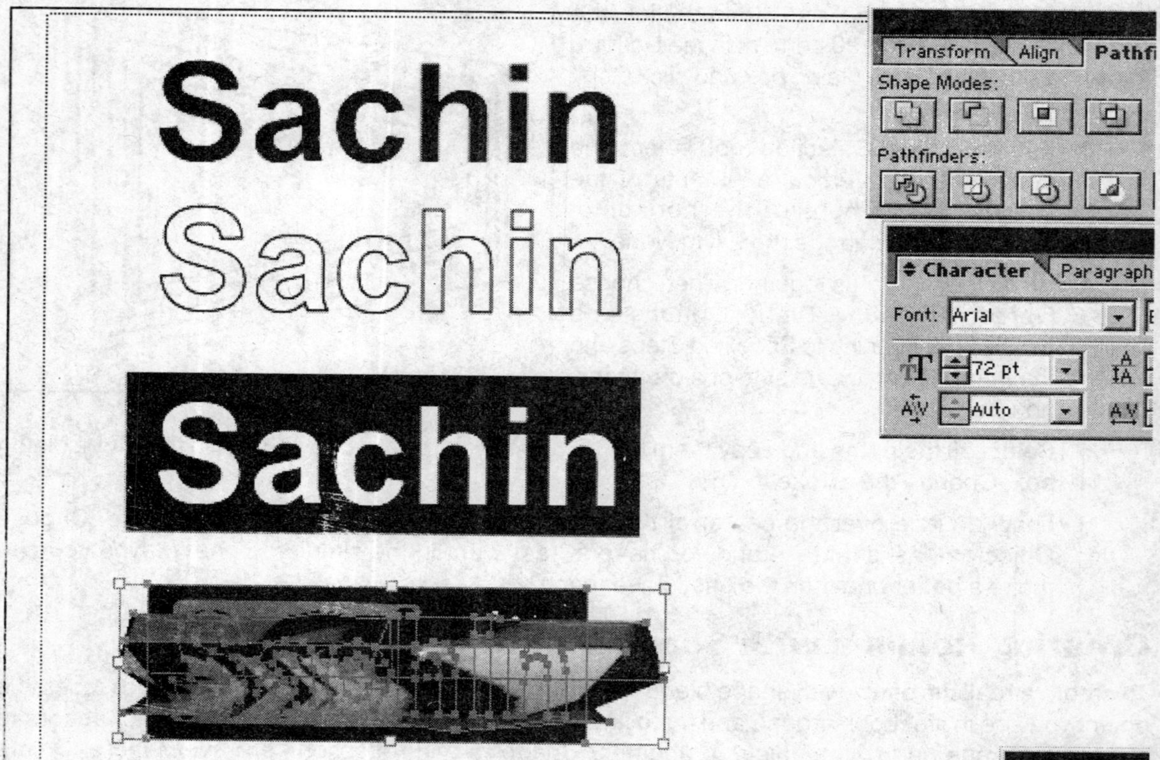

5. Alt + Copy several paths from the original down to bottom of the rectangle. An easy way to copy the paths is to Alt + drag down just a bit and then choose Object>>Transform>>Transform Again (Ctrl + D) several times. In this example, we crated live more paths, with the Direct Several tool, randomly move around individual anchor points and direction points on each path, but try to avoid overlapping paths.
6. Blend the Stroked paths together and mask them with the type outlines. In this example, we did this step twice. The first time, we created the front piece; the second time, we used lighter-color Strokes for a highlight, which we offset slightly up and to the left and placed behind the original type.

In the preceding steps, we Alt + copied the path not only because it was easy, but also to ensure that the end paths in the blends have the same points in the same locations. This technique is much more effective than adding or deleting points from a path.

Compound Paths

Compound paths are one of the least understood area of illustrator, but after you grasp a few simple guidelines and rules, manipulating and using compound path correctly is simple. Compound paths are paths made up of two or more open or closed paths. Where the paths cross or every other Fill area exists, a transparent hole occurs.

You specify which paths create the holes by changing the direction of the paths via the Reverse option in the Attributes palette. The general rule is t hat paths traveling in opposite direction of any adjoining paths from holes. Compound paths can be fun or frustrating, depending on the location of Pluto relative to Saturn, Jupiter and Mickey.

Creating compound paths

You can create all types of compound paths by following the steps describing here. It's a good idea to make sure that none of the paths are currently compound paths or grouped paths before creating a new compound path.

1. Create all the paths that you need for the compound path, including the outside path and the holes.
2. Select all the paths and choose Object>>Compound Paths>> Make (Ctrl + 8). Illustrator now treats the paths as one path. When you click one of the paths with the Selection tool, the other paths in the compound path are selected as well. Fill the object with any Fill.
3. Place the compound path over any other object. The inner paths act like holes that enable you to see the object underneath.

You can select individual paths by clicking them once with the Group Selection tool. As always, you can select points and segments within each path by using the Direct Selection tool.

Masks

In Illustrator, you can masks to mask out parts of underlying objects that you don't want to see. The path that you draw in Illustrator defines the shape for the must. Anything outside the mask is hidden from view in Preview mode and does not print.

Masks are objects that mask out everything but the paths made up by the mask. Masks can be open, closed or compound paths. The masking object is the object whose paths make up the mask and this object must be in front of all the objects that are being masked.

You can masks from any path, including compound paths and text. You can use masks to view portions of multiple objects. Individual objects and placed EPS (Encapsulated PostScript) images.

Crating Masks

To create a mask, the masking object (the path that is in the shape of the mask) has to be in front of the objects that you want it to mask. You select the masking object and the objects that you want to mask. Then you choose Object>>Clipping Mask>>Make (Ctrl + 7). In preview mode, any areas of the objects that were outside the mask vanish, but the parts of the objects that are inside the mask remain the same. Masks are much easier to use and understand in Preview mode than in Outline mode.

If you want to mask an object that is not currently being masked, you need to select the new object and all the objects in the mask, including the masking object. You then choose Object>>Clipping Mask>>Make (Ctrl + 7). The mask then applies to the new object as well as to the objects that were previously masked. The new object, like all others being masked, must be behind the masking object.

Like compound paths, masking does not work in hierarchical levels. Each time you add an object to a mask, the old mask that didn't have that object is released and a new mask is made that contains all of the original mask objects as well as the new object.

Stroking and Filling Masking Objects

Creating a basic mask require four steps:

1. Select the path that you want to use as a mask and bring it to the front.
2. Select the mask and any objects that you want to mask and then choose Object>>Masks>>Make (Ctrl + 7).
3. Group the masked objects with the masks for easier selecting in the future.
4. Using the Group Selection tool, select the mask. Then change the Stroke to 1-point Black. The mask now has a 1-point Black Stroke. The result should resemble step 4 in figure.

Releasing masks

To release a mask, first select the masking object (you may select other objects as well). Then choose Object>>Mask>>Release (Ctrl + Alt + 7) and the masking object no longer is a mask.

If you aren't sure which object is the masking object or if you are having trouble selecting the masking object, choose Select>>All (Ctrl + A) and choose Object>>Mask>>Release (Ctrl + Alt + 7). This action releases any other masks that are in the document – unless they were separate masks that were being masked by other masks.

To release all the masks in the document, even those masks that are being masked by other masks, Select>>All (Ctrl+A) and choose Release Mask repeatedly. Usually three Release Masks get everything, unless you went mask-happy in find particular document.

Masks and Printing

As a rule, PostScript printers don't care too much for masks. They are even less for masks that mask other masks. And they really don't like masks that are compound paths.

Unfortunately, because of the way that Illustrator works, every part of every object in a mask is sent to the printer, even if only a tiny piece of an object is used. In addition, controlling where the masking object slices objects requires a great deal of computing power and memory. You may have a problem, for example, when you have more stuff to mask than the printer can handle.

More important than any other issue involved with masks and printing is the length and complexity of the masking path. The more objects in a mask, the more complex it is. The more anchor points, the more complex it is. The more direction points coming off those anchor points, the more complex the mask is. In other words, your printer would enjoy a mask if the masking object was a rectangle and no objects were being masked.

Using Compound Paths and Masks in an Illustration

We used several compound paths and masks to achieve the effects in figure. The compound paths are the word Tropical and the large strips of film across the lower half of the illustration. The masks are the word Tropical, the binocular shape and the outside frame of the poster.

Creating a film strip

In the first set of steps, you create the strip of film and place the island pictures into the film. You do not use masks in this process. We make this point so that you don't think that you always have to use masks, especially when another method is easier. These steps show you how to create a compound path for a masking effect:

1. To create the film shape, draw a long, horizontal rectangle with the Rectangle tool and place five rounded-corner rectangles inside the long rectangle.
2. To create the sprocket holes in the film, place a right-side-up triangle next to an upside-down triangle and continue placing triangles until you have a row of triangles across the top of the film.
3. After you group all the triangles together, Alt + copy them (drag the triangles with the Alt key pressed, releasing the mouse button before releasing the Alt key to create a second row of triangles along the bottom of the film.

4 Select all the pieces of the film and choose Object>>Compound Paths>>Make(Ctrl + 8). Fill the compound path with a dark purple color that is not quite black.

5. This part looks as if you use a mask, but you don't need to do any masking here. Instead, place one image, size it so that it just covers the hole and Alt + copy it across the remaining holes. Select each image in turn choose File>>Place Art and select a different image for each square. To complete the effect, simply bring the strip of film to the front.

6. Before you place the film into the poster, group the images and the film and rotate them slightly. Grouping them prevents the hassle of selecting each one later if you need to move or transform them.

Instead of making the film a compound path, you can mask each of the photos and place each masked photo on top of the film. The method described in the preceding steps makes changing photos easier and is less taxing on the output device. The next set of steps describes how to use the word Tropical to show the tropical island.

1. Place an image in the document and create a masking path for the top of it. Before you make the object into a mask, select the image and choose Edit>>Copy (Ctrl+C).
2. Select both the masking path and the image and choose Object >>Mask>>Make (Ctrl+7).

3. Choose Edit>>Paste in Back (Ctrl+B) to position the image directly underneath the original image. Choose File>>Place Art and substitute a slightly varied version of the original image. The letters stand out decisively, as figure shows. The image behind the word Tropical was changed in Photoshop using a Mosaic filter.

Flare

The Flare tool creates flare objects with a bright center, a halo, and rays and rings. Use this tool to create an effect similar to a lens flare in a photograph.

Flares include a center handle and an end handle. Use the handles to position the flare and its rings. The center handle is in the bright center of the flare—the flare path begins from this point.

Create a default flare

1. Select the Flare tool .
2. Press Alt and click where you want the center handle of the flare to appear.
3. Flares often look best when drawn over existing objects.

Draw a flare

1. Select the Flare tool.

2. Press the mouse button down to place the center handle of the flare, then drag to set the size of the center, the size of the halo, and to rotate the angle of the rays.
3. Before releasing the mouse, press Shift to constrain the rays to a set angle. Press Up Arrow or Down Arrow to add or subtract rays. Press Ctrl (Windows) or Command (Mac OS) to hold the center of the flare constant.
4. Release the mouse when the center, halo, and rays are as desired.
5. Press and drag again to add rings to the flare and place the end handle.

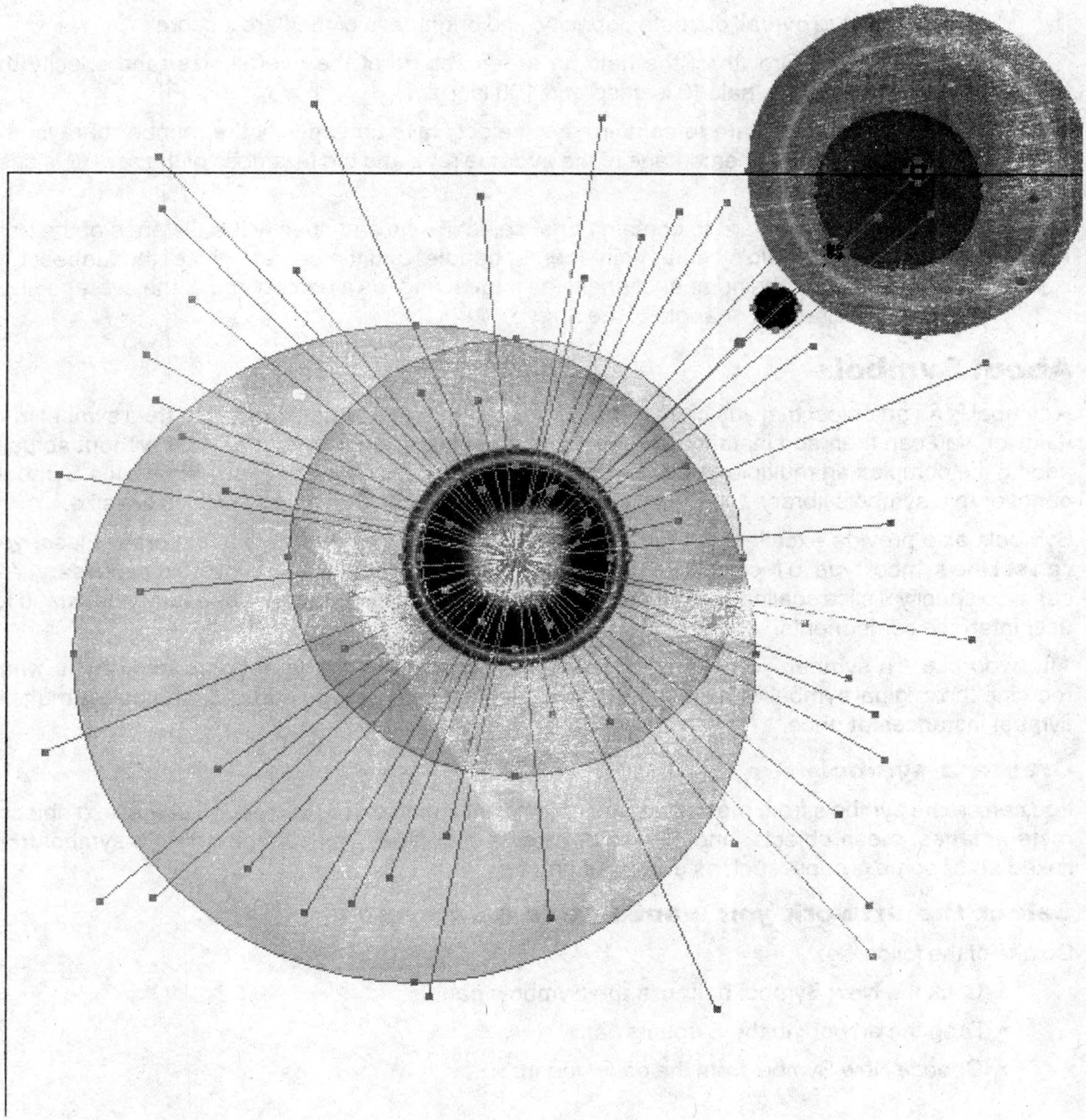

6. Before releasing the mouse, Press Up Arrow or Down Arrow to add or subtract rings. Press the tilde (~) key to randomly place the rings.
7. Release the mouse when the end handle is in the desired location.
8. Each element (center, halo, rings, and rays) in the flare is filled with color at different opacity settings.

Create a flare using the Flare Tool Options dialog box

1. Select the Flare tool, and click where you want to place the center handle of the flare.
2. In the Flare Tool Options dialog box, do any of the following options, and click OK:
   - Specify the overall diameter, opacity, and brightness of the flare's center.
   - Specify the Growth of the halo as a percentage of the overall size, and specify the fuzziness of the halo (0 is crisp and 100 is fuzzy).
   - If you want the flare to contain rays, select Rays and specify the number of rays, the longest ray (as a percentage of the average ray), and the fuzziness of the rays (0 is crisp and 100 is fuzzy).
   - If you want the flare to contain rings, select Rings and specify the distance of the path between the halo's center point (center handle) and the center point of the furthest ring (end handle), the number of rings, the largest ring (as a percentage of the average ring), and the direction or angle of the rings.

About Symbols

A symbol is an art object that you can reuse in a document. For example, if you create a symbol from a flower, you can then add instances of that symbol multiple times to your artwork without actually adding the complex art multiple times. Each symbol instance is linked to the symbol in the Symbols panel or to a symbols library. Using symbols can save you time and greatly reduce file size.

Symbols also provide excellent support for SWF and SVG export. When you export to Flash, you can set the symbol type to MovieClip. Once in Flash, you can choose another type if necessary. You can also specify 9 slice scaling in Illustrator so that the movie clips scale appropriately when used for user interface components.

After you place a symbol, you can edit the symbol's instances on the artboard and, if you want, redefine the original symbol with the edits. The symbolism tools let you add and manipulate multiple symbol instances at once.

Create a symbol

You can create symbols from most Illustrator objects, including paths, compound paths, text objects, raster images, mesh objects, and groups of objects. However, you cannot create a symbol from linked art or some groups, such as groups of graphs.

Select the artwork you want to use as a symbol.

Do one of the following:

- Click the New Symbol button in the Symbols panel.
- Drag the artwork to the Symbols panel.
- Choose New Symbol from the panel menu.

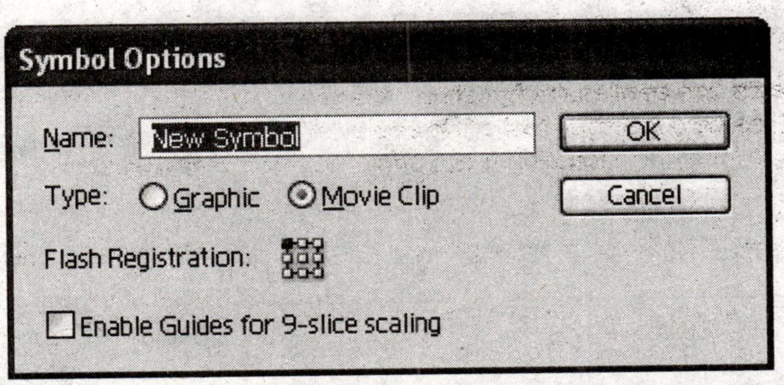

By default, the selected artwork becomes an instance of the new symbol. If you don't want the artwork to become an instance, press Shift as you create the new symbol. In addition, if you don't want the New Symbol dialog box to open when you create a new symbol, press Alt as you create the symbol and Illustrator will use a default name for the symbol, such as New Symbol 1.

In the Symbol Options dialog box, type a name for the symbol.

If you plan to export the symbols to Flash, do the following:

- Select Movie Clip for type. Movie Clip is the default symbol type in Flash.
- Specify a location on the Flash Registration grid where you want to set the symbol's anchor point. The location of the anchor point affects the position of the symbol within the screen coordinates.
- Select Enable Guides For 9 Slice Scaling if you want to utilize 9 Slice scaling in Flash.

Create a Sketch using the Scribble Effect

Do one of the following:

- Select the object or group (or target a layer in the Layers panel).
- To apply the effect to a specific object attribute, such as a stroke or fill, select the object, and then select the attribute in the Appearance panel.
- To apply the effect to a graphic style, select a graphic style in the Graphic Styles panel.

Choose Effect > Stylize > Scribble.

Do one of the following:

- To use a preset scribble effect, choose one from the Settings menu.
- To create a custom scribble effect, begin with any preset, and then adjust the Scribble options.

If creating a custom scribble, adjust any of the following Scribble options and click OK: Angle

Controls the direction of the scribble lines. You can click any point on the angle icon, drag the angle line around the angle icon, or enter a value between –179 and 180 in the box. (If you enter a value that's outside that range, the value is translated to its equivalent in range value.)

Path Overlap

Controls the amount the scribble lines stay within or extend beyond the path boundaries. A negative value constrains the scribble lines within the path boundary and a positive value extends the scribble lines beyond the path boundary.

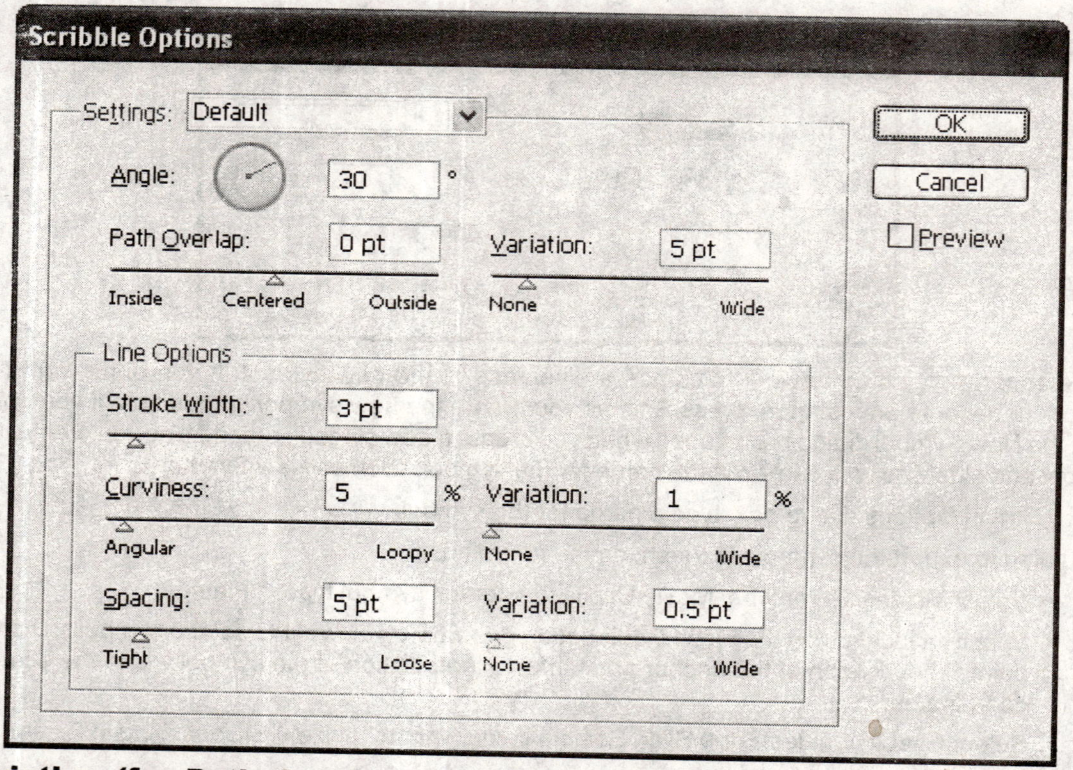

Variation (for Path Overlap)

Controls the lengths of the difference in scribble line lengths relative to each other.

Stroke Width

Controls the width of the scribble lines.

Curviness

Controls the amount the scribble lines curve before they reverse direction.

Variation (for Curviness)

Controls how different the scribble line curves are relative to each other.

Spacing

Controls the amount of space between scribble line folds.

Variation (for Spacing)

Controls how different the amount of space is between scribble line folds.

About Web Graphics

When designing graphics for the web, you must consider different issues than when designing graphics for print.

To help you make informed decisions about web graphics, keep in mind the following three guidelines:

1. Use web safe colors.

   Color is often a key aspect of artwork. However, the colors you see on your artboard aren't necessarily the colors that will appear in a web browser on someone else's system. You can prevent dithering (the method of simulating unavailable colors) and other color problems by taking two precautionary steps when creating web graphics. First, always work in RGB color mode. Second, use a web-safe color.

2. Balance image quality with file size.

   Creating small graphics file sizes is essential to distributing images on the web. With smaller file sizes, web servers can store and transmit images more efficiently, and viewers can download images more quickly. You can view the size and the estimated download time for a web graphic in the Save For Web & Devices dialog box.

3. Choose the best file format for your graphic.

   Different types of graphics need to be saved in different file formats to display their best and create a file size suitable for the web.

Create 3D Objects

3D effects enable you to create three-dimensional (3D) objects from two-dimensional (2D) artwork. You can control the appearance of 3D objects with lighting, shading, rotation, and other properties. You can also map artwork onto each surface of a 3D object.

There are two ways to create a 3D object: by extruding or revolving. In addition, you can also rotate a 2D or 3D object in three dimensions. To apply or modify 3D effects for an existing 3D object, select the object and then double-click the effect in the Appearance panel.

3D objects may display anti-aliasing artifacts on screen, but these artifacts won't print or appear in artwork optimized for the web.

Create a 3D object by Extruding

Extruding extends a 2D object along the object's z axis to add depth to the object. For example, if you extrude a 2D ellipse, it becomes a cylinder. The object's axis always lies perpendicular to the object's front surface and moves relative to the object if the object is rotated in the 3D Options dialog box.

1. Select the Object.
2. Choose Effect > 3D > Extrude & Bevel.
3. Click More Options to view the complete list of options, or Fewer Options to hide the extra options.
4. Select Preview to preview the effect in the document window.
5. Specify options:

   Position

   Sets how the object is rotated and the perspective from which you view it. (See Set 3D rotation position options.)

   Extrude & Bevel

   Determines the object's depth and the extent of any bevel added to or cut from it. (See Extrude & Bevel options.)

Surface

Creates a wide variety of surfaces, from dull and unshaded matte surfaces to glossy and highlighted surfaces that look like plastic. (See Surface shading options.)

Lighting

Adds one or more lights, varies the light intensity, changes the object's shading color, and moves lights around the object, for dramatic effects. (See Lighting options.)

Map

Maps artwork onto the surfaces of a 3D object. (See Map artwork to a 3D object.)

6. Click OK.

5 Keyboard Shortcuts of Illustrator CS 4

Introduction

The working in a software become much easy if you know the various keyboard shortcuts of the commands. Various commands in Illustrator are given below with their respective keyboard combinations.

The File Menu commands

Command	*Shortcut*
New	Ctrl + N
Open	Ctrl + O
Revert	F12
Close	Ctrl + W
Save	Ctrl + S
Save As	Ctrl + Shift + S
Save a Copy	Ctrl + Alt + S
Save for Web	Ctrl + Shift + Alt + S
Document Setup	Ctrl + Alt + P
Page Setup	Ctrl + Shift + P
Print	Ctrl + P
Quit	Ctrl + Q

The Edit Menu commands

Command	*Shortcut*
Undo	Ctrl + Z
Redo	Ctrl + Shift + Z
Cut	Ctrl + X
Copy	Ctrl + C
Paste	Ctrl + V
Paste in Front	Ctrl + F
Paste in Back	Ctrl + B
Clear	Delete

Keyboard Shortcuts	Ctrl + Shift + Alt + K
General Preferences	Ctrl + K

The Object Menu commands

Command	*Shortcut*
Transform>>Tranform Again	Ctrl + D
Transform>>Move	Ctrl + Shift + M
Bring to Front	Ctrl + Shift +]
Bring Forward	Ctrl +]
Send Backward	Ctrl + [
Send to Back	Ctrl + Shift + [
Group	Ctrl + G
Ungroup	Ctrl + Shift + G
Lock>>Selection	Ctrl + 2
Unlock All	Ctrl + Alt + 2
Hide>>Selection	Ctrl + 3
Show All	Ctrl + Alt + 3
Path>>Join	Ctrl + J
Path>>Average	Ctrl + Alt + J
Blend>>Make	Ctrl + Alt + B
Blend>>Release	Ctrl + Alt + Shift + B
Envelope Distort>>Make with Warp	Ctrl + Alt + W
Envelope Distort>>Make with Mesh	Ctrl + Alt + M
Envelope Distort>>Make with Top Object	Ctrl + Alt + C
Envelope Distort>>Edit Contents	Ctrl + Shift + V
Clipping Mask>>Release	Ctrl + Alt + 7
Compound Path>>Make	Ctrl + 8
Compound Path>>Release	Ctrl + Alt + 8

The Type Menu commands

Command	*Shortcut*
Font	Ctrl + Alt + Shift + M
Create Outlines	Ctrl + Shift + O

The Select Menu commands

Command	*Shortcut*
Select All	Ctrl + A
Deselect All	Ctrl + Shift + A

Reselect	Ctrl + 6
Next Object Above	Ctrl + Alt +]
Next Object Below	Ctrl + Alt + [

The Filter Menu commands

Command	*Shortcut*
Apply Last Filter	Ctrl + E
Last Filter	Ctrl + Alt + E

The Effect Menu commands

Command	*Shortcut*
Apply Last Filter	Ctrl + Shift + E
Last Filter Dialog Box	Ctrl + Shift + Alt + E

The View Menu commands

Command	*Shortcut*
Outline/Preview	Ctrl + Y
Overprint Preview	Ctrl + Shift + Alt + Y
Pixel Preview	Ctrl + Alt + Y
Zoom In	Ctrl + Plus Sign (+)
Zoom Out	Ctrl + Minus Sign (-)
Fit in Window	Ctrl + 0
	Double Click Hand Tool
Actual Size	Ctrl + 1
	Double Click Zoom Tool
Hide Edges	Ctrl + H
Hide Template	Ctrl + Shift + W
Show/Hide Rulers	Ctrl + R
Show/Hide Bounding Box	Ctrl + Shift + B
Show/Hide Transparency Grid	Ctrl + Shift + D
Guides>>Show/Hide Guides	Ctrl + ;
Guides>>Lock Guides	Ctrl + Alt + ;
Guides>>Make Guides	Ctrl + 5
Guides>>Release Guides	Ctrl + Alt + 5
Smart Guides	Ctrl + U
Show/Hide Grid	Ctrl + "
Snap to Grid	Ctrl + Shift + "
Snap to Point	Ctrl + Alt + "

The Window Menu commands

Command	*Shortcut*
Show/Hide Align	Shift + F7
Show/Hide Appearance	Shift + F6
Show/Hide Attributes	F11
Show/Hide Brushes	F5
Show/Hide Colour	F6
Show/Hide Gradient	F9
Show/Hide Info	F8
Show/Hide Layers	F7
Show/Hide Pathfinders	Shift + F9
Show/Hide Stroke	F10
Show/Hide Styles	Shift + F5
Show/Hide Symbols	Shift + F11
Show/Hide Transform	Shift + F8
Show/Hide Transparency	Shift + F10
Show/Hide Character Pallete	Ctrl + T
Show/Hide Paragraph Pallete	Ctrl + M
Tab Ruler Pallete	Ctrl + Shift + T

The Help Menu commands

Command	*Shortcut*
Illustrator Help	F1

The Tool Selection commands

Function	*Command*
Select the next pop-up tool	Drag to the right and release on desired tool Alt + click on a tool
Open tool dialog box	Double click on the tool
Hide toolbox and palettes	Tab
Selection tool	V or
	Ctrl + Tab with Direct Selection tool, and then hold Ctrl or
	Ctrl with all other tools if Selection tool was the last tool used
Direct Selection tool	A or
	Ctrl + tab with Selection tool, and then hold Ctrl + Alt with Group Selection tool

	Ctrl with all other tools if Direct Selection tool was the last tool used
Group Selection tool	Alt with Direct Selection tool
	Ctrl + Alt with all other tools if Direct Selection tool was the last tool used
Magic Wand tool	Y
Direct Select Lasso tool	Q

Function	***Procedure***
Select one point	Click with Direct Selection tool
Select one segment	Click with Direct Selection tool
Select one path	Click with Group Selection tool
Select next group up	Click selected path again with Group Selection tool
Select to-level group	Click with Selection tool
Select addtional	Shift + Click
Select specific points	Drag with Direct Selection tool
Select specific paths	Drag with Selection tool
Deselct selected	Shift + click selected
Move selection	Drag
Duplicate selection	Alt + Drag
Constrain to 45^0 movement	Shift + Drag
Duplicate and constrain	Alt + Shift + Drag
Proportionatel resize object	Shfit + drag Bounding Box handle
Resize from center	Alt + drag Bounding Box handle
Resize proportionately from center	Alt + Shift + drag Bounding Box handle
Select all	Ctrl + A
Deselect all	Ctrl + Shift + A
Select all objects with similar Fill, Stroke, Opacity and/or Blending Mode	Click with Magic Wand tool
Add similar colored and stroked objects from the current selection	Alt + Magic Wand tool
Set Magic Wand options	Double click on Magic Wand tool to open the Magic Wand palette

Path Tools

Tool	***Shortcut***
Pen tool	P
Add Anchor Point tool	Alt + Delete Anchor Point tool
	Alt + Scissors tool

Delete Anchor Point tool	-
	Alt + Add Anchor Point tool
Convert Anchor Point tool	Shift + C
	Alt + Pen tool
Pencil tool	N
Smooth tool	Alt + Pencil tool
	Alt + Erase tool
	Alt + Paintbrush tool
Paintbrush tool	B
Scissors tool	C
Function	***Procedure***
Create a straight corner point	Click with Pen tool
Create a smooth point	Drag with Pen tool
Continue existing open path	Click + drag with Pen tool on end point of existing path
Close open path	While drawing, click + drag with Pen tool on the initial end point
	Click + drag with Pen tool on each end point in succession
	Select path and join (Ctrl ÷ J)
Constrain new point to 45 degrees from last point	Shift + drag with Pen tool
Constain control handles to 45 degrees	Shift while dragging handle with Pen tool
Create a path	Click + drag a succession of points with Pen tool
Add anchor points to existing path	Click with the Pen tool on path
Delete achor points from existing path	Shift + click with Pen tool on an anchor point
Convert anchor point to smooth point	Drag with Convert Direction Point tool on existing point
Convert smooth point to corner point	Click with Convert Direction Point tool on smooth point
Convert smooth corner to combination corner	Drag one handle with Direct Selection tool back into the anchor point
Convert somooth corner to curved corner	Drag one handle with Convert Direction Point tool
Draw freestyle paths	Drag with Pencil tool
View Paintbrush options	Double click Paintbrush tool in toolbox
Reshape a path	Select points with Direct Selection, and then drag with Reshape tool
Split path	Click with Scissors tool
Slic multiple paths	Drag wth Knife tool

Constrain Knife slice to straight lines	Alt + drag with Knife tool
Constain Knife slice to 45^0	Shift + Alt + drag with Knife tool

Type Tools

Tools	***Shortcut***
Type tool	T Shift + Vertical Type tool
Area Type tool	Alt + Path Type tool Shift + Vertical Area Type tool Alt + Shift Vertical Path Type tool
Path Type tool	Alt + Area Type tool Shift + Vertical Path Type tool Alt + Shift + Vertical Area Type tool
Vertical Type tool	Shift + Type tool
Vertical Area Type tool	Alt + Vertical Path Type tool Shift + Area Type tool Alt + Shift + Area Type tool
Verical Path Type tool	Alt + Vertical Area Type tool Shift + Path Type tool Alt + Shift + Area Type tool

Function	***Procedure***
Create point type	Click with Type tool
Create rectangle type	Drag with Type tool
Place path type on closed path	Click path with Path Type tool Alt + click path with Type tool Alt + click path with Area Type tool
Place path type on an open path	Click path with Path Type tool Click path with Type tool Alt + click path with Area Type tool
Place area type on a closed path	Click path with Area Type tool Click path with Type tool Alt + click path with Path Type tool
Place area type on an open with	Click path with Area Type tool Alt + click path with Type tool Alt + click path with Path Type tool
Change vertical type to horzontal type	Choose Type>>Type Orientation>>Horizontal

Change horizontal type to vertical type	Choose Type>>Type Orientation>>Vertical
Select entrie text block	Click text block with Selection tool
Select one character	Drag across character with any Type tool
Select one word	Double click word with any Type tool
Select one paragraph	Triple-click paragraph with any Type tool
Select all text in text block	Click in text block with any Type tool, and then press Ctrl + A.
Flip type on a path	Double click the I-bar with any selection tool or just drag it to the opposite side

Line Tools

Tool	***Shortcut***
Line Segment tool	\

Function	***Procedure***
Create line segments using numbers	Click with Line Segment tool
Draw a line segment	Draw with Line Segment tool
Constrain line segments to 45^0	Shift + Drag with Line Segment tool
Create line segment from midpoint using numbers	Alt + click with Line Segment tool
Draw line segment from midpoint	Alt + drag with Line Segment tool
Move line segment while drawing	Spacebar + drag with Line Segment tool
Create multiple line segments	- + drag with Line Segment tool
Create arc segments using numbers	Click with the Arc tool
Draw an arc segment	Draw with Arc tool
Constrain arc segments to circular sections	Shift + drag with Arc tool
Create arc segment from the center	Alt + click with Arc tool
Draw arc segment from the center	Alt + drag with Arc tool
Move arc segment while drawing	Spacebar + drag with Arc tool
Create multiple arc segments	- + drag with Arc tool
Toggle arc between concave and convex	X + drag with Arc tool
Toggle between open and closed arcs	C + drag with Arc tool
Flip the arc	F + drag with Arc tool
Increase arc slope	Up Arrow + drag with Arc tool
Decrease arc slope	Down Arrow + drag with Arc tool
Create spiral using numbers	Click with Spiral tool
Draw spiral	Drag with Spiral tool
Constrain spiral angle	Shift + drag with Spiral tool
Move spiral while drawing	Spacebar + drag with Spiral tool

Create multiple spirals	- + drag with Spiral tool
Decrease spiral decay	Ctrl + drag with Spiral tool
Increase spiral length and size	Alt + drag with Spiral tool
Increase spiral length	Up Arrow + drag with Spiral tool
Decrease spiral length	Down Arrow + drag with Spiral tool
Create a rectangular grid using numbers	Click with the Rectangular Grid tool
Draw an rectangular grid	Drag with Rectangular Grid tool
Constrain rectangular grid to a square	Shift + Drag with Rectangular Grid tool
Create a square rectangular grid	Alt + click with Rectangular grid tool
Draw rectangular grid from the cente	Alt + drag with Rectangular Grid tool
Move rectangular grid while drawing	Spacebar + drag with Rectangular Grid tool
Create multiple rectangular grid	~ + drag with Rectangular Grid tool
Skew horizontal dividers to the left	X + drag with Rectangular Grid tool
Skew horizontal dividers to the right	C + drag with Rectangular Grid tool
Skew vertical dividers to the top of the rectangular grid	F + Drag wtih Rectangular Grid tool
Skew vertical dividers to the bottom of the rectangular grid	V + drag Rectangular Grid tool
Increase vertical dividers	Up Arrow with Rectangular Grid tool
Decrease vertical dividers	Down Arrow + drag with Rectangular Grid tool
Increase horizontal dividers	Right Arrow + drag with Rectangular Grid tool
Decrease horizontal dividers	Left Arrow + drag with Rectangular Grid tool
Create a polar grid using numbers	Click with the Polar Grid tool
Draw an polar grid	Drag wth Polar Grid tool
Constrain polar grid to a circle	Shift + drag with Polar Grid tool
Create a circular polar grid	Alt + click with Polar Grid tool
Draw polar grid from the center	Alt + drag with Polar Grid tool
Move polar grid while drawing	Spacebar + drag with Polar Grid tool
Create multiple polar grid	~ + drag with Polar Grid tool
Skew concentric dividers inward	X + drag with Polar Grid tool
Skew concentric dividers outward	C + drag with Polar Grid tool
Skew radial dividers counterclockwise	F + drag with Polar Grid tool
Skew radial dividers clockwise	V + drag with Polar Grid tool
Increase concentric dividers	Up Arrow + drag with Polar Grid tool
Decrease concentric dividers	Down Arrow + drag with Polar Grid tool
Increase radial dividers	Right Arrow + drag with Polar Grid tool
Decrease radial dividers	Left Arrow + drag with Polar Grid tool

Shape Tools

Tool	*Shortcut*
Rectangle tool	M
Ellipse tool	L
Function	***Procedure***
Create rectangle using numbers	Click with Rectangle tool or Rounded Rectangle tool
Draw rectangle	Drag with Rectangle tool
Draw square	Shift + drag with Rectangle tool
Create centered rectangle using numbers	Alt + click with Rectangle tool
Draw centered rectangle	Alt + drag with Rectangle tool
Draw square from center	Alt + Shift + drag with Rectangle tool
Move rectangle while drawing	Spacebar + drag with Rectangle tool
Create multiple ectangles	~ + drag with Rectangle tool
Create rounded rectangle using numbers	Click with Rounded Rectangle tool
Draw rounded rectangle	Drag with Rounded Rectangle tool
Draw square with rounded corners	Shift + drag with Rounded Rectangle tool
Create centered rounded rectangle	Alt + click with Rounded Rectangle tool
Draw centered rounded rectangle	Alt + drag with Rounded Rectangle tool
Draw square from center with rounded corners	Alt + Shift + drag with Rounded Rectangle tool
Move rounded rectangle while drawing	Spacebar + drag with Rounded Rectangle tool
Create multiple rounded rectangles	~ + drag with Rounded rectangle tool
Create ellipse using numbers	Click with Ellipse tool
Draw ellipse	Drag with Ellipse tool
Draw circle	Shift + drag with Ellipse tool
Create centered ellipse using numbers	Alt + click with Ellipse tool
Draw centered ellipse	Alt + drag with Ellipse tool
Move ellipse while drawing	Spacebar + drag with Ellipse tool
Create multiple ellipses	~ + drag with Ellipse tool
Create polygon using numbers	Click with Polygon tool
Draw polygon	Drag with Polygon tool
Constrain polygon angle	Shift + drag with Polygon tool
Create centered polygon using numbers	Alt + click with Polygon tool
Draw centered polygon	Alt + drag with Polygon tool
Increase polygon sides	Up Arrow + drag with Polygon tool
Decrease polygon sides	Down Arrow + drag with Polygon tool

Move polygon while drawing	Spacebar + drag with Polygon tool
Create multiple polygons	~ + drag with Polygon tool
Create star using numbers	Click with Star tool
Draw star	Drag with Star tool
Constrain star angle	Shift + drag with Star tool
Draw even-shouldered star	Alt + drag wityh Star tool
Move outer points only	Ctrl + drag with Star tool
Increase star points	Up Arrow + drag with Star tool
Decrease star points	Down Arrow + drag with Star tool
Move star while drawing	Spacebar + drag with Star tool
Create multiple stars	~ + drag with Star tool

Transformation Tools

Tool	***Shortcut***
Rotate tool	R
Reflect tool	O
Scale tool	S
Free Transform tool	E

Function	***Procedure***
Moving objects	Drag with the Selection or Free Transform tool
Constrain movements along 45 degrees axis	Shift + drag tool with the Selection or Free Transform tool
Rotate using numbers	Alt + click with Rotate tool
Rotate from center of selection with numbers	Double click with Rotate tool
Free Rotate	Click with Rotate to set Origin, and then drag with Rotate tool
Fre Rotate around selection center	Drag with Rotate tool
Rotate a copy	Alt + drag with Rotate tool
Rotate pattern only	~ + drag with Rotate tool
Scale using numbers	Alt + click with Scale tool
Scle from center of selection with numbers	Double click with Scale tool
Free Scale	Click with Scale to set Origin, and then drag with Scale tool
Free Scale around selection center	Drag with Scale tool
Constrain scaling to 45 degrees	Shift + drag with Scale tool
Scale a copy	Alt + drag with Scale tool
Scale pattern only	~ + drag with Scale tool

Reflect using numbers	Alt + click with Reflect tool
Reflect from center of selection with numbers	Double click with Reflect tool
Free Reflect	Click with Reflect to set Origin, and then drag with Reflect tool
Free Reflect around selection center	Drag with reflect tool
Constrain reflecting angle to 45 degrees	Shift + drag with Reflect tool
Reflect a copy	Alt + drag with Reflect tool
Reflect Pattern only	~ + drag with Reflect tool
Shear using numbers	Alt + click with Shear tool
Free Shear with Shear	Click with Shear to set Origin, and then drag
Free Shear around selection center	Drag with Shear
Constrain shearing to 45 degrees	Shift + drag with Shear tool
Shear a copy	Alt + drag with Shear tool
Shear pattern only	~ + drag with Shear tool

Distortion Tools

Tool	***Shortcut***
Warp tool	Shift + R
Function	***Procedure***
Twirl using numbers	Alt + click with Rotate tool
Free Twirl	Drag with Twirl tool
Reshape distortion brush	Alt + drag with Warp, Twirl, Pucker, Bloat, Scallop, Crystallize or Wrinkle tool
Constrain brush to horizontal or vertical movement	Shift + drag with Warp, Twirl, Pucker, Bloat, Scallop, Crystallize or Wrinkle tool
Set distortion options	Double click on the selected distortion tool

Symbol Tools

Tool	***Shortcut***
Symbol Sprayer tool	Shift + S
Function	***Procedure***
Add a single symbol	Click + Symbol Sprayer tool
Add multiple symbols	Drag + Symbol Sprayer tool
Remove symbols from set	Alt + Symbol Sprayer tool
Move the symbols in a set	Drag with the Symbol Sprayer tool
Change the stacking order of the symbols	Alt + Symbol Sprayer tool
Scrunch the symbols closer together	Drag with the Symbol Sprayer tool
Move the symbols farther apart	Alt + Symbol Sprayer tool

Increase the symbol size	Drag with the Symbol Sprayer tool
Decrease the symbol size	Alt + Symbol Sprayer tool
Rotate the symbols	Drag with the Symbol Sprayer tool
Increase the symbol's transparency	Drag with the Symbol Sprayer tool
Decrease the symbol's transparency	Alt + Symbol Sprayer tool
Change the symbol's colour	Drag with the Symbol Sprayer tool
Restore the symbol's original colour	Alt + Symbol Sprayer tool
Apply a style to the symbol	Drag with the Symbol Sprayer tool
Remove the style from a symbol	Alt + Symbol Sprayer tool

Graph Tools

Tool	***Shortcut***
Column Graph tool	J

Function	***Procedure***
Create a Graph sized by numbers	Click with any Graph tool
Create a Graph sized by dragging	Drag with any Graph tool
Create a square or circular graph	Shift + drag with any Graph tool
Create a Graph from the center	Alt + drag with any Graph tool

Paint Tools

Tool	***Shortcut***
Gradient tool	G
Gradient Mesh tool	U
Paint Bucket tool	K
	Alt + Eyedropper tool
Eydropper tool	I
	Alt + Paint Bucket tool

Function	***Procedure***
Change Linear Gradient direction and/or length	Drag with Gradient tool
Constrain Gradient Direction to 45^0 angles	Shift + drag with Gradient tool
Change Radial Gradient size and/or location	Drag with Gradient tool
Change Radial Gradient origin point	Click with Gradient tool
Sample colour to Colour palette	Click with Eyedropper tool
Change Paint Style of selected objects	Double-click with Eyedropper tool on an object with the desired style
Paint unselected objects	Click objects with the Paint Bucket tool
Measure a distance	Click the start and end location with the Measure tool

Measure a distance by 45^{0} angles	Shift + click the start and end location with the Measure tool

Blend, Auto Trace and Slice Tools

Tool	***Shortcut***
Blend tool	W
Slice tool	Shift + K

Function	***Procedure***
Blend between two paths	Click corresponding selected points on each path with Blend tool
Set Blend options	Double click on the Blend tool
Auto Trace Images	Click area to be traced with Auto Trace tool
Divide artwork into slices	Drag + Slice tool
Constrain slice to a square	Alt + drag with the Slice tool
Slice selected objects	Drag + Slice Selected tool

Viewing Tools

Tool	***Shortcut***
Hand tool	H
	Spacebar (when not enterin text)
Zoom tool	Z
	Ctrl + spacebar
Zoom Out tool	Ctrl + Alt + spacebar
	Alt + Zoom tool

Function	***Procedure***
Reposition the page	Drag with the Hand tool
Fit the page within the document window	Double click on the Hand tool
Moving page boundaries	Drag with the Page tool
Reset page boundaries	Double click on the Page tool
Zoom in	Click with the Zoom tool
	Ctrl + Plus Sign (+)
Zoom Out	Alt + click with the Zoom tool
	Ctrl + Hyphen (-)
Zoom in to a specific area	Drag with the Zoom tool
Move the Zoom Marquee while drawing	Spacebar while dragging with the Zoom tool
Draw the Zoom Marquee from its center	Ctrl + drag with the Zoom tool

TYPE COMMANDS

Type Shortcuts

Action	*Shortcut*
Copy type on a path	Alt + drag the I-bar using any selection tool.
	Spacebar (when not enterin text)
Flip type on a path	Double click the I-bar with any selection tool or just drag it to the opposiete side of the path
Move insertion point to next character	Right Arrow
Move insertion point to previous character	Left Arrow
Move insertion point to next line	Down Arrow
Move insertion point to previous line	Up Arrow
Move insertion point to next word	Ctrl + Right Arrow
Move insertion point to previous word	Ctrl + Left Arrow
Move insertion point to next paragraph	Ctrl + Down Arrow
Move insertion point to previous paragraph	Ctrl + Up Arrow
Select all type in stroy	Ctrl + A when the insertion point is in the story
Select all type in document	Ctrl + A when any tool but the Type tools are selected
Select next character	Shift + Right Arrow
Select previous character	Shift + Left Arrow
Select next line	Shift + Down Arrow
Select previous line	Shift + Up Arrow
Select next word	Ctrl + Shift + Right Arrow
Select previous word	Ctrl + Shift + Left Arrow
Select next paragraph	Ctrl + Shift + Down Arrow
Select previous paragraph	Ctrl + Shift + Up Arrow
Select word	Doble click word
Select paragraph	Triple click paragraph
Deselect all type	Ctrl + Shift + A
Duplicate column outline and flow text	Alt + drag column outline with Direct Selection tool
Insert discretionary hyphen	Ctrl + Shift + Hyphen (-)
Insert line break	Press Enter

Paragraph Formatting

Action	*Shortcut*
Display Paragraph palette	Ctrl + Shift + M

Align paragraph flush left	Ctrl + Shift + L
Align paragraph flush right	Ctrl + Shift + R
Align paragraph flush cente	Ctrl + Shift + C
Align paragraph justified	Ctrl + Shift + J
Align paragraph force justified	Ctrl + Shift + F
Display Tab Ruler palette	Ctrl + Shift + T
Align Tab palette to selected paragraph	Click Tab palette size box
Cycle through tab stops	Alt + click tab stop
Move multiple tab stops	Shift + drag tab stops
Cycle tab measurements	Click

Character Formatting

Action	***Shortcut***
Display Character palette	Ctrl + T
Highlight font	Ctrl + Alt + Shift + M
Increase type size	Ctrl + Shift + >
Decrease type size	Ctrl + Shift + <
Increase type to next size on menus	Ctrl + Alt + >
Decrease type to next size on menus	Ctrl + Alt + <
Highlight size	none
Set leading to Solid	Double click Leading symbol in Character palette
Highlight leading	none
Increase Baseline Shift	Alt + Shift + Up Arrow
Decrease Baseline Shift	Alt + Shift + Down Arrow
Increase Baseline Shift x5	Ctrl + Alt + Up Arrow
Decrease Baseline Shift x5	Ctrl + Alt + Shift + Down Arrow
Kern/Track closer	Alt + Left Arrow
Kern/Track apart	Alt + Rigth Arrow
Kern/Track closer x5	Ctrl + Alt + Left Arrow
Kern/Track apart x5	Ctrl + Alt + Right Arrow
Reset Kerning/Tracking to 0	Ctrl + Shift + Q
Highlight Kerning/Tracking	Ctrl + Alt + K
Reset Horizontal Scale to 100%	Ctrl + Shift + X

COLOUR COMMANDS

Action	***Shortcut***
Show/Hide Colour palette	F6

	Ctrl + I
Rever to default colours	D
Toggle focus between Fill and Stroke	X
Choose current colour in Color palette	Comma (,)
Chang paint to None	/
Apply to inactive Fill/Stroke	Alt + click in colour ramp on Color palette
Apply colour to unselected object	Drag colour swatch from Colour palette to object
Apply colour to selected object	Click swatch in Colour palette
Copy Paint Style from any (source) object to all selected objects	Click source object with Eyedropper
	Shift + drag any Colour palette slider
Tint process colour	Shift + click Colour Ramp
Cycle through Colour modes	

Swatch Palette

Action	***Shortcut***
show/Hide Swatches palette	F5
Toggle focus between Fill and Stroke	X
Add Swatch	Click the New Swatch icon
	Drag from Colour or Gradient palette into swatches
Replace swatch	Alt + drag from Colour or Gradient palette into swatches
Duplicate swatch	Alt + drag swatch onto New Swatch icon in Swatches palette
Delete swatch	Drag to Trash icon in Swatches palette
	Click Tash icon with swatches selected
Select contiguous swatches	Shift + click first and last swatches
Select noncontiguous swatches	Ctrl + click each swatch
Switch keyboard focus to Swatches palette	Ctrl + Alt + click in swatches palette
Apply colour to unselected object	Drag colour swatch from Swatches palette to object
Apply colour to selected object	Click swatch in Swatches palette

Gradient Palette

Action	***Shortcut***
Choose current gradient in Gradient palete	Period (.)
Show/Hide Gradient palette	F9
Apply swatch to selected colour stop on gradient palette	Alt + click swatch
Add new colour stop	Click below gradient ramp

Duplicate colour stop	Alt + drag colour stop
Sqp colour stops	Alt + drag colour stop on top of another
Suck colour for colour stop with Eyedropper	Shift + click with Eyedropper
Reset Gradient to default Black, White	Ctrl + click in gradient swatch
Apply colour to unselected object	Drag colour swatch from Gradient palette to object
Apply colour to selected object	Click swatch in Gradient palette

Stroke Palette

Action	***Shortcut***
Show/Hide Stroke palette	F10
Increase/decrease Stroke weight	Highlight Stroke field, use up or down arrows, press Enter when finished
Increase/decrease Miter account	Highlight Miter field, use up or down arrows, press Enter when finished

Miscellaneous Palette Commands

Action	***Shortcut***
Collapse/display Palette	Click box in upper-right corner
Cycle through Palette views	Double click palette tab
Apply settings	Enter
Apply settings while keeping last text field highlighted	Shift + Enter
Highlight Next Text field	Tab
Highlight Previous Text field	Shift + Tab
Highlight any text field	Click label or double click current value
Increase value by base increment	Highlight field, Up Arrow
Decrease value by base increment	Highlight field, Down Arrow
Increase value by large increment	Highlight field, Shift + Up Arrow
Decrease value by large increment	Highlight field, Shift + Down Arrow
Combine palettes	Drag palette tab within other palette
Dock palette	Drag palette tab to bottom of other palette
Separate palette	Drag palete tab from current palette

Transform Palette

Action	***Shortcut***
Show/Hide Transform palette	none
Copy object while transforming	Alt + Enter
Scale proportionately	Ctrl + Enter

Copy object while scaling proportionately   Ctrl + Alt + Enter

Layers Palette

Action	***Shortcut***
Hide/Show	F7
New Layer	Click New Layer icon
New Layer with Options dialog box	Alt + Click New Layer icon
New layer above active layer	Ctrl + Alt + click New Layer icon
New layer below active layer	Ctrl + click New Layer icon
Duplicate layer(s)	Drag layer(s) to New Layer icon
Change layer order	Drag layers up and down within layer list
Select all objects on a layer	Alt + click that layer
Select all objects on several layers	Shift + Alt + click each layer
Select contiguous layers	Shift + click layers
Select noncontiguous layers	Ctrl + click layers
Move objects to a different layer	Drag coloured square to a different layer
Copy objects to a different layer	Alt + drag colour square to a different layer
Hide/Show layer	Click Eyeball icon
View layer while hiding others	Alt + click Eyeball icons
View layer in Artwork mode	Ctrl + click Eyeball icon
View layer in Preview while others are artwork	Ctrl + Alt + click Eyeball icon
Lock/Unlock layer	Click Pencil tool
Unlock layer while locking others	Alt + click Pencil icon
Delete layer	Drag layer to Trash icon Select layer and click Trash icon
Delete layer without warning	Alt + drag layer to Trash icon Select layer and Alt + click Trash icon

Viewing Shortcuts

Action	***Shortcut***
Zoom In	Ctrl + Plus Sign (+) Click with Zoom tool
Zoom Out	Ctrl + Hyphen (-) Alt + click with Zoom tool
Fit Document in Window	Ctrl + 0 Double click Hand tool
View at Actual size (100%)	Ctrl + 1

	Double click Zoom tool
Artwork/Preview mode	Ctrl + Y
Preview Selection mode	Ctrl + P + Alt + Y
Custom view recall	Ctrl + Alt + Shift + 1 through Ctrl + Alt + Shift + 0
Show/Hide edges	Ctrl + H
Show/Hide guides	Ctrl + ;
Show/Hide grid	Ctrl + '
Show/Hide rulers	Ctrl + R
Hide selected objects	Ctrl + 3
Hide unselected objects	Ctrl + Alt + 3
Show all hidden objects	Ctrl + Shift + 3
Window mode	F (when in Full Screen mode)
Full Screen mode with menu	F (when in Window mode)
Full Screen mode	F (when in Full Screen mode with menu)

Miscellaneous Commands

Action	*Shortcut*
Nudge selection	Arrow keys
See special Status Line categories	Alt + click status bar
Cycle through units	Ctrl + U
View anagram of credits	Alt + click illustrator click toolbox
Speed up credits in About box	Alt
Display context-sensitive menus	Ctrl + Right click
Highlight last active text field	Ctrl + ~

Generic Dialog Box Commands

Action	*Shortcut*
Cancel	Esc
OK	Enter
Highlight next text field	Tab
Highlight previous text field	Shift + Tab
Highlight any text filed	Click labe' or double click current value

6 Questions

ANSWER THE FOLLOWING QUESTIONS

Chapter 1 — Getting to know Illustrator CS 4

1. Describe the contents of the following menus.

   File menu
   Edit menu
   Object menu
   Type menu
   Select menu
   Effect menu
   View menu
   Window menu
   Help menu

2. Describe the contents of the following Preferences:

   General
   Type
   Units and Display Performance
   Guides and Grid
   Smart Guides & Slices
   Hyphenation Options
   Plug-ins and Scratch Disk
   File Handling and Clipboard
   Appearance of Black

3. How would you customize a Palette's Appearance

Chapter 2 — Tools of Illustrator CS 4

1. Describe the various tools on the toolbox.
2. How would you do the colour settings?
3. What do you understand by Points and Segments?
4. What are Strokes and Fills?
5. Describe the various methods of drawing a rectangle.
6. How is an Ellipse drawn in Illustrator?
7. How would you draw different shapes at an angle?
8. Describe the process of creating the followings:

   Stars
   Spirals
   Polygons
   Double Star

9. Describe the working of Arrows and Lassos.
10. What can you do with the Plain Black Arrow Tool?

11. What is Direct Selection Tool? How is it used?
12. How would you select an object using Black Lasso?
13. How would you select with White Lasso?
14. How would you select everything on the artboard?
15. How would inverse all the selection?
16. What do you understand by Dragging?
17. What is the function of Pen tool?
18. Describe the working with the Pen tool.
19. How would you draw curves?
20. How would you convert smooth points to cusp?
21. How would you add points to a path?
22. How would you remove points from a path?
23. Describe the various Redo and Undo Operations.

Chapter 3 — Handling Text in Illustrator CS 4

1. How do you create text objects?
2. How is text created in blocks?
3. How would you resize and reshape the text blocks?
4. How would you select and edit the text?
5. Describe the process of selecting the text with Type tool.
6. How would you add more text to the text block?
7. Describe the process of formatting text.
8. What all you can change at Character level formatting?
9. How can you change the space between characters?
10. Describe the process of changing Height and Width of the characters.
11. How would you create Superscript and Subscript?
12. What sort of alignments are used in Paragraph level formatting?
13. How would you change the letter and word spacing?
14. How would you hyphenate the text?
15. How would you set the tabs in the text?
16. Describe the complete process of sucking attributes from the text and pouring them on another text.
17. What are the type of type effects that you can perform in Illustrator?
18. How can you merge text with the curve?
19. How would you shift the text in relation to its path?
20. Describe the process of typing the text in vertical format.

Chapter 4 — More Commands of Illustrator CS 4

1. Define the various Stroke Types and Text Paths.
2. Define the options of the following terms:

   Line Weight | Line Caps

   Line Joins
3. Define the various Dash patterns.
4. Define the various brushes available in Illustrator.
5. Define the options of the followings:

   Calligraphic Brushes | Scatter Brushes

   Art Brushes | Patterns Brushes
6. How is the colour palette used?
7. How would you apply Colours?
8. How would you use the Slider Bar?
9. Describe the process of creating a colour swatch.
10. How would you adjust colours?
11. How would you apply fills?
12. Describe the process of creating a Gradient Swatch.
13. How do you create a Blend?
14. How would you blend multiple objects?
15. How would you create colour blends?
16. How would you create shape blends?
17. How would you create Masks?

Notes